THE MAKING OF A
PASTRY
chef

THE MAKING OF A
PASTRY
chef

Recipes and

Inspiration

from

America's

Best

Pastry Chefs

Andrew MacLauchlan

Photography by Scott Vlaun

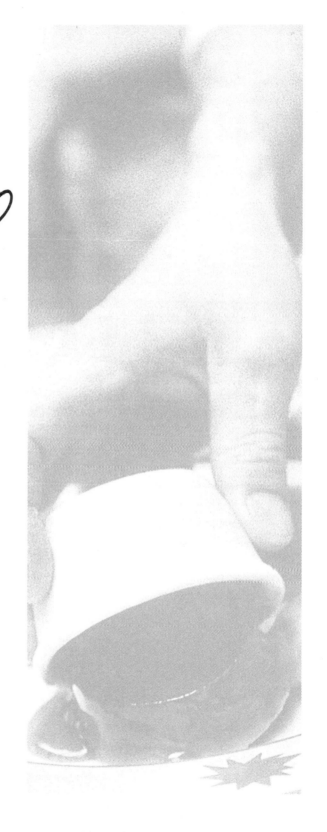

JOHN WILEY & SONS, INC.

NEW YORK CHICHESTER WEINHEIM
BRISBANE SINGAPORE TORONTO

Library of Congress Cataloging-in-Publication Data:

MacLauchlan, Andrew.

    The making of a pastry chef : recipes and inspiration from

  America's best pastry chefs / Andrew MacLauchlan ;

    photography by Scott Vlaun.

        p.   cm.

    Includes bibliographical references and index.

    ISBN 0-471-29320-2 (paper : alk. paper)

    1. Cooks—Training of—United States.   2. Cookery—Vocational

  guidance—United States.   3. Pastry.   I. Title.

  TX649.A1M33   1999

  641.8'65'023—dc21   99-13033

Printed in the United States of America.

10 9 8 7 6 5 4

CONTENTS

RECIPE CONTENTS

RECIPE *contents*

The pastry chef is on the front line of the culinary world. Having risen in importance from a subordinate taskmaster to a prominent leader in America's finest restaurants, cafés, and bakeries, the pastry chef now plays an integral part in many successful restaurant kitchens. Sometimes an independent businessperson or valued manager in a large hotel or catering kitchen, the pastry chef is a confident leader, a craftsperson, and, as his or her career develops, an artist.

The Making of a Pastry Chef explores what it takes to begin on the path of pastry and proceed to the position of pastry chef. All the excitement, technical skill, creativity, and responsibility of pastry chefs at the forefront of the field are forged by their personal paths—their choices, influences, and opportunities for practical training. I have traveled the country and spoken to the best in the business in order to collect their advice, stories, recipes, and formulas for triumph in one of the most exciting and challenging aspects of professional cooking. These are the stories of some of America's leading practitioners in pastry today, stories of discovering the first inklings of their life's work, of decision making that shaped their careers, of everyday experiences creating desserts and pastries for prominent and successful restaurants, hotels, and bakeries.

These are the stories of some of America's leading practitioners in pastry today, stories of discovering the first inklings of their life's work, of decision making that shaped their careers, of everyday experiences creating desserts and pastries.

In addition to possessing specialized technical skills and knowledge of food and flavor, a pastry chef who wishes to become an owner or partner in a bakery, café, restaurant, or cooking school must have business acumen. The growth of the restaurant business and the food industry, as well as its competitive nature, provides enormous opportunity for those dedicated pastry chefs willing to work hard, observe, learn, grow, practice to perfection, continually hone their skills, and develop an appreciation for their endeavor.

Only fifteen or twenty years ago, the job of pastry chef was a marginal career choice in this country, with the best and only lucrative jobs in major cities.

However, the public's evolution as consumers and its demands for freshness, high quality, and flavor fueled the need for meticulously hand-crafted desserts and pastries produced on site. The restaurant and food business remains highly competitive, with a customer base that returns again and again to establishments that maintain consistent food quality. The continued patronage required for ongoing success of a restaurant or bakery can depend on the decisions and skills of the pastry chef. The customer's insistence on high-quality food and the exponential growth of the food business have combined to create many more job opportunities in pastry than at any other time in history.

The pastry chefs who contributed to this project are among the best and most successful in the United States and the world. *The Making of a Pastry Chef* is a captivating collection of inspirational stories, opinions, and detailed musings of these creative, passionate, and driven individuals. The mysteries of their profession are explained here in their own words. Why did they choose to become pastry chefs? Where do their ideas come from? What is the hardest part of their day? What are their thoughts on the future of the discipline? The stories and examples set by these men and women are gathered here as a collective legacy of America's pastry chefs. Which pastry chef, as an apprentice at Lenôtre's Pâtisserie, left in charge of the ovens for the first time, burned an entire rack of pastries (an entire day's work) and, as a result, learned a profound lesson in the ways of managing people? Which pastry chef switched from a career in dance to find fulfillment in the theatre of the kitchen?

> The mysteries of their profession are explained here in their own words. Why did they choose to become pastry chefs? Where do their ideas come from? What is the hardest part of their day? What are their thoughts on the future of the discipline?

The Making of a Pastry Chef explores the history of sweets in many world cultures—the movement of ingredients and development of recipes through wars, migration, and religious crusades. These movements culminated in a diverse range of methods, techniques, and traditions expressed through the personalities and skilled hands of the leading pastry chefs of today's kitchens. What were their early influences? their first memories of something sweet? their very first cooking experiences? What was their first day on the job like?

What programs are available to someone interested in becoming a pastry chef? The paths to success can be as varied as the individuals who pursue them.

The European pastry chefs I spoke with describe their tradition of learning, built on apprenticeships such as the French system of compagnon, in which training begins at age 14 and by the age of 18 has the young apprentice working in a variety of pastry kitchen positions in a dozen or more establishments all over France. Here in the United States, leading pastry chefs recommend that a formal pastry training program, as well as general culinary training, precede a wide variety of experiences and assistant positions in professional kitchens. They also consider continued development vital to maintaining creativity and peak performance long after one becomes a pastry chef.

> Let's go into the hearts, hands, and minds of some of the best and see what it takes to aim high and strive for excellence!

   The Making of a Pastry Chef reflects the real world of the chefs as well as the enormous variety, opportunity, and scope of the profession. Restaurants, bistros, hotels, pastry shops, and bakeries are the platforms for these dazzling performers. This is what it's all about—the ingredients, menu item development, thoughts on traditional recipes, personal styles, working with the chef and owner or being one's own boss, flavor, and future trends. Let's go into the hearts, hands, and minds of some of the best and see what it takes to aim high and strive for excellence!

CHAPTER one

The History of Sweets in Food and Cuisine; The Rise of the Pastry Chef

Within the history of human culture is the fascinating story of the value and development of sweets in societies and the technical evolution of pastry and dessert making. Every present-day pastry chef has a strong link to the discovery of the sensation of sweetness, the contributions of cultural traditions, and the great chefs, cooks, and artistic, skillful pastry innovators of the past. Markus Färbinger, chocolatier/co-owner of L.A. Burdick Chocolates, believes you have to understand the history before you can develop anything new. "You have to understand the masters before you can become one yourself. I think, at the beginning, pastry chefs can be very self-centered, but over the years they begin to open up and they can see more, feel more, and incorporate more. They can better incorporate history with what they are doing, whether from sheer inspiration or by researching traditional recipes."

Prehistory

The first sweet foods known to prehistoric humans were most likely maple or birch syrup, honey, fruits, berries, and nutmeats such as acorns. Charlie Trotter, chef/owner of his namesake restaurant in Chicago, suggests, "Maybe it's a natural thing that people are drawn to sweet and repelled from bitter; maybe that's how they survived. That is a simple way to look at it." The Stone Age diet was based on what was available to prehistoric humans in the regions they inhabited. Hunter-gatherer societies generally had a diet of 50 percent meat and 50 percent foraged foods, such as wild fruits, seeds, nuts, roots, bulbs, and honey.

> Hunter-gatherer societies generally had a diet of 50 percent meat and 50 percent foraged foods, such as wild fruits, seeds, nuts, roots, bulbs, and honey.

Wet, ground cereal grains of wheat or barley left on a rock to ferment and cook in the sun made a crude cracker or pancake, one of humankind's food sources for millennia. Inhabitants of the Swiss Lake Region in 6000 B.C. made a bread of crushed cereal grains and kept dried fruits in their homes, as excavated remains show. Traditional flatbread, such as tortillas, naan, chapati, and pita, remain a staple in the diets of many cultures to this day.

According to James Trager's *Food Chronology,* the first recorded mention of sugar cane is found in the writings of Alexander the Great's admiral, Nearchus, in 325 B.C. Nearchus spoke of Indian reeds "that produce honey, although there are no bees." These "reeds" were soon transplanted to certain wet areas of the Middle East. Herbs and spices were used thousands of years before the Christian era for preserving foods—and during religious observances, for their alleged magical properties.

Ancient Egypt and Greece

Humankind had been consuming the flour of ground grains in many forms such as porridge, or mush, and flattened, dried cakes, but the Egyptians—from 25 B.C. on, as evident from tomb paintings—evolved baking techniques with creative and predictable results. Bread, a basic, delicious, palatable food source, is an important brick in the historical foundations of pastry because many desserts and pastries are just complicated breads. The invention and refinement of bread was the precursor to more elaborate cakes and pastries. The Egyptians kneaded, in large earthenware tubs, a wet dough liquid enough to be poured into heated molds and baked in an oven heated with white-hot stones. Heating doughs in earthen pots placed directly in the fire's hot embers or buried in a stone-lined fire pit were crude baking methods employed in early civilization. The ancient Greeks are credited with inventing the first oven that was preheated and opened from the front, a forerunner of the modern oven.

The ancient Greeks created the art of baking by making specific recipes and shapes of breads appropriate to particular occasions. One ancient treatise on bread making lists over eighty varieties of bread every bit as complex as those available to us today. There were regional specialties as well, such as *boletus,* a mushroom-shaped bread sprinkled with poppy seeds, and *almogaeus,* a coarse rustic bread, and *syncomiste,* a dark bread made with coarsely ground rye flour. Some breads were staples for the poor, such as *maza,* made from easily obtained and therefore cheaper grains, while others made from spelt and the prized flour of wheat were popular with more prosperous customers. The treatise also documents the range of foods these bakers prepared, as they did not confine themselves to bread making. There were no specialist pastry cooks until the end of the Roman Empire, but early Greek bakers produced a wide variety of small cakes and pastries. *Plakon* was one early cake made from cream cheese, oat flour, honey, and spices. The Greeks also made cheesecakes containing dried figs, or other fruits, and walnuts, as well as fritters cooked in oil or honey and an early boiled pudding consisting of lard, brains, eggs, and cream cheese, beaten, wrapped in fig leaves, and boiled in chicken broth and then in honey. Certain recipes came to be associated with special affairs, such as theatrical events, or with the observance of religious festivals. For some early Greek festivals, cakes and pastries were made in the shape of male or female genitals, or into the shape of the breasts of Aphrodite; this was not at all considered indecent. In the upper echelons of Greek society, desserts and pastries came to represent and epitomize the pleasure and abundance of life. The Greeks embellished their food, particularly pastries, to an unprecedented level of sophistication.

The Roman Empire

In 170 B.C. there was a large influx of skilled Greek bakers into Rome who produced much better bread than the slaves. These commercial bakers, who were employed by the nobility and the emperor, became the first-known professional cooks. Average Roman families still ground their own flour and baked their own bread. Breakfast may have included an unleavened bread-cake cooked on cinders and dipped in milk or honey. The Greek idea of traditional specialty cakes and pastries caught on in Rome. For example, in celebration of a person's fiftieth birthday—a rare occasion in this period—a cake consisting of honey, wheat flour, grated cheese, and olive oil was served and enjoyed with wine sweetened with honey. Another Roman confection, this one of distinctly Arabian origin, was a flaky pastry made by stretching individual sheets of dough (perhaps a distant cousin of phyllo) and filling them with cheese and honey.

Before the days of the Roman elite's famed, lavish feasts, cooks were slaves of the lowest price, but they slowly became more valuable and thus better compensated. Cooking, up to that time considered a lowly job, became known as high art and was heavily influenced by the food of its conquered territories. Early Roman feasts included many new tastes as trade with Asia, Persia, and the Middle East introduced apricots, peaches, plums, quinces, and raspberries to Rome's orchards, spawning the first international cuisine. The convergence of many ingredients gave rise to a culturally specific and complex cuisine. Food and dining held significant meaning beyond mere sustenance; they now related to celebration and revelry in the form of banquets and festivals.

The documentation of these new foods and methods of preparation began in this period of Roman history. The first known cookbook was made by Archestratus in the fourth century B.C. Later cookbooks written by Apicius and

Athenaeus were the authority for many centuries. This is significant for the pastry chef, as the first formulas and quantified ingredients led to increasingly better recipes and, in turn, to standards in baking.

India, Japan, China

Sugar cane was introduced to India from New Guinea in neolithic times. It is here, in India around 100 B.C., that the earliest methods for refining sugar by extracting and processing the sweet juice of sugar cane are thought to have been invented.

Sweets in ancient India were intertwined with Hinduism and the divine. For thousands of years, Hindus have offered sweet things to the gods and goddesses to please them and show their devotion. The worshipper's idea of the sacred is said to reside in the center of a sea of nectar, where the individual earthly self and the cosmic self are one. This union is compared to the taste of honey or some divine nectar. The use of sweetness in this analogy shows deep cultural and spiritual reverence for sweets in Hindu society. To Indians, sweets also meant fun and festivity, as a wide variety of traditional recipes were prepared only for specific holidays and observances.

> For thousands of years, Hindus have offered sweet things to the gods and goddesses to please them and show their devotion.

The Chinese learned the Indians' sugar refinement technique in the seventh century and began intensive sugar cane cultivation and sugar manufacturing for their own use and for trading. They also imported honey from the mountains of Tibet and sweetened some foods with a malt sugar made from germinating barley. Their most prized fruits were peaches, bananas, cherries, kumquats, loquats, lychees, citrus, quinces, persimmons, plums, and apples. They also harvested almonds, pine nuts, pistachios, and walnuts. A tenth-century Japanese text mentions a possible precursor to all frozen desserts, ice creams, and sorbets as "chips of ice mixed with fruit juice and served in a new silver bowl." During the same period of China's Tang dynasty, which influenced and promoted the arts, *mi-king,* a bread of wheat flour and honey, was invented. This nutritious, high-energy food staple was carried in the thirteenth century by Genghis Khan's horsemen across Mongolia to the Arabs, Persians, Turks, and, eventually, to pilgrims of the Holy Land.

The Arabs, in their conquest of Spain, planted citrus and almond trees from their native Persia. These foods became commercial crops, supporting Roman and, eventually, European tastes for common Middle Eastern sweets such as marzipan (sweet almond paste) and nougat (egg white, honey, and nut candy). Passed down through the ages from mother to daughter, many early Middle Eastern

Black mission figs

confections from a thousand years ago remain unchanged. One such confection is *ghorayebah* (lover's pastry, named for its heart shape), made of nutmeat-filled dates sprinkled with salt and candied in honey. Although it originated in Syria, it can be found in Morrocco, Tunisia, and Iran. Perhaps the most famous of these handed-down confections is *baklava,* traditionally consisting of forty layers of pastry. Mentioned in Armenian folklore writings of the tenth through twelfth centuries, baklava spread throughout the Arab world and the Balkans during Ottoman rule.

The cuisine of the Arab world, like most cuisines, is based on regional and local specialties. The mountainous north is known for sweets made with honey, fresh and dried fruits, almonds, and walnuts. The south is known for its dates as well as milk-based puddings. The west, from southern Turkey to northern Egypt, is famous for its fine pastries, which incorporate local products like pistachios, pine nuts, sesame seeds, and fruits. In the east, rice with spices such as saffron, cardamom, and dried fruits, are prevalent. To this day, the influence of these recipes and ingredients appears in European and, consequently, the world's desserts, pastries, and confections in the form of crispy, flaky breakfast pastry and delicious ground nut fillings. Mark Miller, chef/owner of Coyote Cafe and Red Sage restaurants, believes there is much to be learned from studying Middle Eastern and Indian desserts. "A lot of our desserts are not aromatic or spicy enough. People think they can just add ancho chile or black pepper to something, but that's not it. There's a whole tradition to explore." Including ethnic techniques and flavors in the desserts pastry chefs make can elevate them to a higher level. Pursuing these cuisines can also increase a chef's marketability and open doors for jobs in Indian, Asian, and Southwestern-influenced restaurants.

Religious Crusades, Middle Ages, Europe

The Crusades were undertaken by the Christians of Europe during the eleventh through thirteenth centuries to wrest the Holy Lands from the Muslims. In their travels and warfare, a clash of cultures, traditions, customs, and food ensued and many Crusaders returned home to Europe with exotic new foods and notions of diet.

Frumenty

A simple porridge or gruel, Frumenty was a staple of the European diet in the Middle Ages. First mentioned as a dessert in one of the earliest known cookbooks, Le Menagier de Paris, *from the fourteenth century, Frumenty consisted of cracked wheat cooked in milk in which almonds had been boiled. It was then sweetened, spiced, and served warm or cold during winter.*

Yield: 6 servings

1¼ cups cracked wheat (bulghur)

3 cups water

4 cups milk

1 cup raw almonds

½ teaspoon salt

½ cup honey

1 pinch saffron strands, lightly toasted (or 8 whole cloves)

2 tablespoons butter, or ½ cup cream whipped with 2 teaspoons sugar

1. Combine the cracked wheat and water in a saucepot and bring to a boil over medium heat. Turn off the heat and let sit for ½ hour or until all the water is absorbed.
2. In a separate pot, combine the milk, almonds, salt, honey, and saffron and bring to a boil over medium heat. Turn the heat down and simmer the mixture for 5 minutes. Strain the mixture into the cracked wheat, removing the almonds and whole cloves (if used).
3. Place the pot of cracked wheat mixture over medium heat and stir for 1 minute. Serve in bowls with butter or slightly sweetened whipped cream.

Simple spiced breads, biscuits, and hardtack were food ideas imported from the Middle East that were embraced throughout medieval Europe, becoming popular among the nobility and more prosperous peasants. Over time, successive generations altered hardtack, biscuit, bread, and cake recipes to incorporate new imported or traded ingredients that were suddenly available to them—particularly fruits, such as dates or raisins, spices, local nuts, and dairy products, such as butter or cheese.

Dried Fruit and Nut Scones

by Nancy Silverton

Yield: 12 scones

1 cup (5½ ounces) whole raw almonds, skins on

½ cup plus 6 tablespoons unbleached pastry flour

¾ cup whole wheat flour

1 teaspoon baking powder

¾ teaspoon baking soda

¼ teaspoon kosher salt

¼ cup plus 2 tablespoons granulated sugar, plus extra for sprinkling

1¼ cups rolled oats

5 ounces unsalted butter, cold and cut into ½-inch cubes

2 teaspoons orange zest (from 1 orange)

½ cup currants

1 cup yellow raisins, coarsely chopped

1 cup dried cherries, coarsely chopped

½ cup flax seeds

½ cup buttermilk

Confectioners' sugar for finishing

1. Preheat the oven to 325°. Spread the almonds on a baking sheet and toast in the oven until browned, 10 to 12 minutes. Coarse chop the nuts and set aside.

2. Turn the oven up to 350°. In a mixing bowl fitted with the paddle attachment or in a food processor, combine the flours, baking powder, baking soda, salt, sugar, and oats and mix on low or process until incorporated.

3. Add the butter to the bowl or food processor and mix on low, pulse until the mixture is pale yellow and the consistency of a fine meal.

4. Transfer the mixture to a large mixing bowl and add the almonds, zest, currants, raisins, cherries, and flax seeds and mix by hand, tossing and turning the ingredients together. Mix just until combined.

5. Make a large well in the center of the mixture and pour in the buttermilk. Draw in the dry ingredients by hand, mixing just until combined.

6. Turn the dough out onto a lightly floured work surface and gently knead it to gather it into a ball. With a rolling pin or by hand, press the dough into an 11-inch circle.

7. Cut the circle in half, then cut each half into 6 pie shaped wedges. Place them at least 1 inch apart on a parchment-lined or stickless baking sheet. Brush the tops with water and sprinkle lightly with the extra sugar. Bake for 35 to 40 minutes until firm and well-browned.

8. When scones are cooled, sift a light layer of confectioners' sugar over the top.

In the Middle Ages in Europe (marked from the fall of the Roman Empire in the fifth century to the fifteenth or sixteenth centuries), the development and expansion of food and cooking knowledge suffered a disastrous setback at the hands of the church and ruling classes when centuries of Roman and Greek writings were kept as sole property of the scholarly church-run universities, the monasteries, and the castles. The freewheeling pleasures known in the Roman and Greek periods were viewed with suspicion, fear, and condemnation. The church regarded earthly pleasure as sin and the nobility felt their power could become threatened by a population given to self-gratification. These factors, in addition to increasing class differences, contributed to the great rift between the foods and cooking techniques used by the commoners and those reserved for the nobility.

The invention of spice bread *(pain d' épices),* one of the earliest of the more complex confections, is credited to a pastry cook of Bourges, France, who made it to honor King Charles VII. It was made of black rye flour, dark buckwheat honey from Brittany, and available spices of the time. As in ancient Rome, the bread bakers of France also made pastries and cakes, at least until 1440, when a loose guild called the Cooperation of Pastry Cooks broke away from the bread bakers. This early pastry cook guild began to standardize recipes. They made meat and fish pies, marzipan turnovers, cream cheese tartlets, cream darioles (puff pastry filled with almond cream), sponge cakes, biscuits, and a pear tart that had *crème pâtissière* (pastry cream) underneath the fruit. In setting themselves apart from the bread bakers, pastry cooks set the stage for the growth and refinement of their craft.

Trays of finished brownies, meringues, and cookies.

In fourteenth-century England, King Richard II invited two thousand of the country's wealthiest barons to dine with him. Two hundred cooks prepared peacock, roasted boar, oxen, venison, small birds baked in pies, and, for dessert, a marzipan castle, four feet square, three feet high, with two drawbridges, all surrounded by a moat. Even at this early stage in confectionery history, the pastry chef's creation expressed not only the festive spirit of the moment, but also, having been left to his whimsical and creative abandon, his own talents as trickster, magician, chemist, and artist.

One of the great turning points in the history of pastry and cuisine was the arrival in France of Catherine de Medici from Italy in 1533. Destined to wed the heir to the French throne, she brought with her many of her own chefs and pastry cooks who introduced *frangipane* (an almond cream invented by a member of the Frangipane family of Rome), *macaroons* (cookies made with egg whites, sugar, and almonds), and a form of flaky pastry. This pastry, probably the predecessor of puff pastry, was made with a new method of adding butter, folding, and rolling, quite different from the Roman method of stretching individual sheets of dough. These basic recipes, among many others, inform the repertoire of every pastry cook since that time.

In the sixteenth century, French nuns began selling biscuits and fritters to benefit charities. By the seventeenth century, a group of talented nuns in a Parisian convent had invented crispy puff pastries called *feuillantines*. At this time, chocolate and sugar also became available in small quantities. Although they were treated as delicacies, sugar was gradually replacing honey as a sweetener. The croissant and viennoiserie arrived in France from Austria, bringing new methods and techniques for the French pastry cook. The conflict between bread bakers and pastry cooks in France was not yet resolved. The bread bakers were still hanging on to the baking of simple traditional cakes, such as *Twelfth Night cakes*. The bakers' guild sent one to the king of France every year. This seriously offended the pastry cooks who, in the early 1700s, took the bakers' guild to court and were granted a ruling stating that "no one who was not a pastrycook might use butter, eggs and sugar in making cakes for sale." By now, the wedding cake, intricately constructed with ornate, individual candies, was the architectural masterpiece of the pastry cook's world. A decorated cake was also in vogue for the occasion of a child's christening. Regional specialties included simple cakes, seasonal fruit tarts, and custard-based desserts. Sweetened, yeast-leavened cakes came from the East, Viennese-style pastry from Austria, and the popular *kugelhopf* from Poland.

Mark Miller points out the class difference between those who could enjoy sweets and those who could not. "Desserts equaled status and people who ate foods that normally were not eaten had a higher status in society. Desserts became more popular in the Renaissance when attention turned to art, music, and cooking. Western society became more affluent through trade, and in Venice, Rome, and Paris, cuisine developed and became distinctive to particular countries and regions."

> No one who was not a pastrycook might use butter, eggs and sugar in making cakes for sale.
> —Eighteen-century French law

Restaurants, Grand Cuisine, Great Chefs

The ingredients chefs and pastry cooks use have been the same for several hundred years. With the convergence of trade, war, migration, and shared, borrowed, inherited, worked, and reworked techniques, a consensus began to emerge within certain cultures from the seventeenth century onward. Over the centuries, regional foods, passed-down cooking methods, discoveries, and inventions were distilled into recipe form. Within each culture, like a language that becomes familiar to inhabitants of a region, distinctive cuisines developed and grew.

Today, people often take for granted the idea of a restaurant. How is it possible that you can open up a directory, such as the Zagat Survey, or the Yellow Pages, and choose from an incredible array of foods and ethnic dining experiences? It is important to remember why people go out to restaurants and cafés. For all dining customers, at one point or another, it is not only the food. Certainly customers expect the food to meet or exceed their expectations. Perhaps equally as important as getting something to eat, people go out to restaurants to participate in a living theatre, to interact with others, to play at being an honored guest, a king or queen for an evening.

In the guild system of medieval France, butchers, bakers, distillers, and pastry cooks belonged to separate unions but worked together to provide food and drink at banquets and weddings. By necessity, a traiteur (caterer) often organized such occasions. Seventeenth- and eighteenth-century Paris had a large number of taverns, inns, and hotels that featured a common table, or *table d'hôte,* where travelers ate together, often in great conflict, greedily gobbling up the food intended for all. Innkeepers vying for patrons began offering increasingly better food. A reputation for good food became vital to remaining in business. In 1765, a French baker set up a business selling "restaurants" (literally, meat broths or soups) on his own premises. In the nineteenth century, cuisine flourished. The kitchens of royalty, formerly the only employer of the professional chef, began to lose some of their greatest cooks to this novel idea—the restaurant.

> Carême's talent was apparent to his master early on. He began to copy architectural drawings in the library and base pastry creations on these ideas.

One of the great French chefs of the post-Renaissance era was Marie-Antoine Carême. Born in 1783, he was put out in the street at the age of 10 and taken in by the owner of a lower-class restaurant, where he began to learn about cooking. At 16 he became apprenticed to one of the best pastry cooks in Paris. Carême's talent was apparent to his master early on. He began to copy architectural drawings in the library and base pastry creations on these ideas. In his fifty years, Carême worked for princes, kings, a tsar of Russia, the Viennese court, and the British embassy, among other noble positions. He recognized the need for ceremony and entertainment of his elite clientele and he dazzled them with elaborate constructions, garnishes, and decorations, as well as refined recipes.

Carême was concerned with every area of cooking. He designed kitchen equipment and elements of the chef's uniform. He invented saucepans and molds, as well as many formulas and techniques that are still in use today. He was a prolific writer, took notes constantly, and created four books; the last, *L'art de la cuisine*, was published in five volumes. Carême made considerable contributions to cuisine and the credibility of chefs by combining his multiple talents as visionary, artist, and designer, his work ethic, his sense of style, and his flamboyant presentation.

To understand the role of dessert in today's menus, it is important to understand the historical development of dining and menu design. The menu and style of service touted and refined by Carême was to create an impression of luxury and abundance by serving numerous dishes simultaneously. This idea comes from the traditions of the medieval banquet, which were often displays in overabundance and downright gluttony. Many dishes were brought at once, feasted upon, and cleared, and yet another display of extravagantly garnished creations arrived. This style of three or four changes of the dishes constituted the courses of the meal and was called *à la française*.

In the early nineteenth century, these courses became grouped in an increasingly logical order. The first courses consisted of appetizer and main courses, during which four different soups and lighter dishes such as fish were served. While these were being consumed, platters of salted and cured meats or hot dishes of kidneys and liver were offered. These were considered extras and rather than being placed on the table, were passed around much like *hors d'oeuvre*. Main courses were grandiose presentations of game birds, poultry, large roasts on the bone, salads, and elaborate vegetable garnishes. Next came an assortment of cold meats, more vegetables, aspics, shellfish, egg dishes, cakes, and other dessert items known as *entrements,* or "between courses," which spanned a broad spectrum of items both savory and sweet. At this time, what we consider dessert was offered alongside the savory items—lobster au gratin, pineapple cream, liqueur-flavored jelly, oysters, scrambled eggs with truffles, genoise cakes with coffee filling, and potato or chocolate soufflés. Accompanying these dishes, at the most lavish dinners, were numerous majestic pastry centerpieces made of sugar paste—for example, models of great palaces or Turkish mosques, decorated at their bases with such edibles as cheese brioches, nougat, and biscuits. Pastries, ices, coupes, and bombes were eventually served last and became increasingly separate from the *entrements.*

Pouding de Cabinet
(Raisin Pudding)

by Marie-Antoine Carême (1833)

The English word pudding comes from the French pouding, of the same meaning.
This dessert, which today would be considered a type of bread pudding,
reflects Carême's sense of the elaborate, as it is constructed layer by layer
rather than just being mixed together.

Yield: 6 servings

2 cups milk

1 vanilla bean, split and scraped

1 cup sugar

2 whole eggs

5 egg yolks

1 tablespoon flour

¼ cup dried currants

¼ cup sultanas (golden raisins)

¼ cup dark raisins

1 large lemon (peeled with a potato peeler)

2 cups water

¾ cup sugar

1 tablespoon vanilla-flavored sugar

⅓ cup brandy

One 1-pound loaf of brioche or egg bread

1. Place the milk and vanilla bean pod and scrapings in a saucepot over medium heat. Bring to a boil while stirring with a wooden spoon.

2. Add ⅔ cup of the sugar; stir until dissolved. Remove the pot from the heat and remove the vanilla bean pod.

3. In a bowl, beat the eggs and yolks. Gradually stir in the the sweetened, aromatized milk. (Do not beat; this causes foaming, which creates an unpleasant spongy texture.)

4. Preheat the oven to 425°. Place the flour in a bowl with the currants, sultanas,

and raisins. With the hands, roll the raisins and currants in the flour until coated.

5. Julienne the lemon peel into ¹⁄₁₆-inch-wide strips. Over medium heat, bring the water and the lemon zest to a boil, reduce heat to low, and simmer the mixture for 14 to 16 minutes. Add the sugar and continue to simmer for 18 to 20 minutes, or until zest is translucent; strain the zest from the syrup. Add the lemon zest, remaining sugar, flavored sugar, and brandy to the bowl of currants, sultanas, and raisins.

6. Cut the brioche to fit a single cake mold (8 inches × 4 inches × 4 inches) or individual timbale molds. Brush the mold with melted butter and place a piece of fitted brioche into the bottom of the mold. Spread a layer of raisins over the brioche, then top with another slice of brioche. Continue to alternately layer the raisins and brioche until all is used up.

7. Pour three quarters of the cream mixture over the layers and let sit for 10 minutes while the brioche soaks up the mixture.

8. Place the mold in a larger pan with a water bath and bake for 40 minutes.

9. Heat the remaining cream mixture over medium heat, continually stirring, to a point just before boiling. Mixture will be thickened. Cool the cream.

10. Unmold the pudding and serve with cream.

Service *à la francaise,* though opulent in some ways, was also awkward for the guest. As this style of fine dining moved from palaces to the homes of nobility, it became even more cumbersome. Entertaining became a competitive endeavor and homes of the wealthy were staffed with butlers, stewards, and less experienced servants who needed training to execute properly a twenty-five- or thirty-dish meal for eighteen people.

In this style of service, the soup was removed and the next side courses presented. The guests helped themselves to the dish closest to them and offered some to the person beside them. If they wanted something different, they had to cross the table or send their server for it. When servers tried to offer dishes to everyone, confusion ensued and guests were offered the same thing more than once. Even the best-trained staff could not prevent such problems. Refinement was necessary.

After Carême's death in 1833, there was a movement toward simpler, less opulent decoration. In Russia, Carême had come across a style of service that eventually replaced *à la francaise.* In service *à la russe,* which survives to this day, courses are served consecutively rather than all at once. This approach did not appeal to Carême's sense of spectacle. He admitted its merits but did not let go of his belief in the importance of dramatic presentation. "This manner of service is certainly beneficial to good cooking," he said, "but our service in France is much more elegant and of a far grander and more sumptuous style." But progress demanded something simpler. The advantages of service *à la russe* were at once obvious. Food could be served and enjoyed at its best, right from the pans and grills of the kitchen. This not only simplified service but also greatly reduced waste. It became the tenet embraced 165 years later by chefs cooking *à la minute.*

Enter Auguste Escoffier (1846–1935), whose achievements in the annals of cuisine are legendary. He is credited for advancing the concept of "menu" to the orderly list of offerings we know today. Escoffier's innovative menu planning perfected the idea of one course or dish at a time. By the 1870s, service *à la russe* was considered the norm, and the number of dishes served in a single meal was drastically reduced, enabling Escoffier to concentrate on individual dishes. Escoffier documented his principles for a well-planned meal in 1912, and his advice can be followed and embraced by any successful chef today. "[The menu] should be appropriate to the occasion and to the guests. The season should always be borne in mind. If the time is limited, the menu should be as well, and in any case an exorbitant number of courses should be avoided."

Escoffier saw simpler as better, and he proposed that the simplification of cuisine was development and not regression in the discipline of cooking. Escoffier's belief still has relevance for today's chefs. "What already existed in the time of Carême, which still exists in our time, and which will continue as long as cooking itself, is the foundations of that cooking," he said. "Because it is simplified on the surface, it does not lose its value. On the contrary, tastes are constantly being refined and cooking is refined to satisfy them."

Escoffier did away with elaborate garnishes and instead embellished dishes with simply cooked vegetables and a sprinkling of parsley. He championed the idea that everything on the plate be edible. He thought food should look like food and not necessarily be sculpted or in any way made to look like something else. At the time, these ideas were revolutionary in upscale fine dining. Escoffier believed in high-quality ingredients and avoided numerous competing flavors in one dish, aiming instead for balance. He abhorred the swearing and brutality of the kitchen he experienced as a young apprentice and determined to change the stereotype of the loud-mouthed chef. He was the original proponent of calm in the kitchen and believed that brutality had no place in the well-run kitchen. His professionalism, brilliance, and grace changed the way the public perceived the chef.

Escoffier's influence behind the scenes was a more rational and intellectual approach than the cooking world had ever known. His practical, simple style of presentation was a drastic improvement over the highly decorative, multi-ingredient dishes of the time. He revolutionized the way kitchens were organized, the first reordering since medieval times. Before Escoffier, the kitchen had several sections made up of several cooks; each section produced all the items needed for its particular dishes, so basic preparations were duplicated throughout. Sauces and pastry items, for example, were made several times over. This production process made quality difficult to control. Escoffier separated the kitchen into designated areas, each one responsible for different items and interdependent with the others. Thus the pâtissier produced the basic pastry preparations needed by the other stations. The garde manger area prepared the cold dishes. Another section made soups, vegetables, and desserts—still another, roasted, broiled, and fried items. The saucier, second in command under the chef, produced all stocks and finished sauces. This system expedited the production of dishes and made it easier for the chef to see the process and the finished product.

> Escoffier separated the kitchen into designated areas, each one responsible for different items and interdependent with the others. Thus the pâtissier produced the basic pastry preparations needed by the other stations.

At age 34, Escoffier met Cesar Ritz and began a legendary partnership heading up the kitchens of the great Ritz hotels in Monte Carlo and Lucerne, Switzerland. Between 1880 and 1919, Escoffier presided over the kitchens of all the luxurious Ritz hotels. The king of chefs and the chef of kings cooked for vacationing royalty and the wealthiest chic of his day and left a remarkable culinary legacy that persists through the livelihood of all chefs, pastry chefs, restaurants, and the heart of cuisine's great past and future.

Peach Melba

by Auguste Escoffier

It was after a performance by the opera singer Nellie Melba in 1890s London that Escoffier invented and dedicated to her the first version of this famous dessert. The early rendition was composed of poached peaches on vanilla ice cream set in an ice carving of a swan. Years later, Escoffier added the crowning touch of puréed raspberries and served it in a glass.

Yield: 6 servings

6 ripe freestone peaches

1 lemon, cut in half

Sugar for sprinkling

4 cups fresh raspberries

½ cup confectioners' sugar

1½ pints vanilla ice cream

1. Pour boiling water over the peaches. Let stand for 30 seconds, then transfer the peaches to a bowl of ice water. The skin should loosen. Peel the skin from the peaches and immediately rub the peaches with cut lemon and sprinkle with the sugar to prevent browning.

2. Purée the raspberries in a blender with ¼ cup confectioners' sugar, adding more to taste. The purée should be fairly tart. Strain out the seeds and chill the purée. Chill 6 coupe glasses.

3. To serve, scoop vanilla ice cream into each coupe glass. Settle a peach into the ice cream. Spoon the raspberry purée over the peaches. Serve at once.

Gaston Lenôtre is one of the most famous and influential French pastry chefs of the latter half of the twentieth century. Markus Färbinger was a fan of Lenôtre from an early age. "Lenôtre was an inspiration to me when I got my first foreign book," Färbinger says. "Even back then, he had his own farm where he got his dairy products. He really inspired the last grand revolution of pastry. Over the

THE MAKING *of a* PASTRY CHEF

years, I have been able to appreciate what he did. He was so strong in getting the word out, in publishing, writing and documenting recipes, making volumes of books, and organizing things. It's not enough to make your pastries in your little shop and get your recognition and do your thing; it's bigger than that and that's how Lenôtre inspires me."

America's Food Scene— Past and Recent History

To trace the roots of American food and the history of our dessert traditions, it's fitting to look at the food traditions of England and other European countries, as early settlers and immigrants brought with them their recipes and familial cooking customs. These customs were influenced by the New World's original inhabitants, Native Americans. In England, as in many countries, domestic recipe writing and preservation was achieved exclusively by women. Hannah Glasse (1708–1770) wrote the most successful English cookbook of the eighteenth century, *The Art of Cookery Made Plain and Easy*. In the following recipe, it is interesting to note that over 250 years ago, Hannah Glasse found that certain herbs usually reserved for savory foods are wonderful in desserts.

Peaches

Sherry Yard of Spago Beverly Hills notes that very little is new in pastry innovation: "We think we are so brilliant when we come up with something we think no one has done before, and then we go back and read a book from the 1700s and find that someone has already put chamomile in an ice cream. We discover that we are really not so innovative because so many things have already been done, so I think that the history of cooking is very important to us today."

When we look at the wisdom of history, we find familiar patterns. Roland Mesnier, White House pastry chef, reminds us, "You have to realize that we create nothing new. All the things you think of as new, they're as old as can be. They were done many years ago. There's absolutely nothing new in our business, nothing at all. It's just turning in circles."

While she feels certain flavor combinations may be new, Lindsey Shere doesn't think that much is new under the sun. "There's no point in reinventing the wheel. You may think that you're doing something new, but often you're not. Someone has probably already thought about it."

Chocolate Rosemary Cream

by Hannah Glasse (1741)

Although this recipe is from 1741, it could be from the latest issue of Art Culinaire. *Here we find, as Hannah Glasse did, that chocolate and aromatic rosemary go surprisingly well together.*

Yield: 6 servings

¾ cup sugar

1 cup sweet white wine (such as muscat)

1 lemon, juiced

2 cups heavy cream

One 6-inch sprig of rosemary

4 ounces bittersweet chocolate, grated

1. In a thick-bottomed saucepan over medium heat, stir together the sugar, wine, and lemon juice until sugar dissolves. Add the cream and rosemary sprig and, while stirring, bring mixture to a simmer. Reduce heat to low.

2. Add the chocolate and cook, while stirring, for 5 minutes or until it has the consistency of thick cream.

3. Strain the mixture and pour into individual ramekins or small cups. Chill and serve.

The early colonists' reliance on England for food imports gradually faded, giving way to native food such as corn, local fish, and game. Hoecakes, or simple cornbreads, were made by cooking batter over an open fire on the blade of a hoe.

Other early bread items of young America include corn pones, corn sticks, johnnycakes, and hushpuppies. Mark Miller reminded me of some important points with regard to our dessert history: "Americans didn't really eat desserts in colonial America. They didn't have refined cane sugar, they had maple sugar which they learned about from Native Americans and then molasses later on with the rum trade. It was also a puritanical thing; it wasn't part of their life to eat things that were sensual or delightful. Food was there to nurture the soul and body and desserts were not seen as nurturing, they were seen as sinful."

America's food includes the traditions of many cultures. Generations of immigrants brought with them foods and familial traditions from France, Italy, Ireland, The Netherlands, Germany, Eastern Europe, Africa, Asia, and Central and South America. Markus Färbinger makes an important distinction between the origins of European and American pastry and baking traditions: "In the United States, [baking] is a profession that came out of domestic help, while in Europe, it has always been part of guilds and crafts that are deeply rooted in many centuries past."

Affluent Americans have long been heavily influenced by Parisian cooking. Thomas Jefferson was a connoisseur of fine wine from Bordeaux. As Minister to France, he traveled through southern France and Italy taking notes on the crops and agriculture of the area, which included olives, almonds, pistachios, walnuts, figs, strawberries, and pomegranates. He was so interested in raising the American awareness about food that he returned to the United States with extensive writings on Italian and French wine, a rice-husking machine, and tools for making pasta.

Jefferson raised many experimental vegetable crops, which he brought back from his European travels, both at his home in Monticello, Virginia, and at the White House. For making elegant desserts at the White House, he imported a *sorbetière*, an ice pail with a hand crank, using ice and salt.

Because of French settlement, New Orleans became known for its French-trained cooks, but dishes that were classically French in origin took on an inescapably American style. These dishes and their influence spread and became evident in the repertoire of cooks in other parts of America.

The first cookbook to be published by an American was *An American Orphan* by Amelia Simmons in 1796. It went through four revisions, contained Native American specialties such as spruce beer, Indian pudding (made with cornmeal), pumpkin pie, gingerbread, and rice pudding.

The expansion into the frontier of the American West made for tough times for the average settler, and dessert was all but absent for most. Miller, who looks to the West for inspiration for his great American restaurant Red Sage, comments, "Obviously they didn't have ingredients available. People were poor, and they also came as immigrants from culinary backgrounds where they didn't have any knowledge of desserts. Desserts were not commonplace in the expansion of the West in the nineteenth century. My mother, who was born in 1924, remembers as a child that people got apples at Christmastime."

By the early to mid 1800s, hotels and inns were popular tourist destinations and cooking was necessary, professionally and competitively. In 1831, the famous Delmonico's Restaurant was opened in New York City by a French-speaking Swiss family. They offered the first American menu, which they printed in French with corresponding English translations. Delmonico's food was essentially continental, based on different dishes from around Europe and the world, and it continued to popularize the French influence on American food.

Apple Fritters

by Alexander Filippini,
chef of Delmonico's (1906)

This recipe from Filippini's book of 3,300 is reproduced the way it was
written. Note the loose, inexact style of the writing. Ingredients and amounts
are written in the body of the recipe, not in a list at the beginning,
and old measurements such as gill and saltspoon are used.

Yield: 4 servings

Batter for fritters:

Place half pound sifted flour in a large bowl. Add two tablespoons olive oil, half teaspoon salt, one tablespoon powdered sugar, three egg yolks, half gill cold water, and a gill cold milk, also a teaspoon vanilla essence. Briskly stir with a wooden spoon for five minutes. Just before serving, beat the white of the three eggs. Add to the batter and gently mix for one minute. It will then be ready for use. (The same quanity of butter can be substituted for oil if preferred.)

Rum sauce:

Place in a very small, clean saucepan a quarter pint of cold water, two ounces of fine sugar, the rind of one sound lemon, three tablespoons good Jamaican rum, one teaspoon cognac, one teaspoon good butter, four drops vanilla essence, and a very small piece of cinnamon. Mix well, then let it come to the simmering point. Thicken the same with a saltspoon of arrowroot. Gently mix while allowing to simmer for one minute and a half. Remove the lemon rind and cinnamon. Set aside.

For the finished dish:

Peel and core three good-size, sound apples. Cut each apple in four even slices. Lay them on a plate. Dredge a tablespoon of fine sugar over. Pour in two tablespoons of rum then repeatedly turn the apple slices in the seasoning and let infuse for one half hour, turning them in the rum once in a while. Dip the slices of apple in the frying batter, then gently drop them one by one into boiling fat and fry for eight minutes, frequently turning with a skimmer. Take them up, and let drain on a wire grater. Neatly trim them all around. Pour rum sauce on a hot dish. Arrange the fritters over the sauce, one overlapping another. Sprinkle a little powdered sugar over and serve.

Although Delmonico's was associated with excellence, as many of its chefs went on to establish grand cuisine in far-flung hotels in other great American cities, it also represented a decline in the importance of continental cuisine and the quality of food it came to represent, with some of their more unsophisticated dishes in chafing dishes, perhaps on the cook's night off.

In the great hotels and haute cuisine restaurants of the nineteenth century, even through the 1970s, the predominant grand, flamboyant presentation of dessert was fulfilled by the pastry cart and the dessert tray. The pastry cart was wheeled tableside and diners chose from perhaps a dozen or more tortes, cakes, tarts, puddings, poached and candied fruits. The waitperson sliced off the customer's selection, maybe poured a sauce on the plate, and presented the dessert.

Pastry tray presentation was executed in one of two ways. Desserts were prepared on plates, filling each tray, and the customer's choice was taken directly from the tray. Alternatively, the trays were decorated with miniature versions of each dessert being offered. Occasionally, if an ice cream were served with a dessert, it was imitated with a nonmelting facsimile. After the selection was made, the tray was returned to the kitchen and the real desserts assembled and served. Though some restaurants still exhibit desserts in this fashion, feeling that the immediacy of desserts on trays creates more sales, the quality and freshness of the dessert often

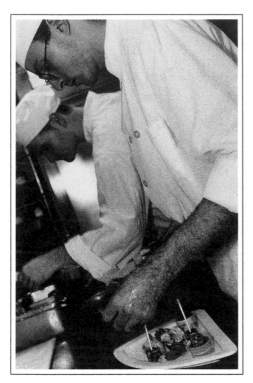

*Dessert service at
Park Avenue Café*

suffers. Richard Leach of Park Avenue Café was inspired by the switch from the pastry cart to plated desserts. "I've done a little tray work, but it's nice to see dessert treated as another course instead of as a big display all the time." The demise of the pastry cart method of presentation increased the potential and credibility of pastry chefs in the United States, not only making them more important than ever before to restaurants but also establishing them as masters of their own course in the guest's experience of a meal. A pastry chef can now create a dessert menu containing hot and cold combinations and much more complicated and interesting desserts.

America's Cuisine Awakens

Fannie Merritt Farmer is an important figure in American cookery, particularly baking, of the late nineteenth and early twentieth centuries. She promoted good food and cooking for all Americans. "Cookery," she said, "is the art of preparing food for the nourishment of the body." But she also saw its connection to something greater when she said, "Progress in civilization has been accompanied by progress in cookery." Farmer brought cooking and baking to millions of Americans by removing the guesswork and standardizing measurements into cups, tablespoons, and teaspoons. She also eliminated the haphazard language in recipes of the period, such as "heaping" and "lump of butter the size of an egg." Farmer authored *The Boston Cooking School Cookbook* in 1896; it subsequently sold three million copies. Her fame at the time was unparalleled. Her demonstrations and lectures attracted two hundred people twice a week and, in one year, she lectured in over thirty cities, even as far away from her native Boston as California.

At this time, cooking on a wood- or coal-fired range became more commonplace than the colonial method of cooking in the fireplace. Testing the heat level of the oven was done by holding a hand inside until the heat forced one to pull it out: 20–30 seconds for a "quick" oven, 45–60 seconds for a "slow" one. Fruits and vegetables began to arrive in American cities by train, and the domestic refrigerator, or icebox, became common. Classic American home baking and cooking products were on the horizon as well, such as Knox Gelatin, Quaker Oats, and Baker's Chocolate, making desserts at home more popular than ever.

Chocolate Fudge

by Fannie Farmer (1896)

Chocolate fudge is a favorite homemade American confection popularized by Fannie Farmer.

Yield: One 8-inch-square pan

5 tablespoons butter

1 cup milk

3 cups sugar

10 tablespoons cocoa powder

or 4 ounces (4 squares) unsweetened chocolate, chopped

2 teaspoons vanilla

1. Melt 4 tablespoons of the butter in a large saucepan over medium heat. Add the milk and sugar. Cook, stirring, until the sugar dissolves. Rub an 8-inch-square pan with the remaining butter.

2. Add the cocoa and reduce heat to low; continue stirring. Bring to a boil and boil steadily for 12 minutes, stirring occasionally.

3. Remove from the heat and add the vanilla. Beat the fudge for 1 to 2 minutes or until the mixture loses its shine and begins to stiffen. (Do not overbeat or the fudge will harden.) Pour at once into the prepared pan and leave to cool. Cut into 1¼-inch squares and serve.

The single most important transformation in the way Americans ate in fine restaurants and the way chefs approached food was brought about by a handful of chefs in the early to mid-1970s. Before this time, America's dining scene consisted of ethnic restaurants, continental cuisine or steak and seafood restaurants, and proliferating fast food. On an international level, American restaurants, and certainly American chefs, were not highly regarded. America was lucky to have celebrity chef personalities like Julia Child and James Beard promoting good food and cooking, but when they became famous in the 1940s and through the next two decades, for many Americans, what they did was some complex novelty that was more about entertainment than food. The average American had little experience with the culture of food.

Plums

In one 1950s-era episode of *I Love Lucy,* Lucy is in a Chinese restaurant desperately trying but unable to use chopsticks while she tries to hide her inability from the other diners. That was funny then because most Americans had never used chopsticks. It's not as funny now, in an age when local supermarkets carry wasabi (Japanese horseradish), tofu, lotus root, different grades of miso (fermented grain paste) and wakame (seaweed), and delis supply hand-rolled sushi. In the early 1970s, the reputation of American chefs began to improve with the opening of Chez Panisse. Chef Alice Waters and her employees, including chefs Jeremiah Tower and Mark Miller, were highly influenced by the writings of earlier chefs Richard Olney, James Beard, and Julia Child, but the cooks at Chez Panisse didn't do anything complex with respect to cooking techniques or methods. Instead, Alice Waters and her team at Chez Panisse borrowed from the French Nouvelle approach of regionalism, using impeccably fresh, locally obtained organic produce, meat, fish, and game. They prepared food with reduced cooking times to retain flavors. Local, small growers harvested and delivered baby lettuces and other vegetables and fruits that were prepared and served the very same day. These simple ideas were unheard of in this country at a time when frozen vegetables and processed foods were promoted as the sustenance of the future.

Strongly rooted in classical French cooking methods, the curriculum at The Culinary Institute of America and other respected schools began to evolve, in the late 1970s and early 1980s, to include this new vantage point, which respected both seasonal and regional ingredients. A new sense of pride and reverence developed for the bounty of regional ingredients available to American chefs. American regional cuisine had arrived.

Miller points to a time when attitudes toward dessert in this country were changing. "The idea of candy being readily available was not around even in the twenties," he says, "and then came the Depression. The whole idea of sweets, candy, and desserts in the diet is really a post–World War II phenomenon. Candy was around on special occasions, like cotton candy at the fair, or candy apples. These may have been the only times of year people actually saw candy."

Nick Malgieri, director of the baking program at Peter Kump's New York Cooking School, credits a better-educated, more sophisticated, and well-traveled population for the dessert boom: "There was a gradual expansion from World Wars I and II onward, when the first soldiers went to Europe and discovered different types of food. They were ready for food that wasn't just well-done meat and iceberg lettuce. Also, people were interested in hand-crafted foods produced in small quantities and the back-to-the-farm movement. Because of this general interest in food, once Americans started thinking about how to improve food quality, baking and pastry became part of the puzzle. I don't think it's a separate revolution, although pastry and dessert-making have gained a little momentum in the past five to ten years. Lately we have been hearing a lot more about pastry chefs and what it means to be a pastry chef. Journalists have suddenly discovered that there are pastry chefs, which I think they really didn't care about before."

Park Avenue Café's "Opera in the Park"

Michael Schneider, editor-in-chief of *Chocolatier* and *Pastry Art and Design* magazines, looks back a short time to the days when desserts and, therefore, pastry chefs were first becoming noticed. "The day that the concept of dessert went from being a single taste sensation to a multisensory experience where the visual plays a tremendous part was the beginning of the realization that dessert is not just simple food—it's entertainment. Up until that time, I saw chocolate as food. Now I look at it as an emotion. No doctor ever said, 'You need more dessert in your diet.' You have it because it's an indulgence, because you wish to feel good, because you feel it's deserved and there's a certain emotion inside of you that finds it hard to resist. In the old days a great compliment was, 'It tastes homemade.' Today most pastry chefs are not looking for their signature desserts to be described as 'good as homemade' because they hope to be beyond that level. The taste of desserts is always paramount, but when the quality level and entertainment value supersedes taste alone, it can no longer be avoided by food critics. I think magazines and books like mine have given desserts more of an identity. Therefore, what you have is a natural extension of the media picking up on it. Go back fifteen years and read reviews in the *New York Times* and see how little space was devoted to desserts. Today it is completely different."

> No doctor ever said, "You need more dessert in your diet." You have it because it's an indulgence, because you wish to feel good, because you feel it's deserved and there's a certain emotion inside of you that finds it hard to resist.
> —Michael Schneider

Pear Financier with Hazelnut Praline Ice Cream

by Sebastien Canonne

Yield: 6 servings

For the poached pears:

6 Bosc pears, peeled

1 quart white wine

1 quart water

3½ cups water

2 bay leaves

1 branch rosemary (6 inches long)

1 branch thyme

5 black peppercorns

1 cinnamon stick

1 vanilla bean

2 lemons

For the financier:

½ cup butter

¾ cup finely ground almonds

1½ cup confectioners' sugar

½ cup cake flour

10 egg whites

1 cup applesauce

For the hazelnut praline ice cream:

1 cup sugar

1½ cup toasted hazelnuts

1 teaspoon vegetable oil

4 cups milk

1 cup cream

10 egg yolks

½ cup sugar

For the poached pears:

1. In a large saucepot over medium heat, combine all of the ingredients and bring to a boil.

2. Turn heat to low and simmer the pears until they are easily pierced with the tip of a knife. Turn off the heat and set aside to cool.

For the financier:

1. In a saucepot over medium heat, cook the butter until it browns and begins to emit a nutty scent. Turn off the heat and allow it to cool.

2. In a large bowl, stir together the almonds, the sugar, and the flour.

Continued on next page

3. Add the egg whites and applesauce and whisk in the still-warm browned butter. Cool the batter in the refrigerator.

For the hazelnut praline ice cream:

1. Caramelize the 1 cup of sugar in a thick-bottomed saucepot over medium heat, stirring occasionally to melt the sugar to an amber color.

2. Stir in the hazelnuts and pour the mixture onto a sheet tray that has been lightly rubbed with vegetable oil, and allow to cool thoroughly, about 20 minutes.

3. Pulverize the nut and sugar mixture in a food processor until finely ground.

4. In a saucepot over medium heat, heat the milk and cream to scalding.

5. Whisk the egg yolks in a large bowl and whisk in the ½ cup sugar.

6. Temper one-third of the hot milk mixture into the yolks while stirring, then return this to the main milk mixture.

7. Stir constantly over medium heat until thickened enough to coat the back of the spoon. Do not boil.

8. Whisk in the pulverized nut and sugar mixture and cool.

9. Spin in an ice cream machine. Store in the freezer until use.

Final assembly:

1. Preheat the oven to 375°. Halve and core the pears. In a large ramekin or other ceramic dish, place a pear half core side down and lean another half upright against that one.

2. Put the financier batter in a piping bag equipped with a ½-inch plain tip. Pipe the batter around the pear halves in the ramekin.

3. If desired, garnish each dessert with a sprig of thyme, rosemary, cinnamon stick, or vanilla bean.

4. Bake the desserts for 10 to 12 minutes.

5. Sprinkle with confectioners' sugar. Place 1 scoop of ice cream next to the pear halves on each dessert. Place each dish on a plate with a folded napkin and serve.

Mark Miller delineates pivotal times in America's collective cultural perception of dessert. "Prior to 1970, desserts were in two catagories: American home desserts and European-style restaurant desserts, meaning French or Viennese style. By the 1970s, most people weren't cooking dessert in their homes anymore. They had some memories of what their grandmothers made, but their mothers were all part of the workforce. Homemade dessert was lost. Then with James Beard and the advent of American regional food, people like Larry Forgione (of the Coach House in New York City) brought back things like shortcake. That was the first time someone said that American home desserts could be served in a restaurant. It was a major change."

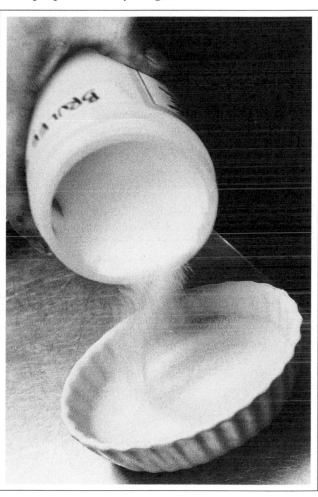

The impact of upscaling traditional American home-style desserts for restaurants created a new range of acceptable desserts for pastry chefs to serve. No longer was it acceptable to serve only French classical desserts, such as tarte tatin or napoleon, but now there were new and creative ways to incorporate American desserts, such as apple pie or peach cobbler, in an upscale restaurant's menu. This is a valid and growing style of dessert making to this day.

Lindsey Shere reflects on her early days as pastry chef at Chez Panisse. "We were home cooks. I had cooked and baked all my life and I was 35 years old by that time. I had three children and the youngest was in school, so I was ready to do something, and then Alice [Waters] asked me to do the pastries for the restaurant. I really didn't have any idea what that might mean, but I thought, 'Why not? I'll try it and see what it's like.' I was a real babe in the woods—we all were. None of us had any training in restaurants. We didn't have people there who had gone to culinary school. All we had was our cookbooks to depend on. So we were cooking from one day to the next, learning on the job as quickly as we possibly could."

Sprinkling sugar over a crème brûleé

Blackberry Soup with Noyau Ice

by Lindsey Shere

*This dessert can be made ahead of time and assembled at the last minute.
It's the essence of summer flavors and requires ripe, sweet, full-flavored fruit.
It can be made with just one of the fruits if you can't get both peaches
and strawberries; either one would be delicious. You can get the noyau nuts,
or kernels, out of the pits of the apricots or peaches by folding the pits
in a towel and tapping them with a hammer.*

Yield: 6 servings

For the noyau ice:

1 cup sugar

½ cup peach or apricot kernels

4 cups milk

Almond extract to taste

4 egg whites

Pinch of cream of tartar

For the blackberry soup:

3 cups blackberries

½ cup water

6 tablespoons sugar

¼ teaspoon kirsch or to taste

2 ripe peaches

3 cups ripe strawberries

Crisp cookies such as gaufrettes or tuiles

For the noyau ice:

1. Grind the kernels with ¾ cup of the sugar until finely ground in a food processor and combine with the milk in a stainless steel saucepan.

2. Stir the mixture over medium heat until the sugar dissolves. Remove from the heat and let the flavor steep for 15 minutes.

3. Taste the mixture. If the flavor isn't strong enough, reheat and let stand again. Add almond extract, if necessary.

4. Strain the mixture into a bowl and place in the refrigerator until chilled.

5. Beat the egg whites until foamy. Add the cream of tartar and beat until soft peaks form. Beat in the remaining ¼ cup of sugar. Whip for 30 seconds more.

6. Fold the egg whites into the chilled milk mixture and spin in an ice cream machine, or freeze the mixture in a pan until solid, then pulverize until smooth in a food processor.

For the blackberry soup:

1. Combine the blackberries in a stainless steel saucepan with ½ cup of water. Cover and bring to a simmer over medium heat. Cook for 5 minutes.

2. Press through a strainer or put through a food mill to remove the seeds.

3. Add 3 tablespoons of the sugar (or to taste). Add the kirsch and chill the soup.

4. At serving time, or an hour or two before, halve, pit, peel, and slice the peaches. Gently toss them with 2 tablespoons of sugar (or to taste).

5. Into another bowl, slice the strawberries and sweeten them with the remaining tablespoon of sugar (or to taste).

Blackberries

To serve:

Ladle ¼ cup of the soup into a soup bowl, arrange the peach and strawberry slices in it, and add a scoop of noyau ice. Serve immediately with crisp cookies.

Mark Miller continues, "People liked to have desserts in restaurants because they were made with better ingredients and techniques. Then author Maida Heatter popularized home-style recipes with her popular cookbooks and became the queen of the baking world. People then began to go back and look at Shaker recipes like Brown Betty, shortcake, and lemon meringue pie. Professional chefs began to work with the American repertoire."

From the beginning, desserts at Chez Panisse were driven by fruits—the very best at their peak of ripeness—a simple premise that made sense and melded perfectly with the preceding courses and the philosophy of the restaurant. Miller comments, "At Chez Panisse, they didn't just rely on cream, butter, and sugar. It was more nuts, more fruit. Fruit was the basis, with different flours and honeys and things that became a little more dynamic in taste—bitter honey, nougatine, that sort of thing. They weren't just sweet or chocolate." He adds, "People were sometimes disappointed at Chez Panisse because they felt what they got wasn't big enough or grand enough. "I think Americans felt that birthday cake, apple pie, and Twinkies were the three classic American desserts.

"Nancy [Silverton] took a lot of what Chez Panisse was doing and crossed it with French and Italian traditions and emphasized California fruits. She would use something classic like puff pastry with bitter prunes and Armagnac, or a shortcake with different kinds of berries instead of strawberries. People began to borrow from those ideas. She was at Spago in the 1980s and I think she became the most important pastry chef for that generation. Her desserts tasted good, but they were still simple and American in spirit."

Nancy Silverton, pastry chef/owner of La Brea Bakery and Campanile restaurant, recalls the days before creativity with desserts on America's restaurant menus. "When I returned to Los Angeles from the Cordon Bleu Cooking School in Paris, I wanted to get a job as a cook," she says, "but the only job was dessert making at Michael's Restaurant. So I thought I'd hang out in that area of the kitchen until something opened up on the hot side. I got to work with Jimmy Brinkley, who was throwing together desserts that didn't have names. I never realized you could do that. Until that time, all dessert menus had familiar dessert names. People who ordered desserts in restaurants wanted recognizable dessert names that they'd heard about or read about. Jimmy would call something 'lemon mousse cake with poppy seeds and candied zest.' That just wasn't done, but he was doing it. That's when I realized the importance of the ingredients themselves and ways of combining them. I didn't have to stick to the rules. That's when the whole world of pastry opened for me and, as simple as that seems, twenty years ago, it was revolutionary." When Silverton started at Michael's, it was one of the few places in Los Angeles that had a pastry chef. Through the late 1970s, it was not uncommon for good restaurants to buy their desserts from a bakery or wholesale operation. Now customers expect that a chef or pastry chef makes the desserts.

In the mid- to late 1980s, desserts became more architectural. Chefs like Richard Leach and Dan Budd, lecturing professor in baking and pastry arts at The Culinary Institute of America, popularized this movement. "People began to have such a high level of expectation," says Miller. "The corner shop was selling better breads and pastries, but that meant the restaurant had to do something that was even more specialized."

Throughout the 1980s, the demand for skilled pastry chefs increased drastically. The country was enjoying an economic boom, and many restaurants were featuring architectural desserts and other multifaceted desserts. Timothy Moriarty, managing editor of *Pastry Art and Design* and *Chocolatier* magazines, looks to that time when the pastry chef became more popular in the food writing media. "I believe it had to do with the showiness of the desserts at the time, and the rising importance of dessert as a course of the meal, one that was just as important as the others. So many things started to happen at once. Restaurants started to see the pastry kitchen as a profit center and began to feature their desserts more. I don't know if one led to the other or if it all came at once, but now pastry chefs get their names on the menu. Dessert menus weren't always separate and now they almost always are." Today's restaurants feature the dessert course and rely on the pastry chef to carry a perfect meal to its finale.

Bruno Feldeisen at work at the Four Seasons

Dan Budd was able to reap the benefits of this new-found pastry popularity. "When I went to New York City in 1987," he says, "desserts seemed to be very simple. The classic French restaurants were still doing very well. Places like the River Café, where I was, were popular also. Larry Forgione [The Coach

House] had made his start there; then Charlie Palmer [Aureole] was there when I started. I guess we wanted to make something new, something different. So we went out on the edge and took from history and from all the elements of pastry we worked with and tried to combine as much as we could into each plate. At one point, we had a menu of about twenty-six desserts. We had seven pastry cooks and we were going crazy. An interview with the *New York Times* featured the first-ever photograph of any food in a *New York Times* review. It was one of our desserts from the River Café, and food critic Bryan Miller said, 'Desserts are worth coming across the river for.' All our hard work was recognized and people just started flowing to the River Café for dessert. I think all of New York at that point was in a surge of making better desserts."

Preparing apple tarts

It was an exploratory time and pastry literally reached new heights. Budd reflects realistically on the architectural approach and the interest in desserts it helped foster. "I think a lot of things we did were mistakes. I think the whole architectural thing went crazy with desserts that were beautiful to look at but difficult to eat. We were going out on a limb in all directions. Then, on top of that, things came out that were just phenomenal and that would sell incredibly. We were open to a lot of things. I think the smart pastry chefs learn how to apply everything that they've learned."

Emily Luchetti, pastry chef of Farallon in San Francisco, and author of *Stars Desserts* and *Four-Star Desserts,* points to the mid- to late 1980s as a time when chefs and restaurants finally began to focus on dessert as an important course that should intermingle with and complement the preceding courses. "Back then, with American regional cuisine, chefs concentrated on the first courses and the main courses," she says. "It wasn't until chefs were done with that that they started to pay attention to desserts. I think it was about 1987 when we started waking up to this. We hadn't gotten to dessert yet. Everyone was preoccupied with the American regional fish or vegetable course. If you look at the dessert menus from then, they were much simpler. The evolution made sense; it just worked its way down."

Charlie Trotter emphasizes the importance of the entire menu for today's dining experience and the sense of cohesiveness that must extend through the dessert course: "I think it's important that desserts don't act as stand-alone entities with regard to the whole menu. That would be like having appetizers with a Chinese flair and then serving French food. It wouldn't really make sense. I think sometimes chefs don't collaborate with their pastry chefs enough, or there isn't enough cohesion with the other courses. The whole menu needs to flow. First and foremost is a flow of flavors. If the style of cuisine is soft and delicate, then the style of dessert needs to be soft and delicate. If the style of the cuisine is fiery with chilies and herbs, the desserts must too reflect that."

A great awakening has taken place. Customers are more sophisticated, more attuned to the culinary world and they notice when things are not in balance. This awakening has come after a time of exploration, when pastry chef and chef learned to work together to make the whole dining experience flow. Now customers and chefs alike are aware of the power of dessert, of the extreme satisfaction that a great dessert can deliver.

America's Cuisine in Motion

The tenth anniversary issue of *Food Arts* magazine, in September 1998, summed up a decade of pastry in a feature article titled "10 Years on the Front Burner: The Hottest Trends and Remarkable Advances to Steam Up the Industry's Windows." Here are some highlights: "From crème brûlée to verbena sorbet, biscotti to brownies, towering skyscrapers to banana bread pudding, old-fashioned s'mores to exquisite petit fours, this has been the decade of dazzling desserts. The blitz began when creative young confectioners started composing pastry fantasies

> It just exploded. We're finally on par with the potato-peelers and the bone-burners.
> —Nick Malgieri

that were playful, colorful, and complicated. Richard Leach, dubbed the 'Pythagoras of pastry,' constructed chocolate pyramids. Other visual artists painted intricate sauces on their plates or sculpted miniature buildings and bridges. The last ten years have witnessed a lot of twists on the classics: Le Cirque's sublime crème brûlée was cloned with variations ranging from cappuccino to ginger to corn. Bananas, coconuts, and exotic tropical fruits appeared in puddings and pies and inventive ice cream concoctions ranged from [San Francisco chef] Elka Gilmore's chocolate 'sushi' with green tea ice cream to Wayne Brachman's cinnamon-cayenne snickerdoodle and cinnamon ice cream sandwich. Pastry chefs have also restored respect for homey American desserts—crumbles, puddings, pies and layer cakes—upgraded, of course, to improve flavor and appearance. Charlie Trotter's 'surprise dessert wave,' a carefully

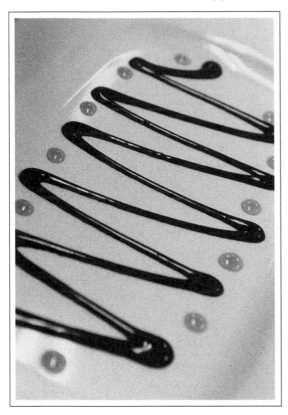

Chocolate and caramel sauce awaiting a dessert

orchestrated plethora of sampler plates, attests to our ongoing sweet-tooth syndrome. Still not enough? Pre-desserts—fruit soups, sorbets with spirits, herbs, or spices, and miniature custards—provided a smooth transition from savory to sweet. Post-prandial friandises encourage even more nibbling. Pastry chefs have risen from supporting roles to star status. They're getting spiffy new kitchens, larger staffs, higher salaries, fame, TV gigs, and much more attention." "It just exploded," says Nick Malgieri. "We're finally on par with the potato-peelers and the bone burners." *Food Art's* summation proclaims the strides pastry has made in recent history. It provides a glimpse of how pastry got to where it is today, an important player in the exciting evolution of cuisine.

America's pastry chefs are part of a long chain of knowledge that stretches through the centuries. The demand for great desserts by savvy, discerning customers makes our use of that knowledge critical in the midst of our daily work. Bill Yosses, whose desserts have followed the acclaimed food of chef David Bouley at Bouley in New York City for many years, embraces the public's scrutiny of desserts. "I draw inspiration from this explosion of interest from the general public," he says. "I think the public has gotten pulled along in the interest of good food and cooking. They are more demanding now. I don't think it matters whether they are looking for a spectacular, tall dessert or a painted plate, but they do want something special and they aren't going to be satisfied with something less."

Emily Luchetti agrees that customers have become knowledgeable about what they are getting. "People may not know how to make a true crème brûlée or puff pastry," she says, "but they know what good is and I think that's really exciting. On the one hand, we don't want everyone going around making their own puff pastry. We want them to come eat ours, but we want them to be educated consumers. People say, 'That's not a good crème brûlée. It's supposed to have a thin, crisp caramelized crust. It's supposed to be nice and creamy.' But you ask them how to make it, and they wouldn't know where to start. It's not their job; it's ours. I love that they are savvy enough to know." Does increasing customer dessert knowledge have implications for the work of the professional pastry chef? "On the one hand, it's going to be dangerous because of all the armchair pastry chefs out there," says Luchetti, "but on the other hand, it's going to be really exciting too, because they will keep us on our toes."

*Filling ramekins
with flan*

I think desserts and the dining public could be compared to the American automobile industry in the late 1970s and early 1980s, when the American consumer recognized the low quality of cars manufactured by U.S. companies and the low level of repair service those companies offered. Consumers turned to the Japanese, who were producing dependable, affordable cars, who stood behind them, and who offered personalized, caring service. Savvy restaurant or bakery patrons are going to seek out the businesses with the best product. The work of the pastry chef can have enormous impact on the perceptions of the customer and, therefore, add value and dollars to the bottom line of the business. Remember, dessert is the last course served—perhaps the final memory of the meal. It could be a determining factor in whether or not a customer will return.

The knowledge and awareness of food history is the foundation on which modern pastry stands. From this body of knowledge and technique, pastry chefs make their statements, passionately preparing backstage, drawing inspiration from the greats who have gone on before them. Then comes their cue, the end of a meal, when their creation takes center stage as the grand finale.

I think the best pastry chefs get at the heart of an old recipe or technique they use and are able to understand it in a personal way. They make a particular recipe or perform a certain technique so many times that it becomes their own. Judy Contino, proprietor of Bittersweet Bakery in Chicago, concurs. "Historical techniques have given me a lot of inspiration," she says. "It amazes me how old a technique can be and how creative you can be with it."

Placing a quenelle of sorbet on a dessert

"We've seen a lot of evolution in pastry in the last ten years," says Jacques Torres, pastry chef at Le Cirque 2000. "I've been in New York for nine years now and I've seen a lot of change. I hope I've contributed to that by bringing in other pastry chefs. I hired François Payard as sous chef at Le Cirque when he was in France. I advised Andre Renard to come work at Essex House. Other people who worked with me are now pastry chefs and pastry instructors around the country."

The work of today's leading pastry chefs is influenced by a wide variety of arts, culture, history, and philosophy. Each chef's work is also inextricably linked to the other's because of the high level of communication in the industry. It is simple for a chef to open a magazine or book, surf the Internet, or watch a cooking show and be exposed to new techniques, ideas, or foodstuffs. Gale Gand, pastry chef and co-owner of Brasserie T, north of Chicago, recalls her backround in fine arts. "I don't have a culinary backround," she says. "I went into this as an art student, so a lot of my work has been influenced by the Russian painter Wassily Kandinsky, an abstract expressionist. I think some of the people I studied in art history and art design really influenced my work in pastry more than anything."

Elizabeth Falkner, pastry chef and owner of Citizen Cake in San Francisco, has a degree in film from The San Francisco Art Institute. She believes pastry can be a medium through which passion is communicated. "If you pay attention to things that inspire you," she says, "whether it's films or furniture or demolition sites or music or the work of other pastry chefs, those can all be reflected in your work."

Chocolate Piñon Cookies

by Andrew MacLauchlan

These are the best Southwestern chocolate cookies of all time— dark, rich, and studded with roasted piñons. Be sure to choose a high-quality bittersweet chocolate. This simple recipe can be made quickly and, once in the oven, the cookies fill your home with an irresistable chocolatey aroma.

Yield: 20 to 25 cookies

8 ounces bittersweet chocolate, chopped

½ cup butter

2 eggs

¾ cup sugar

¼ cups all-purpose flour

1 teaspoon baking powder

¼ teaspoon salt

1 cup toasted piñon nuts

1. Preheat oven to 325°. Melt the chocolate and butter together in a double boiler, then remove from heat. Whisk in the eggs.

2. Sift the sugar, flour, baking powder, and salt separately into a mixing bowl. Stir together, then stir into the chocolate mixture until thoroughly combined. Stir in the piñon nuts.

3. Grease a cookie sheet and drop 1-tablespoon dollops of the batter onto the sheet, at least 2 inches apart. Bake for 18 to 20 minutes or until the cookies puff up and the tops crack. Remove from the oven and let cool. Store in a sealed airtight container.

The wide variety of cuisine in America's finest restaurants, bakeries, and hotels—Lespinasse, Campanile, Chez Panisse, Charlie Trotter's, Aureole, Gramercy Tavern, Farallon, Park Avenue Café, Spago, City Bakery, Four Seasons, Citizen Cake, Citronelle, Coyote Café, Le Cirque—represents the many directions America's cuisine has taken. Pastry chefs, perhaps more now than in past centuries, must make a dazzling statement. They must be able to adapt to their restaurant's style of cuisine, to distinguish what will sell, to create uniquely flavored compositions, and to follow the produce availability of the seasons. The distinguishing style expressed through the desserts and pastry items of each establishment is the culmination of many historic factors and includes the perfection of recipes from trial and error throughout the ages.

Passing vanilla ice cream base through a fine strainer

Maury Rubin, of City Bakery in New York, expresses reverence for pastry making's long history. "I take ornate work and process it through me into a cake with practically nothing on it but a straight line and maybe a few dots," he says. "I am very aware of what I would call historical references, especially those referring to French Pastry. Those references are in me, but you don't always see them in my work. I learned in France with people who were very mindful of tradition. I revere it. There is a reason why City Bakery makes croissants the way we do, why we make puff pastry the way we do. Because my teachers were faithful to the process used five hundred years earlier. I am faithful to that process."

For Sebastien Canonne, who once worked for French president François Mitterand, a look to the past is inspirational. "In the 1600s," he says, "chefs spent enormous amounts of time preparing for the buffets for the kings and queens. It was very detailed work even then."

Sherry Yard looks to local history to establish the restaurant's context. "When I started at Catahoula restaurant in Napa Valley, it was right next to the Mountain View Hotel, the oldest hotel in Napa Valley," she says. "I had to find out more about its history. I went to the libraries in San Francisco and pulled out the oldest cookbooks I could find. The recipes were a dash of this and a handful of that. It was very homespun, but the important thing was that they featured indigenous ingredients. They made things based on what was available to them. It was interesting to create a menu based on that history. That, for me, was the best part."

Later in her career, Yard took her "out of history" approach to Wolfgang Puck's Spago, where she connected inspiration from the Renaissance period in Vienna to Spago's flavorful modern California cuisine. "That's why I went back to Vienna before we opened up Spago," she said. "It was just incredible to be there with the history of all those pastry shops. I went to one shop that had been owned by five generations of pastry chefs; it was two hundred years old. It was amazing to hear these stories and then bring them back with me to the States. When we opened up Spago, I said this is what I have to do; this is what it's all about."

Viennese Café Glacé

by Sherry Yard

Yield: 8 servings

For the cream topping:
1 cup heavy whipping cream
¼ cup crème fraîche
1 tablespoon sugar
1 quart vanilla ice cream, homemade or store bought, softened
at room temperature for about 20 minutes
1 cup fresh-brewed, chilled espresso
2 tablespoons Amaretto or Tia Maria (*optional*)

For garnish:
¼ cup chocolate shavings
8 pirouette cookies, homemade or store bought

Continued on next page

For the cream topping:

1. Combine the whipping cream and the crème fraîche in a mixing bowl. Mix on medium speed while sprinkling in the sugar.

2. Whip to stiff peaks and reserve for serving the desserts.

To serve:

1. With a rubber spatula, transfer the softened ice cream to a bowl and stir in the chilled espresso and optional liqueur.

2. Spoon the ice cream into chilled glasses and top with a scoop of the cream topping, a pirouette, and a sprinkle of chocolate shavings. Serve at once.

Dessert ideas may turn in circles like the seasons, but there is always that new customer to please and the new day ahead, or evening's service to be ready for. That allows the opportunity to do better than the day before, to learn, to improve. This is how we participate and find our place in the long process of history and make a personal contribution to better pastry.

Pastry chefs must take the responsibility to seize their own destiny and forge ahead. Those who truly love their work are the most successful. Nothing and no one can stop them because they are not really working. They are doing what seems to them a natural expression of who they are. Nancy Silverton reveals the strength of her driving passion. "I've always said that I wake up in the morning and never go to work. I wake up and do what I was meant to do in life. I am so happy that I found food and dessert making because it allows me to do what I truly love."

> I've always said that I wake up in the morning and never go to work. I wake up and do what I was meant to do in life. I am so happy that I found food and dessert making because it allows me to do what I truly love.
> —Nancy Silverton

CHAPTER two

ORIGINS OF INSPIRATION

Early Influences on the Palate

There may be no definitive course of early sweet experiences that leads people to devote their life to dessert and pastry making. Tracing back to first memories is interesting because these varied encounters with sweets and baking are the beginnings of the pastry chef's dessert and sweets dictionary. They use this dictionary throughout their lives to form their ideas and areas of emphasis within the field. These are the first experiences from which they draw inspiration.

The experience that created my first memory of something sweet happened when I was three or four years old. I was riding in the back of a pickup truck with a group of other children. We were on our way to a Vermont country fair and were eating spice cookies and drinking grape soda. I've never forgotten those cookies, though I'm not sure why. It might have been the cinnamon. I just know they were delicious.

I truly believe that desserts appeal to us as adults because of an association with a feeling of reward, perhaps from childhood, and the pleasures of a sense of indulgence and satisfaction. The first bite of a crisp Winesap apple just off the tree or the first taste of fresh blueberries can be the memory, the source of passion, that drives pastry chefs to make their apple desserts explode with flavor or to intensify the flavor of their blueberry ice cream, resulting in the ultimate accompaniment to a blueberry or lemon tart.

When I was five or six years old, my mother and grandmother sent me out into the woods on our land in Vermont armed with containers to be filled with all the wild blackberries and raspberries I could gather. They served them either as a simple dessert with cream and a sprinkle of brown sugar or made a pie or preserves. When my mother baked pies, she gave the trimmings to my sister, Lynn, and me. We sprinkled them with cinnamon and sugar and made twists or little jelly turnovers.

Richard Leach's first memories of sweets involve the commercial products of suburban Long Island, like Entenmann's cakes. He also recalls cooking with his mother and being drawn to his family's kitchen. "They baked cookies and I just ate them," he says. "I remember everyone hanging out in the kitchen. It was the best room in the house. My family was always in there. We had a big kitchen. They cooked every night and everyone lent a hand. It was nothing too wonderful— basic meals—but it was fun."

Iced Raisin Squares

by Nancy Silverton

Nancy Silverton says that when she was growing up, the only cookies her mother would buy were the wholesome ones like Fig Newtons or raisin bars, "those long flat cookies whose ends fit together like a jigsaw puzzle and came layered in a long, cellophane package. As a child I resented her health-conscious choices, but now I can finally appreciate the pure delicious simplicity of this cookie." To keep the pretty, zig-zag edges, don't cut them, instead, break them along the scored marks.

Yield: 2 1/2 dozen

For the dough:

1¼ cup unbleached pastry flour or unbleached all-purpose flour

½ teaspoon kosher salt

⅛ teaspoon ground cloves

1 teaspoon ground cinnamon

3 tablespoons granulated sugar

2 tablespoons light brown sugar, packed

½ cup (4 ounces) almond paste

5 extra-large egg yolks, hard-boiled

2 tablespoons vanilla extract

4 ounces unsalted butter, chilled and cut into 1-inch cubes

For the filling:

1¼ cups currants or raisins

¾ cup water

For the egg wash:

1 egg yolk beaten with a splash of water

For the glaze:

3 tablespoons confectioners' sugar

1 tablespoon heavy cream

Continued on next page

For the dough:

1. In a food processor, pulse together the flour, salt, clove, cinnamon, and sugars. Crumble in the almond paste and process until combined.
2. Sieve the egg yolks into the mixture and pulse just until it comes together.
3. Add the vanilla extract and butter and pulse just until it comes together.
4. Turn the dough out onto a lightly floured work surface and knead a few times to gather the mixture into a ball, then divide the dough into quarters.
5. Form each quarter into a rectangular bar about 1 inch thick and 2 inches wide, wrap each bar in plastic and chill in the refrigerator until very firm.

For the filling:

1. In a small saucepan over medium high heat, combine the currants or raisins and the water. Bring to a boil, stirring to keep the currants or raisins from sticking.
2. Cook until the liquid is reduced, about 5 minutes. Remove from heat and allow to cool.

For the glaze:

Whisk the confectioners' sugar and heavy cream together and set aside.

Assembly:

1. Preheat the oven to 350°. Place 2 bars of dough onto a lightly floured work surface and cut both in half crossways.
2. Using a sprinkling of flour as needed to keep the dough from sticking to the work surface or rolling pin, beat one piece of the dough to soften it. Roll it out lengthwise to 8 or 9 inches long, then turn the dough sideways to roll it 5 to 6 inches wide and ⅛ inch thick.
3. Slide a metal spatula underneath the dough and carefully move it onto a parchment-lined or nonstick baking sheet. Repeat the process with the remaining 3 pieces of dough.
4. Place 2 of the chilled dough strips onto a lightly floured work surface and, using a pastry wheel or paring knife, trim the edges to 8 inches long and 4 or 5 inches wide.
5. Evenly distribute the raisin filling over the surface of the two strips of dough, to ½ inch from the edges. Brush the edges with the egg wash.

6. Place the other two strips of dough over the filling, aligning the edges with the bottom layer of dough.

7. Dust the surface of the dough and roll over the surface of the two doughs to seal them. Chill in the freezer for several minutes.

8. Trim the edges of the dough with a fluted wheel to even and seal them. With the wheel, score the dough down the center (not cutting all the way through). Then score the dough horizontally at 2-inch intervals to form small rectangles.

9. Brush the entire surface with egg wash and, using a toothpick, dot each rectangle 4 to 6 times.

10. Bake for 20 to 25 minutes until firm to the touch and lightly browned. Remove from the oven and allow to cool.

11. Brush the surface of the bars with the glaze.

12. Break the cookies at each scored mark on the edge of a counter.

Nancy Silverton grew up in Los Angeles and remembers commercial products as well. "I didn't come from a household with generations of dessert makers," she says. "If we ever had dessert with dinner it was usually ice cream, but I do have memories of products that I thought were really great at the time, like Sara Lee pound cake. I remember eating it out of the freezer."

Bill Yosses recalls his first sweets from his Ohio youth. "My mother baked a lot—not every day, but she really enjoyed it and a baked dessert was often part of the meal. So probably my best dessert memories are of cheesecake, pineapple upside-down cake, chocolate fudge, and, of course, Halloween candy and Three Musketeers."

> My mother was a pie baker. . . . When she made pies there would always be some dough left, and she rolled out a little individual pie for me. I still have the glass dish she used to make it in.
>
> —Gale Gand

Michelle Gayer of Charlie Trotter's has similar memories. "My first memories were cookies baked at home. There were always so many, like my grandmother's sugar cookies, with the sugar on top and the fork pressed into each one, and peanut butter cookies with the Hershey's Kiss in the middle. My mother baked all the time. I grew up on strawberry-rhubarb crisp, apple pie, and pumpkin pie."

Gramercy Tavern's Claudia Fleming remembers sitting on her grandmother's couch with a box of Whitman's Sampler chocolates. "I would sneak away with the box and taste them all," she says. "Also, I grew up in Hicksville, Long Island, the same town where the Entenmann's factory was, so we always had cake in the house and we had to have ice cream with cake." Another memory she has is of a sweet detour she and her father consistently made coming home from Sunday mass. "He would get the *Sunday Times* and a Three Musketeers bar and I would get a Milky Way. It was before Sunday dinner and, of course, we would never tell Mom. So for me it was always caramel and milk chocolate. That is actually a very dear memory, sharing candy bars with Dad."

Maury Rubin vividly remembers his favorite childhood pastry. "I grew up eating Pop Tarts. In my book [*Book of Tarts*], I write, 'Pop Tarts were the formative pastry of my youth.' American kids in the suburbs grew up eating Pop Tarts."

Elizabeth Falkner recalls soufflés. "My mom cooked a lot when we were growing up," she says. "We watched Julia Child all the time and laughed. My mom made things from magazine recipes and cookbooks, but more than anything I remember the soufflés because I thought they were miraculous. My grandmother is from Missouri and I remember picking wild blackberries there for canning or making pies."

Gale Gand tells of her mother's grip on pie making. "My mother was a pie baker. She was the pie baker in the neighborhood. No one dared bring a pie to the block party because my mother, Myrna, was going to make the pie. She used to make cherry pies with the lattice. She had really cold hands, which is why she was so good at pies—the butter in the dough didn't melt in her hands. That's the secret to being a pastry chef—poor circulation [laughter]. When she made pies there would always be some dough left, and she rolled out a little individual pie for me. I still have the glass dish she used to make it in. She rolled out a little bit of pie dough, put cinnamon and sugar on it, then she put my initial on it and baked it. That little pie came out of the oven before the big one was done. We poured milk or cream over it and ate it hot."

Sherry Yard had palate coaching at a very early age. "My grandmother made my sister and me ice cream sodas. She went to the store for strawberry and vanilla ice cream and she took coffee or cocoa and swirled the flavors into it. Then she had us close our eyes, taste the ice cream, and guess what flavors they were. 'Guess what this is. Guess what that is.' The experience was profound. When we were little, we didn't know the difference between cocoa and coffee because they look kind of the same, but the flavors were the amazing thing."

Persian Mulberry~Poached Fiori Figs

by Sherry Yard

Yield: 8 servings

4 cups Persian mulberries or blackberries, plus 2 cups for garnish

1 Valencia orange

½ lemon

½ lime

1 vanilla bean, split and scraped

4½ cups good-quality Merlot wine, such as Ravenswood

1 cup sugar

1 tablespoon cassia buds or 4 cinnamon sticks

8 Fiori figs or other large ripe figs

Sacristain cookies

1. In a thick-bottomed saucepot, pour ¼ cup water and add the mulberries. Cut the skin and pith from the citrus and discard. Slice fruit ¼-inch thick and add the slices to the pot.

2. Add the vanilla bean and Merlot and place the pot over a low flame. Bring to a simmer, then stir in the sugar. If using cassia buds, heat them in a saute pan over medium heat for 30 to 45 seconds. Add the cassia buds or cinnamon sticks to the mulberry mixture and remove from heat. Let the mixture steep for 30 minutes.

3. Remove the cassia or cinnamon, citrus slices, and vanilla bean pod. Strain the cooked mulberries and juice into a bowl, pressing the berries with the back of a ladle to separate the pulp from the seeds.

4. Pour the strained mixture back into the saucepot and place over medium-low heat. Simmer for 10 minutes or until reduced by one quarter.

Continued on next page

5. Peel the thin skin from the figs with a sharp paring knife.

6. Add the figs, continue simmering for 10 minutes, then remove from heat.

To serve:

1. Ladle 2 ounces of mulberry sauce in each bowl and spoon one fig into each.

2. Cut the top ½ inch off each fig to show some of the inside.

3. Drop several mulberries around each fig and serve with sacristain cookies or other crisp puff pastry cookies.

Ann Amernick, pastry chef/owner of Amernick in Wheaton, Maryland, was interested in pastry at a very young age. "Ever since I was really, really small, I have been fascinated by cakes, petit fours, and pastry. But when I was young my favorite books were always the ones that had descriptions of food, especially pastry. When I was eight, I got this book called *Pantaloon*. It was about a little French poodle that wanted to be a baker. It was filled with drawings of little petit fours, éclairs, and little cakes, and I still have that book. It meant so much to me. When I walked home from school I passed the dairy store. In those days—back in the late 1940s and early 1950s—there were stores that sold just dairy. They used to sell chocolate bars, too. I saved my money up and bought a black-and-white-labeled chocolate bar for 35 cents. It was years later that I realized I was buying Lindt chocolate and I knew the difference at eight years old."

Judy Contino recalls a regional treat from her childhood. "I am from New Mexico and I remember eating cajeta (traditional Mexican caramelized goat's milk) that came in little boxes. We used to drive to El Paso on Easter weekend and get these little wooden boxes, filled with the candy, that we would peel apart and eat with a spoon."

Dan Budd recalls his memories of local childhood treats. "I have specific memories of things in Vermont that always inspire me, like the maple candies and syrup, and apple-picking. There was nothing like eating a McIntosh apple with the dew still on it, right off the tree on a frosty, cold morning. They were all so good you wanted to take just one bite, throw it away, and get another one—one bite each, like Montezuma drinking his chocolate."

Mary Bergin, Wolfgang Puck's longtime pastry chef, recalls, "I grew up in a family with six kids and my mother used to buy these brownies in a tin. She didn't bake at all and if she tried, she usually burned whatever it was. So all eight of us had to share the brownies and I always wanted the corner piece. We make brownies every day at Spago and I still cut out the corner piece and it makes my day."

In most American families, cooking was and seems to remain the domain of wives and mothers and grandmothers. This makes lasting impressions on those women who choose cooking as a profession. Gale Gand thinks back on her Hungarian and Jewish roots. "There is a kind of great Eastern European baking tradition in my family. We made strudel and, because of my grandmother, I have a love for poppy seeds. My mother was a typical 1950s mother. She was into convenience food. As much as she liked cooking, she hated it. There was a lot of ambivalence about food in my family. Food was love, yet there was an understanding that it harnessed women to the kitchen."

Winesap apples

Emily Luchetti thinks back. "I would say my first dessert memory is coming home from school and seeing the kitchen counter lined with chocolate chip cookies. I always thought it was amazing how my mom timed it so perfectly; the moment we walked through the door, they were warm out of the oven."

Nick Malgieri remembers a lot of home baking from his childhood. "My grandmother lived with us and she liked to bake almost every day. That was my main influence, seeing it at home so often. My grandmother had to learn how to cook at an early age because her mother had died very young. My grandmother and her niece were interested in baking and trying different things. When they were in their twenties, a pastry chef from Naples retired to their town and they actually took lessons from him. They learned a lot of techniques that your typical southern Italian home cooks didn't know. So although she wasn't a professional, my grandmother had a little professional training in her youth, which meant that the desserts she made were a little more finished than the usual home cooking. I'll never forget standing next to the stove on a little stool watching what was going on. Although I never learned a recipe from her, the influence of all that baking stuck with me."

Markus Färbinger grew up in Austria and was close to baking from the beginning as well. "I grew up in a bakery, but I was not into sweets. We ate a lot

Satisfied customer enjoying dessert

of bread. To me, sweet was the raisins in the rolls we ate only on Sundays, or a big bowl of strawberries from the garden with milk and sugar. I'll never forget the smell of the sourdough in the steam from the oven when it came up through cracks in the floor from our bakery below."

Amernick may have been drawn to pastry because she was not allowed to have dessert as child. "When we went out to dinner as a family," she said, "we were never allowed to order dessert. My mother said, 'You can get dessert at home.' It wasn't because we didn't have the money, but that was the way people were brought up during the Depression. And they passed on these frugal habits to their families. So when I grew up, I always ordered all the desserts just to taste them. I so regretted not having been able to have them as a child."

The first memory of sweets made a major impression on the creative minds of the pastry chefs I interviewed. In the formative years of a person lies the blueprint of the person-to-be. The memories associated with cumulative food experiences from a very young age are the most important prerequisite for success as a cook, chef, or pastry chef because it is from these memories that dessert inspirations arise. This is how chefs acquire the most crucial tool in their profession—the palate. For a chef, constantly tasting and relating to the nuances of the food that one makes is a prerequisite for making delicious food for other people.

From the early encounters with flavors in infancy and childhood through the often finicky years of adolescence, widening food adventures lead a young potential pastry chef to gain a full spectrum of flavor cognizance. All successful pastry chefs continue to widen this flavor background throughout their careers. In this way, they develop their own palate and begin to understand the palates of the customers they serve. Chefs' taste experiences, collected and mentally recorded from infancy on, work themselves either consciously or unconsciously into every dessert, cookie, or chocolate they make. This flavor background is a crucial ingredient in building dessert creations that go beyond the expected or mundane.

First Cooking and Baking Experiences

Most pastry chefs I interviewed had amusing stories about their first cooking and baking experiences. My personal challenge at the age of eight was perfecting the Toll House cookie. My older sister, Lynn, always made apple crisp with apples from trees on our family's land and it was delicious.

Lynn's Apple Crisp

by Andrew MacLauchlan

Yield: One 8 x 8 x 2-inch pan

1 cup rolled oats
½ cup flour
½ cup brown sugar
¼ teaspoon salt
1 teaspoon cinnamon
½ cup butter, softened
4 tart apples, peeled and sliced
Whipped cream, lightly sweetened, or vanilla ice cream

1. Preheat oven to 350°F. In a mixing bowl, combine the oats, flour, brown sugar, salt, and cinnamon. Mix with a fork until blended.

2. Add the butter and mix with the fork until mixture appears crumbly.

3. Spread the apples into the bottom of a greased 2-quart casserole dish or an 8 × 8 × 2-inch pan.

4. Sprinkle the oatmeal mixture over the apples.

5. Bake for 30 minutes or until topping is brown and apples are tender.

6. Serve with lightly sweetened whipped cream or vanilla ice cream.

I was always competitive with Lynn at this age. I probably felt starved for attention, as siblings often do. I realized she already made the best apple crisp, so I had to make the best chocolate chip cookie. I must have made them a hundred times in the next six years, altering the recipe with different kinds of nuts or trying different spices from my mother's cupboard. I remember having a breakthrough by closely watching the baking time, and shortening it slightly.

At an early age, through trial and error with a single recipe, I learned a significant amount about the science and processes of baking. I can remember

Chopping chocolate

the disasters of not preheating the oven or not mixing the ingredients thoroughly, and the difference in the finished product when I tried using shortening or margarine instead of butter. Even then, I began to insist on using only butter—without it, I wouldn't bother baking. I remember making cupcakes at school in the third grade. I mistakenly used baking soda when the recipe called for baking powder. They tasted bitter and I remember feeling panic, knowing that soon everyone would know that my cupcakes were a total loss. I also remember doing food experiments, like whipping cream into butter by hand and then adding just the right amount of salt to make it taste like store-bought butter, and the old science experiment—a baking powder and vinegar volcano.

Claudia Fleming remembers making chocolate pudding at age seven or eight. "It must have been the instant kind. I misread the directions; they said to put plastic wrap on top so it would not form a skin. I lined the cups with plastic wrap instead and wound up making a mess. It wasn't a great first experience."

Chocolatier Jim Graham of Le Français in Wheeling, Illinois, remembers one of his first adventures in the kitchen. "I had a friend when I was twelve who I knew had a real love for chocolate. My mom was out of town and I invited my friend over for dinner with my dad. I decided to make an entirely chocolate dinner. It seemed like a perfectly acceptable thing to do. I pulled out one of my mom's cookbooks; maybe it was *The Joy of Cooking*.

I made a chocolate éclair, chocolate mousse, and a chocolate soufflé, and that was dinner."

Cinnamon Ganache Moussée

by Jim Graham

This makes a fantastic filling for molded, hand dipped, or rolled chocolates and truffles. Cassia is available at Asian markets; it's darker and more fragrant than Indonesian cinnamon. Mexican canela would also work well in this recipe.

Yield: 1 quart

2 tablespoons glucose or light corn syrup

1¼ cup heavy cream

½ ounce cassia cinnamon or Mexican canela cinnamon (crumbled sticks)

1 pound plus ½ ounce high-quality milk chocolate (coarsely chopped and placed in a bowl)

¼ cup plus 2 tablespoons softened butter

1. Combine glucose and heavy cream in a thick-bottomed saucepot and bring to a boil over medium-high heat.

2. Remove from the heat and add crumbled cinnamon sticks, cover and leave for 20 minutes to infuse the cinnamon flavor into the cream.

3. Strain the hot cream into chopped chocolate, pressing the cinnamon well to extract as much cream as possible. Whisk the cream and chocolate together until chocolate is completely smooth.

4. Add the butter and whisk into the chocolate thoroughly. Cover the chocolate with plastic wrap directly in contact with the surface of the ganache and allow to set at room temperature for 18 hours.

5. In a mixer equipped with a whip, whip the ganache starting on low speed to soften the ganache. Gradually increase the speed to high until the mixture becomes fluffy and holds peaks. Ganache may be piped into chocolate centers or spread in a uniform layer and cut into shapes for dipping.

"I don't think I woke up one day and said, 'I want to become a pastry chef,'" says Jacques Torres. "I've always loved sweets. When I was a kid, I remember this chemistry kit I had. One of my favorite experiments was making caramel. To me it was amazing to put sugar on top of that little lamp and have the sugar turn to caramel. That was my first experience with pastry."

When Gale Gand was six years old, she was featured in *Life* magazine for a children's book that had just come out called *The Art of Mud Puddle Cookery*. "I was one of the children picked to be photographed for the book's illustrations. So I was in *Life* magazine making mud soup and mud meatballs. As for real cooking, I think I made Toll House cookies with my mom and made the recipe wrong. I measured teaspoons instead of tablespoons and had difficulty following the directions. It didn't come out right and my mother said, 'You can't change a recipe; you have to follow it verbatim.' It turned out that they came out sort of lacy and they were great, but they weren't Toll House. So that was my first I-didn't-follow-directions-but-it's-not-the-end-of-the-world experience."

> I've always loved sweets. When I was a kid, I remember this chemistry kit I had. One of my favorite experiments was making caramel. To me it was amazing to put sugar on top of that little lamp and have the sugar turn to caramel. That was my first experience with pastry.
>
> —Jacques Torres

Michelle Gayer recalls cooking at home with her mother. "I remember making a chocolate cake. I just put every ingredient into the mixer and didn't read the directions. I didn't know that you had to read the instructions. When I was ten, I tried to make these petit fours from a women's magazine that my mom had lying around. Little squares of cake with green fondant poured over them. It was probably the biggest disaster of my life."

Mary Bergin created a disaster of her own. "My younger sister and I once made a packaged brownie. We had it in what we thought was the oven. I didn't realize we really had it in the broiler. Once we actually put it in the oven, I couldn't figure out why, after twenty minutes, it was still soupy, and then I remembered we forgot to add the eggs, which are probably the only thing you needed to add besides water."

Peanut Butter Cookies

by Jackie Riley

"I have this memory of sitting on the kitchen counter with my mother making these peanut butter cookies—you know, with the fork impressions."

Yield: 30 cookies

1 cup butter
1 cup brown sugar, packed
1 cup granulated sugar
2¼ cups peanut butter
2 eggs
1½ tablespoons vanilla extract
1½ cups bread flour
1½ cups all-purpose flour
½ teaspoon salt
½ teaspoon baking soda
½ teaspoon baking powder

1. Preheat oven to 350°. In a mixing bowl, beat the butter until creamy. Add sugars and beat until light and fluffy. Scrape the bowl down often during the creaming process.

2. Add the peanut butter, eggs, and vanilla extract. Mix until ingredients are well incorporated.

3. In a separate bowl, sift together flours, salt, baking soda, and baking powder. Add to the peanut butter mixture; mix just until cookie dough comes together. Scrape down the bowl and mix for 10 more seconds to be sure all ingredients are well incorporated.

4. Roll the cookie dough into 1½-inch-diameter balls and place them on a nonstick cookie sheet or parchment-lined sheet tray. Using the back of an entreé fork dipped in flour, press a criss-cross pattern on each cookie.

5. Bake for 12 to 14 minutes. Remove from oven and cool.

Family and Cultural Influence

We learn how to relate to the world by observing the attitudes and experiences of those around us. That means we learn how to eat, how to treat food, and how to experience flavors as children from our parents, grandparents, other relatives, or family friends. A pastry chef's family life, and America's collective food consciousness formulated throughout this century, are major influences on the work of these chefs.

The American public has lived through drastic shifts in popular opinion regarding food and eating. A brief look at the changes in American perceptions of food is key to understanding our present cultural fascination with cuisine. The first half of the century saw most Americans living a rural farm life. Those were days when organic farming was the rule because there was no other way to farm. Fruits and vegetables tasted better in their natural state. Dairy products were fresher and tasted better because they were produced on one's own farm or at least one nearby. The 1950s brought mass-produced and shipped frozen and canned food, TV dinners, and candy bars. Though these were incredible feats of engineering and manufacturing, in many ways this technology dulled, or perhaps tranquilized for a time, the American palate. The late 1960s and 1970s, in some areas of the country, brought movement back to organic, unprocessed foods and sparked an awareness of healthful eating. Growing public awareness and preference for fresh organic foods, along with the advent of Europe's nouvelle cuisine, led restaurants and chefs to serve lighter, more flavorful, and healthier food. The restaurants and food of the 1980s reflected popular culture, with an emphasis on opulent presentation, while the 1990s saw some movement away from nouvelle cuisine, a shift toward value consciousness, further refinement of chefs' personal styles, and an emphasis on ethnic food and highly specialized restaurants. Elaborate grocery stores and gourmet specialty food shops flourished. These decades formed America's current pastry chefs—years of ever-changing popular culture and learning about food through family and friends.

Emily Luchetti had close ties to cooking from early on. "My first job in the business was in a cookware store in Florida that my parents owned. So I was brought up with a love for food." Dan Budd recalls lots of food activity in his childhood home. "My mom loved to bake. Our kitchen at home always had great things going on. Mom canned and made cookies and pies. I had great home economics teachers in junior high and high school who really helped me. We actually pretended to have a restaurant in home economics class and took turns cooking and serving. I found I was very confident, even back then."

Ideas of working in a restaurant begin very early in a person—sometimes directly, as with Budd's experience in school, and other times indirectly—for example, by the sheer importance our parents placed on mealtimes.

Michelle Gayer grew up with a strong sense of the importance of dessert as part of a meal. "When I was growing up, there were three meals a day. My father had dessert at lunch and dinner. It was part of the meal."

For some pastry chefs, an absence of interest in food in their family life sparked the discovery later on. This was the case with midwesterner Jim Graham. "Food did not occupy a big place in our family life at all. When I was a teenager, I traveled to the West Coast and tasted all kinds of foods for the first time. Someone there asked me, 'Well, what do you eat at home?' I sat there for a long time and thought, 'I don't know what we eat at home!' It wasn't bad, but it was no more than nourishment. I guess that is why my first trip to France was such a revelation."

> When I was growing up, there were three meals a day. My father had dessert at lunch and dinner. It was part of the meal.
> —Michelle Gayer

As children, we may have disliked some foods because of their flavor; with maturity, we rediscover these foods. For Gayer, black walnuts were one such food. "My grandmother had a black walnut tree in front of her house. So there were black walnut brownies and black walnut chocolate chip cookies; it was black walnut heaven. Only a few years ago did I finally start liking them again."

By contrast, Claudia Fleming remembers, "The most exciting things about my grandmother coming to visit were pomegranates, fennel, and fresh ricotta that she would bring from the Bronx. She was originally from Sicily. We ate very well growing up. It was relatively sophisticated for the sixties. There was never a frozen or canned vegetable in the house, no iceberg lettuce, no TV dinners, no Chef Boyardee—never. There was a huge farmer's market in the next town that we went to every week. I remember Saturday mornings being like a food odyssey. First it was the Italian delicatessen, then it was the German delicatessen, because they had the best potato salad, and we picked up rye bread and kaiser rolls. Then we were off to Entenmann's and the soda place. It was unbelievable! I was never too intimidated to taste something new or eat something unfamiliar. I was fortunate in that way."

Elizabeth Falkner recalls comparing the gourmet chocolate chip cookies that became the rage in southern California when she was in high school. "I really liked the ones with big chunks in them," she said, "but I noticed that some companies used lower-quality chocolate. I decided I needed to figure out what my own ultimate chocolate chip cookie was, so I spent a long time during high school working on the recipe in my mom's kitchen." She discovered that she could make a superior product and developed a passion for baking.

Mocha Sorbet with Toasted Cocoa Phyllo

by Dan Budd

This light dessert features rich chocolate and coffee flavors, simply presented on a crispy, toasted phyllo nest.

Yield: 6 servings

For the mocha sorbet:

2 cups water

1½ teaspoons finely ground espresso beans

2 tablespoons high-quality, dark cocoa powder

1 cup sugar

2 tablespoons corn syrup

2 ounces bittersweet chocolate

For the cocoa phyllo nests:

6 sheets of phyllo

2 tablespoons high-quality cocoa powder

2 tablespoons sugar

2 tablespoons water

¼ cup confectioners' sugar

For the mocha sorbet:

1. Combine all sorbet ingredients in a saucepot over medium heat. Whisk the mixture until it is warm and ingredients are incorporated.

2. Pass the mixture through a fine strainer into a container and cool it on an ice bath.

3. Churn the base in an ice cream machine. Store in the freezer until serving time.

For the cocoa phyllo nests:

1. Preheat oven to 350°. Roll the phyllo sheets up together and, starting from one end, with a French knife, cut ¹⁄₁₆- to ⅛-inch strips until the sheets are completely shredded.

2. Over medium heat, dissolve the sugar in the water to form a syrup.

3. Toss the shredded phyllo, syrup mixture, and remaining ingredients together in a large bowl.

4. Place a 3-inch round pastry cutter on a parchment-lined or nonstick baking tray. Settle a small amount (1 ounce) of the mixture into the bottom of the pastry cutter, then pull the cutter up and repeat the procedure, leaving 1 inch between discs.

5. Bake the shredded phyllo discs for 14 to 16 minutes, or until they are crispy. Allow them to cool.

Assembly:

Place a toasted cocoa phyllo disc on each plate and top each disc with a generous scoop of the mocha sorbet.

François Payard, pastry chef/owner of Payard Patisserie and Bistro, grew up in a family that owned two pâtisseries in the south of France, one in Nice. "Jacques [Torres] used to go there to practice when he was learning to work with chocolate. My parents pushed me to be a caterer. I started by working for a caterer, making napoleons and canapés, and realized then that I liked it. It was something different. I never worked for my parents. I always saw my father bake, but my father is tough.

He never allowed me to work with him, so my parents sent me to apprentice and it was better that way. It's too easy to work for your parents. You can do what you want. When you work for someone else, you have to be quiet. You have to listen and learn everything." Jacques Torres was heavily affected by his family's love of food. "We all love to eat in my family. My brother is a chef and I wanted to be a chef. I love the ambience of dining. I love the action of a kitchen. When I was thirteen, I asked my older brother for advice and for my summer vacation I went out to get a job in a restaurant—busboy, dishwasher, or whatever job people would give me. My brother told me there wasn't a good restaurant in town but there was a good pastry shop that I should try." Jacques immediately found himself at home in the rigorous work environment of that first pastry kitchen.

Dan Budd remembers his introduction to the business. "My sister wanted to get a job. She saw an ad in the newspaper for a breakfast and lunch place opening in Killington, Vermont. The ad said, 'Hostess and dishwasher needed. No age requirement.' I was fourteen and she was fifteen, and we went up there and met the people who were opening Marge and John's Country Breakfast. We opened that restaurant with them as kids. We were dishwashers there on weekends and I worked there for about four and a half years, all through high school. After a while, I became a short-order cook. People used to come in and request things from me, and I would think, "Wow, that's kind of cool." I began to understand how each customer wanted their food and I could make it, whether it was cooking a Western omelette sandwich or doing the eggs just right. My sister wanted only me to make her French toast because I knew exactly how she liked it. I felt like I had a lot of control over how to make things the way people liked them. This was a lot of inspiration for me early on. I bring those experiences with me even today. Working with food, learning how to cook different parts of a meal so that they are ready at the same time, being efficient, and bringing out the best in the dishes was always the challenge. And whether it's cooking breakfast or it's making pastries, or working as a saucier or poissonier in New York (I haven't always been in pastry), it started back when I was fourteen years old."

Budd's attitude was a prelude to his success. He had his mind set on quality from the beginning and treated each job in the business with a seriousness and intensity that carried his career to new heights.

"Everyone on my mom's side of the family liked to cook," muses Emily Luchetti. "My grandfather was one of these people who cut food articles out of the newspaper and kept them in piles and boxes, all of which I have. I don't know what I'm going to do with them, but I have them. My grandfather didn't necessarily make the recipes in them, but he collected them because he had a real passion for food."

Elizabeth Falkner grew up in a family whose artistic leanings influenced her approach to becoming a pastry chef. "Nobody in my family really talked about being a professional chef. It wasn't something that really occurred. My father is an abstract painter and I have one brother who is a rock star and another brother who is getting into acting. Art seems to run in my family. I think growing up going to museums and art galleries definitely influenced my style."

Children assimilate both positive and negative attitudes and opinions about food from the role it plays in family life. The negative perception of cooking as drudgery work for the oppressed housewife is a stigma that Gale Gand had to overcome in her family. "My mom was the original feminist and she spent her whole life trying to get out of the kitchen, trying not to be a housewife. I was a starving art student when I was nineteen and I couldn't really afford food, so I started working in a restaurant as a waitress because I could get the meal prepared for the staff every day. I got thrown into the kitchen one day because one of the cooks didn't show up. I just loved it. I instantly found my home; I found my medium. I was so excited, I called my parents and said, 'Guess what? I'm cooking in a kitchen and I just love it.' My mother was disappointed because she had spent her whole life trying to get out of being a housewife and there I was marching right back in and celebrating it. They were

> Pastry chefs are in the business of making people happy. This is a profession of festivities. We rarely see people sad. They come to us in the best of times.
> —Sebastien Canonne

paying for my art school and they envisioned my becoming a sculptor or something. My father's response was, 'Well, Gale, I guess everyone's got to eat.' So they were very disappointed that I finally found my love at nineteen."

Sebastien Canonne recalls cooking at home with his grandmother. "When I got into the professional kitchen it was just like going to the next step, like playing baseball for fun and then getting on the team. I loved it right away. I was born into it." Canonne attributes his career choice to family influence. "For my parents and grandparents, the making of a meal was something really special. Pastry chefs are in the business of making people happy. This is a profession of festivities. We rarely see people sad. They come to us in the best of times."

Mrs. Essam's
Mince Pie

by Gale Gand

*This recipe is from a ninety-two-year-old woman Gand lived
next to in the row cottages of the English countryside. Sometimes her
work starts from something traditional passed down in this way.*

Yield: 1 large pie

1 pound green apples (about 4 to 5 apples)

1½ cups raisins

1 cup golden raisins

1½ cups currants

1 cup candied citrus rind

1½ cups shredded beef suet (or lard)

½ lemon, grated and juiced

½ orange, grated and juiced

½ teaspoon cinnamon

½ teaspoon mace

½ teaspoon nutmeg

2 cups brown sugar

½ teaspoon salt

½ cup rum

¼ cup apple juice concentrate

1 recipe simple pie dough (see below)

For the simple pie dough:

4½ cups all-purpose flour, sifted

2 teaspoons kosher salt

2 teaspoons sugar (optional)

1½ cups (3 sticks) cold, unsalted butter, cut into pieces

½ cup ice water

2 teaspoons red wine vinegar

1. Peel, core, and chop the apples and place in a large bowl. Chop all the dried fruit and stir it, along with the remaining ingredients (except the pie dough) into the bowl.

2. Place the mixture in a large pot over low heat and cook for 1 hour, stirring occasionally.

3. Remove from the heat and chill overnight. (This mixture can be refrigerated for up to a month.)

For the simple pie dough:

1. In the bowl of a mixer fitted with a paddle attachment, combine the flour, salt, and sugar. Mix 1 minute. Add the butter and mix just until the mixture resembles coarse crumbs.

2. Stir the water and vinegar together, then gradually add to the flour mixture. Mix at medium speed just until a dough forms. Do not overmix; the mixture may still have bits of butter. Wrap the dough in plastic and refrigerate.

To assemble the pie:

1. Preheat the oven to 450°. Roll out two pieces of pie dough slightly larger than the diameter of a deep-dish pan. Line the deep-dish pan with one piece, letting the dough hang over the edge.

2. Brush the edge with water, fill the pie with the mincemeat, and top with the second piece of rolled dough. Press the edges together, trim off the excess dough, and cut a few vents in the top.

3. Bake for 10 minutes, then turn the oven down to 350° and continue baking for about 30 minutes. You should see the pie filling bubbling from the vents. Remove from the oven and cool.

Jacquy Pfeiffer, owner and instructor of the French Pastry School in Chicago, grew up in a family that owned a bakery and he remembers taking breads out of the big brick oven at the age of seven. His attraction to the ovens served a practical purpose as well. "As a child, I was drawn to the oven because of the cold winter mornings of northern France. The bricks were hot, so I would stand near the oven and watch the bakers, or sometimes I would help my father."

Nancy Silverton recalls her early food experiences and how she got her start in the kitchen. "My mother loved to cook. She didn't cook elaborate meals all the time, but when she did, she liked to cook ethnic meals. I used to really hate her cooking and wonder why she couldn't just make creamed tuna on toast. We used to eat out a lot when we traveled and my parents would always search out the little ethnic spots. I was always saying, 'Why can't we go to Denny's?' I loved Denny's. I loved the overcooked hamburgers. That kind of food was all I wanted to eat. I didn't have much of a food sense. When I moved from Los Angeles to northern California to go to school in Sonoma, I lived in the dorms. I fell in love with a guy who was heading a vegetarian food service program. I needed to meet him so I walked up to him and told him that I loved to cook. I told him that I was a vegetarian and asked if I could I help out in the kitchen. So one day a week I was responsible for the vegetarian meal, both lunch and dinner, and I absolutely loved it. It was very heavy, plain food, but I had a great time. I did it for only a year, but sometime in those first few months, I knew this was what I wanted to do, because I loved cooking. For summer breaks, I worked in what was popular at the time, pseudo French bistros, then I dropped out of college my senior year. That's when I thought to myself, 'I'm going to get a job in the best restaurant.' " Silverton went on to make her

Richard Leach and assistant

mark at Wolfgang Puck's Spago, where she met her husband, Mark Peel. The couple opened the acclaimed Campanile and LaBrea Bakery in 1989.

Dan Budd's large family shares a playfulness about food. "One of the things my family does, even to this day, is get together, sometimes as many as twenty of us, and have an apple pie baking weekend. I built my house and when we finished the kitchen, we said, 'All right, we're ready for apple pies.' We baked sixty-seven apple pies in one day and everything was done by hand. Each individual pie crust was mixed by hand and flour was everywhere. The uncles all peel and the moms make the dough and I don't say anything. I just enjoy it. Sometimes they get mad at me and say, 'Hey! The pastry chef's not making enough pies.' But sometimes I just like to make the soup for lunch and enjoy the day."

Bruno Feldeisen, pastry chef/owner of Senses Bakery & Restaurant, Washington, D.C., reflects on his childhood and the culturally ingrained love for food that many families in his native France exude. "Cooking is such a big part of the culture. Every Sunday is a big meal. Even during the week, people take off at noon to go home for an appetizer, entrée, cheese, and dessert, then go back to work. You are surrounded by it all the time; you breathe it. People pay so much attention to food. I remember my grandmother saying, 'What am I going to cook today?' That was her big question. It wasn't 'What kind of bills do I have to pay?' or 'What kind of shopping should I do today?' "

Your food experiences from your family and surrounding environment may be memorable and include preparing food from scratch or picking fruits or berries and baking pies with your grandmother. Or you may have no such early feelings of connection with cooking and food, as they may develop later, once you leave college or start your first job. Your attraction to cooking and pastry is an individual experience rooted in your own life. Your connection with and attitudes toward food are something worth pondering. Consider your attraction to this field by looking at your past, because that is what will propel your creative ideas for the future.

Mentors—Influence from Chefs and Food

A mentor is a wise and trusted teacher, guide, and friend. All chefs have a mentor, someone they looked to at some point in their career and perhaps still do. I could name many who influenced me in different areas of my professional life that needed development. I continue to find new mentors in some of the incredibly talented, focused, and driven people I meet and work with on various projects. I believe that chefs who deny having mentors negate both the past and future possibility of continuous learning. Mentors are part of a great tradition of passing on precious knowledge, which is a vitally important way the profession stays alive and grows. Those who recieve mentoring must remember to carry on that tradition of generosity by passing on knowledge whenever possible. In my mind, this is as much a part of the profession as whipping cream. Pastry chefs must continue to share recipes and techniques with subsequent generations of pastry chefs who will carry on the business and tradition of providing customers with a delicious experience, a memory, a brief, pleasurable, flavorful interlude.

Nick Malgieri serves as a mentor for many future pastry chefs. As a culinary educator, he stresses the importance of having a mentor. "Identifying with a mentor gives you a chance to to be exposed to different styles of work and to codified personal styles. It gives you exposure to a coherent body of work that helps you to build your own personal style. It's hard to do that in a vacuum, without looking at the work of other pastry chefs. We are all influenced by things we see in books, but one person all alone with a pile of books and a bunch of ingredients isn't going to come up with much except a carbon copy of what is in the books. Pastry chefs who have a well-rounded background, have been exposed to different mentors and different styles, and have evolved their own style as a result. They can then go to a restaurant and see a particular pastry chef's work and say to themselves, 'This combination of tapioca and coconut is really great.' Then they can go back and, instead of making a carbon copy of that dessert, draw on that experience as an influence and make something of their own that relates to the original." Lindsey Shere agrees. "I think by working with someone you respect, or even working with several people, if at all possible, is a really good idea, because you always learn something. From that you can develop your own style."

Claudia Fleming identifies strongly with the work of Chef Tom Colicchio, chef of Gramercy Tavern. "My style has really developed as a result of watching him cook. My desserts are derivative of what he does. I draw on other pastry chefs' use and combinations of flavors, but in terms of composition and the way I put things together, I think more about cooking savory food than making dessert." Fleming also counts among her mentors Alice Waters, Lindsey Shere, and Nancy Silverton. "Nancy and Lindsey were definite inspirations to me as women. I read their books over and over again, and because the books had no pictures, I was allowed to use my imagination. I love to look at pictures in cookbooks, but at the same time it is fun to imagine what it might look like. You don't feel as though you have to make it look like whatever their dessert looked like. You can interpret because it is left up to your imagination."

Richard Leach was introduced to the restaurant business and the diverse tasks involved in running restaurants while working as a teenager on Long Island. "Peter Visero, who owned the Armenian restaurant I started in, could do everything. He went from working in hospital incinerators to owning his own restaurant." Visero showed Richard the resourcefulness necessary in this business and the ability to learn and grow with the job. "Later on, Charlie Palmer, chef at Aureole, introduced me to fine cuisine. David Burke at the River Café influenced my work as well. Half of the cooks I knew at that time were pretty inspiring. Jerry Hayden was the first pastry chef at Aureole. He would get me pumped up about trying new things. I'm not sure if he was encouraging me or if he was just trying get out of the position, but he used to push me to do more. He had a great work ethic."

A mentor can become important to you at different times in your career, even years after the actual work association. You may notice subtle things in the way a mentor works or how he or she handles a specific situation. Later you may find yourself in that same situation and the memory of your role model's methods come back to you. From this memory comes guidance, a voice, and you have solutions to apply to your own set of inevitable problems or obstacles. Dan Budd relates his belief in mentors. "Mentors inspire you in ways that you don't even realize. Something about them is special and it begins to be something that helps you along in your career. Even if you don't know you have a mentor, you probably do. Chef David Burke was the first person who showed me how important desserts are. At the time, I was grateful that he was willing to teach me everything he knew if I was willing to learn it. At the River Café, before he became the chef, he used to come in late at night after dinner service. At that time I was plating desserts and it would be two o'clock in the morning and I had been there since seven o'clock in the morning. He would say, 'Stick around. We're going to cook sugar and make chocolates. We're going to practice all these things so when I come here as the chef, we're ready.' And so I used to stay until the wee hours of the morning with him making liquor candies, cooking sugar, and pouring sugar. I would go home, sleep for a couple hours, and come back. He was definitely a great inspiration."

> Chefs know how to mix flavors but pastry chefs often don't. French pastry chefs often use too much mousse and mushy things. They often create desserts with no flavor that look good to the eye, but don't taste very good.
> —François Payard

Chefs and pastry chefs must work together closely, so the chef is very often the role model, leader, and influential mentor for pastry chefs. François Payard is more often inspired by chefs than pastry chefs. "Chefs know how to mix flavors but pastry chefs often don't. French pastry chefs often use too much mousse and mushy things. They often create desserts with no flavor that look good to the eye, but don't taste very good."

Tropical Fruit Spring Rolls

by Andrew MacLauchlan

Asian spring rolls earned their name because they were originally served
during new-year celebrations, also known as spring festivals in China and Vietnam.
Although typically filled with vegetables, seafood, and meats, this playful version
of spring rolls bursts with fresh tropical fruits, vanilla, and a hint of allspice.
Any assortment of tropical fruits, other than those listed below, can be used.
They make a perfect ending to an Asian meal.

Yield: 6 servings

6 leaves of rice spring roll wrappers

1 mango

1 papaya

2 kiwis

2 figs

1 banana

2 tablespoons brown sugar

1 teaspoon vanilla extract

2 tablespoons sake or white wine

½ teaspoon ground allspice

1. Preheat oven to 325°. Soak the leaves of rice spring roll wrappers in cold water.

2. Prepare the fruits by peeling the mango, papaya, kiwi, and banana, and cutting the hard stem from the fig.

3. Cut the flesh from the mango and cut into matchstick-sized julienne. Cut the papaya in half from top to bottom, remove the seeds, and julienne.

4. Julienne the remaining fruits, and toss all the fruit in a bowl with the brown sugar, vanilla extract, sake, and allspice.

5. Place a soaked leaf of rice wrapper on your work surface and spoon some of the fruit off center in a 1-inch-thick line across the lower half of the circle.

6. Roll the bottom edge over the fruit and begin rolling the circle halfway up, then fold the excess rice wrapper on the sides over the fruit into the center, then continue rolling to form the spring roll.

7. Repeat the process with remaining rice spring roll wrappers and fruit.

8. Place the spring rolls in a pan and drizzle with a little water and heat in the oven for 12 minutes.

9. Cut them in half crossways and place 2 halves on each plate, propping one half up against the other.

Judy Contino also found support from the chefs she worked with. "I took a class from Albert Kumin that I loved. I was in one of his very first classes. There were only three students and we couldn't have had more individual attention. He took us home half the nights for dinner. I remember him taking me to the train station when I was leaving and I had asked about a recipe that wasn't included in his class. He suddenly pulled out his recipe bible and, right there in the train station, he shared it with me. I'm sure he has shared it with a lot of people but just the way he did it was very special."

Nancy Silverton, who has inspired me and so many people in the world of cooking, has her own source of influence. "Alice Waters is my true mentor. From reading about her and then eating at her restaurant, I know that, like me, she is never satisfied. You can tell she is passionate about cooking, eating, and sharing. The way she chooses what ingredients to use and how she uses them has influenced me."

Silverton recalls arguing with Mark Miller over whether a good chef needs to show his or her technical skills by making something complicated or whether a good chef is someone who can pick out a perfect tomato, slice it up, and put some salt on it. "Mark says, 'Picking out that tomato is fine, but that doesn't make a great chef. A great chef has to do something with that tomato.' That's just a funny little ongoing argument I have with Mark, but I believe that a great chef can make the decision to say, 'This is a truly great tomato and it can be left the way it is,' or, 'This tomato isn't so great, so we need to roast it.' I think Alice Waters is one of the few people who can really do that. She is also someone who is firm in her beliefs and has been able to stick to them rather than make compromises."

Jim Graham speaks of his mentor. "I always come back to the pastry chef at Taillevent in Paris, Gilles Bajole. He is a remarkable person. I can't say that I came away from working with him with a lot of technique—it was more an attitude, a spirit. I have drawn a lot of inspiration from that as well as the pastry chef I worked with at Lenôtre in Houston, Gerald Gautheron. He was a good first person to work for. He had a good attitude. A lot of the chefs who come out of the classical French tradition are really rough on beginners, but he wasn't. He was much more sympathetic. He appreciated the enthusiasm I showed, and as I wasn't as young as a lot of the other apprentices, he gave me credit for having a little bit more maturity. He took me under his wing and allowed me to do a lot of things that typically a person at my stage in training wouldn't have been allowed to do. He was very forgiving of mistakes and got me off to a good start."

Maury Rubin found personalized guidance in an intensive six-day training course. "My mentor is Denis Ruffel, the chef at Pâtisserie Millet. He taught my first course. I found his range of ability captivating. I realized, watching him in the first two days, that his creative framework was one I could work in, very broad and open to a person's imagination. I didn't spend that much time working directly with him, but he is what I consider a legitimate inspiration."

Rubin questions the necessity of personal mentorship for every student of pastry. "I am not sure that having a mentor is as important as having the proper training. You might be a natural at pastry, or you might be phenomenally motivated, and if either one of those is the case, the question is, 'Are you getting enough of a reference to great pastry work in formative, early stages of your training to develop real quality in your work?' "

A mentor provides a model of excellence to strive for. By actually mimicking the traits in your mentor that you admire, you come to absorb them into your own way of being. At first this may seem unnatural, but if you can absorb these good qualities that you see, believe it or not, over time, you will also begin to experience some or all of the success that your mentor has created in his or her life and career.

Emily Luchetti has had many mentors, resulting in many areas of growth. "Jeremiah Tower was an incredible mentor for me with respect to quality. He had a very big influence on me. Being around that environment for so long, you just pick up on it. As far as baking, I think I kind of pull from everybody. I pull from people like Julia Child, Jacques Pepin, and Nancy Silverton. I look at everybody and think, 'What do they do that I respect and admire?'" Richard Leach remembers an eye-opening turning point. "I had a memorable meal at Mondrian before I worked there. Tom Colicchio's desserts involved herbs I still draw from—the raspberry-thyme combination, chocolate with bay leaf, and rosemary with different things. I liked his desserts because he managed to combine savory cooking techniques and ingredients in fantastic desserts."

Espresso Shortbread Cookies

by Emily Luchetti

Yield: 2 dozen

1 cup cold sweet butter

½ cup sugar

1¾ cups flour

Pinch of salt

¼ cup freshly ground espresso

1. Preheat the oven to 250°.

2. Combine the butter and sugar in an electric mixer bowl. With the paddle attachment, mix on low speed for 15 seconds.

3. Add the flour, salt, and espresso grounds and mix on low speed for 3 to 5 minutes. It will look dry just before it comes together.

4. Put the dough on a lightly floured board and roll it to ¼-inch thick.

5. With a 3-inch star cutter or other desired shape, cut out the cookies and chill them for 1 hour in the freezer or refrigerator.

6. Line a baking sheet with parchment paper and place the cookies on the sheet so they are not touching.

7. Bake the shortbread for about 45 minutes or until firm. The cookies should remain white in color.

Roland Mesnier feels strongly about mentors. "It's very important to have somebody that you can look up to. Let's say you get into a difficult situation. For myself, I always think back. 'How would so-and-so have handled that?' Sometimes I see young people in difficult situations today. They just throw their arms up and don't know which way to go. Maybe they're too young to be in the position they are in, or perhaps they don't have a mentor. I've had at least ten mentors in my life, people I regard very highly, people I've stayed friends with all of my life, people I make sure I stay friends with because they've done so much for me. They've shown me what to do and sometimes what not to do. They were not perfect. They made mistakes too, and sometimes I learned from their mistakes. I always tell young people, 'Don't take a pastry chef job too early in your life. Go work with some great people. Stick with them. See everything and honor them. Don't just take from them and act like you don't know them after that because someday you will be in the shoes of that mentor."

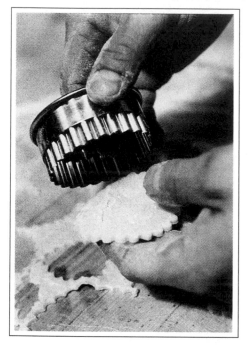

Cutting dough with a fluted cutter

Jacques Torres looks to mentors as a vital part of the world of pastry. He considers direct influence and the passing on of technique from pastry chef to novice central to the continuity of the craft. "When I started in this profession, I was inspired by teachers, friends, and people I worked with. Once you start to know your skill and profession, you have to become an inspiration to other people. You have to become the driving force for other people. You have to be the engine. I use the engines of other people like Jacques Maxim and Louis Franchin, people who really helped me in my career. Now I feel I have the responsibility for taking that leadership to help other people. That is why I work with the French Culinary Institute and accept a lot of inexperienced people in this kitchen."

Many of Gale Gand's mentors are from outside the culinary world, from her days in art school. "I had a drawing teacher with whom I spent a lot of time. He was the person who taught me how to discover more than just the obvious, how to go beyond just the normal surface ideas. He used all sorts of techniques. He'd take away all color, allowing us only to work in black and white for a day. It would push us past our boundaries. You know when you have to come up with a dessert idea, you've got your top ten, but if someone took away your top ten, it would force you to go beyond where your comfort is. He really gave me that as a way of working and developing myself."

Passing on of the craft is a way of connecting us all as pastry chefs. Jaques Torres speaks passionately on this topic. "I think, as a pastry chef, you have to be a giving person. You have to give away the things you like. I always tell people who come to see me, 'If I help you or give you something, I don't expect anything back from you, but I do expect you to help another person. And you have to get that same commitment from the person you help.' I think if we all do this in our profession, it will be a lot easier for the younger generation to approach us and work with us."

Apple Apple Apple

by Jacques Torres

"This dessert presents apples in three different ways—as apple syrup, apple sorbet, and apple chips," says Torres. "I usually make it in the fall when the countryside smells of apples, but it makes a refreshing summer dessert too. I prefer to use Granny Smith apples because of their tart flavor and crisp texture."

Yield: 8 servings

For the sorbet:
2 tablespoons water
2 tablespoons sugar
2 cups apple juice

For the apple chips:
1 large apple

For the syrup:
½ teaspoon powdered gelatin
2 tablespoons plus 1 cup water
½ cup sugar
Juice of 1 lemon
1 large apple

Continued on next page

1. Combine the water and sugar in a saucepot over medium heat and bring to a simmer (this is called a simple syrup). Prepare the sorbet by whisking together the juice and the simple syrup. Spin in an ice cream machine until smooth and creamy. Place in a covered container and store in the freezer until ready to use.

2. Prepare the chips by preheating the oven to 250°. Peel the apple and save the peel to make the syrup. Core the apple and lay it on its side.

3. Using a sharp knife, cut the apple into ⅟₁₆-inch-thick slices, or use a mandoline slicing tool. Place the slices side by side on a nonstick baking sheet, a sheet of parchment brushed with vegetable oil, or a Silpat (a rubber nonstick baking sheet) and bake until golden brown and dry, about 1½ hours. Remove the chips from the oven and let them cool.

4. Prepare the syrup by pouring the 2 tablespoons of water into a bowl. Sprinkle the gelatin over the water to let it bloom, let sit for about 1 minute. Combine the reserved apple peel (see step 2), remaining water, sugar, and lemon juice in a non-reactive saucepot and bring to a boil over medium-high heat. When mixture boils, stir in the gelatin. The gelatin will thicken the syrup as it cools. Strain the syrup through a fine mesh strainer into a container. Cover and refrigerate until ready to use.

5. Assemble the dessert by pouring the chilled syrup into the bowls to fully cover the bottom. Peel and core the apple and, with a sharp knife, cut it into matchstick-size pieces. Divide the pieces among eight bowls, placing them in the center of the syrup. Place a large scoop of the sorbet atop the cut apple and top each with four apple chips. Serve immediately.

For the pastry chef, much passion for the craft can be stirred by looking at and tasting another chef's food and by examining classic desserts and recipes. These observations can be even more powerful than direct encouragement from a mentor. Emily Luchetti draws inspiration from the fundamentals. "I think of puff pastry. I think of tart doughs. Those fundamental things that are in both American and European desserts are the backbone. You take those and you turn them into your own creation, your own idea, but it's really just the fundamentals that you begin with."

Sebastien Canonne cautions against blindly incorporating ingredients and techniques. "Here in the States, everyone influences someone else because we are free to do so much more than in Europe. I hope the strongest influences come from those who do the right things with strong base recipes and ingredients. Your type of work may not be what I do, but I look at it, try some recipes, and it influences me somewhere."

Richard Leach stresses the importance of seeing everything that surrounds you in the kitchen. "There should be a definite influence from the chefs around you, the way they do things, the way they handle food—different techniques for making sauces, for instance. Every chef is different and, if you are observant, you will continually learn."

Particular ingredients can be especially inspiring for a chef or pastry chef—for example, the first black Mission figs that arrive in the kitchen, ripe and sweet, or the first frais de bois (wild strawberries) of spring. Canonne recalls the excitement brought about by seasonal foods. "I was brought up in a little town where, when the first strawberry came into season, there was all this excitement. Here it's pumpkin pie. Everyone's excited and then it's gone, but then next year everyone's excited again. Nobody's excited about raspberries anymore because they're here all year round. That's one reason people lose their taste for something or don't like it anymore. When you have the right fruit at the right time of year, then you don't have to do much to it to serve it."

Pineapple

Nancy Silverton looks to the ingredients as well. "I think my inspiration has always come from the ingredient itself. I don't get inspired from photographs so much, although sometimes I enjoy looking at them. My inspiration comes from tasting, especially tasting fruit."

Charlie Trotter remembers the point at which he began to view desserts as an integrated part of the meal that could be as moving an experience as any of the preceding courses. "I think back to my San Francisco days. I had a dear friend out there, Robert Morris, who I used to cook with almost every day. What began as two cooking buddies getting together to have fun, practice cooking, and experiment with recipes, quickly turned into a friendly competition, who-could-make-the-next-best-course kind of thing. I remember trying to do some elaborate desserts back then. One day, Robert did something so simple with some tropical fruits that were just warmed up—some mangoes, pineapple, a little vanilla, some black pepper. He deglazed the pan with a little Sauterne wine, made a little juice sauce, and literally scooped Häagen Dazs vanilla ice cream out of the container. The fruit was perfectly ripe and it was just warmed through. The sauce had the flavor of the fruits and the heat of the pepper. I thought to myself, 'The flavors here are as profound and sensual as the most elaborate concoctions I've seen at any restaurant or hotel.' At that time, it occurred to me that desserts were more about flavor and purity of ingredients than anything else."

> The fruit was perfectly ripe and it was just warmed through. The sauce had the flavor of the fruits and the heat of the pepper. I thought to myself, "The flavors here are as profound and sensual as the most elaborate concoctions I've seen at any restaurant or hotel." At that time, it occurred to me that desserts were more about flavor and purity of ingredients than anything else.
>
> —Charlie Trotter

Claudia Fleming also strives to stay open to new ways of looking at the same ingredients or desserts. "At any given point, whatever your frame of mind, you have to look at things differently. I pore over the same things again and again and again, and I continue to be inspired and have a different viewpoint, even though it's the same thing."

Being inspired by food itself is something great pastry chefs share. Trotter speaks about foodstuff as inspiration. "How do you improve on a perfect peach? It's harder to leave it alone than it is to build a bunch of stuff around it. It means waiting for the right season. It means having a brief window of opportunity in which to work. It means celebrating flavor in a way that allows that food to just sing with its own flavor, beauty, and texture."

No matter how long you have been a pastry chef, finding the best way of preparing and serving a perfect peach or strawberry in its prime season and peak flavor is an inspirational, creative journey. Classic or memorable dessert experiences can be used to create your own desserts that bear the mark of your own personal approach. Jaques Torres prefers simple things done to perfection. "I don't have just one dessert I really like. I like figs if they're done well. You can impress me with an apple tart, if the color is there, if the flavor is there, if the crunchiness is there, if there's a nice cream under it. You can impress me with simple things that are made to a high standard, to a standard not many people can accomplish. That's when I am impressed. When someone serves me a napoleon and it's so crunchy, so light, so flavorful that I can taste the flavor of the butter from the puff pastry, I can taste the flavor of the vanilla, I can feel the smooth texture of the cream, then I'm impressed. If there's a balance of creaminess, crunchiness, temperature, and pure flavor, that's when I'm impressed. Give me a big sugar presentation or a big chocolate centerpiece and I'm not impressed because I know with time and hard work anyone can do that. You have to be really talented to do something simple and extremely good."

Why a Pastry Chef? Why Not a Chef?

In a restaurant or hotel, the chef is the undisputed leader of all food operations, management, supply, and equipment costs. In a restaurant owned by the chef, add to those responsibilities business expertise such as contract negotiation, finance, accounting knowledge, and public relations ability. A pastry chef generally works under the chef in a hotel or restaurant, although every situation is different. A pastry chef is most often an acknowledged leader and department head and shares a cooperative vision with the chef and the management team. The best pastry chefs, in my view, have a sense of the entire operation. They have an acute awareness of how their job or area contributes to the whole. Charlie Trotter agrees. "I always love it when I see a pastry chef who actually has some experience with savory food. I think it gives them a better understanding about the dynamic of the rest of the kitchen. I have seen pastry chefs who couldn't care less about what is happening around the kitchen, as opposed to taking an interest in understanding how what they do fits in."

> I always love it when I see a pastry chef who actually has some experience with savory food. I think it gives them a better understanding about the dynamic of the rest of the kitchen.
> —Charlie Trotter

Trotter believes that with cross-training and appreciation for all food and savory cooking, a pastry chef only makes him- or herself better. "Sometimes we try to rotate some of our personnel. I don't always like to saddle a pastry chef with a line cook that we're just moving to a position to help out. That person generally has to be interested in being in the pastry department. I think the best pastry chefs are ones who have experience outside the world of pastry and the best chefs are chefs who have spent some time working with desserts and pastry and don't regard it as a foreign world."

Nancy Silverton agrees and emphasizes the similarities of chef and pastry chef techniques and products rather than the differences. "The successful pastry chef is one who also cooks and understands food. A successful cook is one who also understands pastries. The pastry chef who has cooking experience has the capacity to understand many dimensions of flavor. Desserts don't have to be one-dimensional. They don't have to be just sweet. For example, there's a lemon meringue tart here at Campanile that's very successful. It has a champagne vinegar sauce made with caramelized sugar and vanilla, and built up with butter. It comes from my days of making duck sauce. I think that this sauce has more play with the lemon than an anglaise or a raspberry sauce. The vinegar brings a new dimension to the dessert, adds another layer. It comes from my cooking experience and I think the dessert is more interesting because of it. Sometimes taking those sweet edges off really enhances a dessert. You can borrow many things from cooking if you do them properly. Roasting, braising, and poaching are all borrowed or collective cooking techniques that you have to know. Those pastry chefs who don't know these methods are more limited."

> The pastry chef who has cooking experience has the capacity to understand many dimensions of flavor.
> —Nancy Silverton

Markus Färbinger sees the similarities between chefs and pastry chefs. "I don't think a pastry chef and a chef are all that different, really. If you look at hot desserts, they require 90 percent of the skills and knowledge that the hot food chef is using. If you make hot desserts and soufflés, your work style on the line is similar. You finish off the sauce. You finish off the fruits you have flambéed. You taste everything that you make. You are flavor sensitive and you work closely with the taste of everything. As a hot dessert maker, you are also able to adjust the flavor of things at the last minute, just like the savory food chef. In the traditional pastry chef sense, you make the taste and then you put it away in the oven or refrigerator and there is little you can change at that point. Chefs today emphasize ingredients more than before and make decisions about quality and taste earlier. Like apples chosen for their special texture and flavor that apples from somewhere else don't have. It's the same thing with meat, fish, vegetables, and herbs. I don't think there is that much difference between the pastry chef and chef."

Though the output of chefs and pastry chefs should be essentially the same—great food, a delicious, seamless meal down to the last chocolate or petit four—the means of a pastry chef may be somewhat different than the means of chef. Mark Miller addresses these different paths. "I think that the best pastry chefs have the same aptitude as chefs, but a good pastry chef is not necessarily a good chef, and a good chef is not necessarily a good pastry chef. It can happen, but it doesn't happen very often. In order to be a pastry chef, you have to be more exacting and patient. People who aren't patient make terrible pastry chefs. Most chefs are used to controlling their ingredients a lot more by adding them and seeing the effect and building up flavors. But in pastry, for the most part, you don't see the effect until later. For example, you make the recipe and put it in the oven; once the cake is baked, it's done. You get a deferred kind of result. If you don't like it, you have to throw it out and start over.

"Most chefs don't like to measure anything when they cook, but pastry work is more exact. Pastries don't reflect anything in the natural world. When you make a white sponge cake, it doesn't really resemble anything else; it doesn't have a model. When you work with salmon, you have models. You have raw salmon, baked salmon, cured salmon, smoked salmon,

Pastry cook hard at work

but eventually it still tastes like salmon. You can start with wheat and think about making a cake, but cake doesn't exist in that way. There is more chemistry involved than in cooking. There is also more of what I would call transformation. It's true that chefs also transform things from one state to another. Some people are not comfortable taking the guts out of animals, boning them, skinning them. Cooking has a visceral quality—dealing with wild mushrooms, confit, garlic, thyme, chile—that pastry doesn't. Pastry deals more with refined sugars, fruits, honey, and flours. Pastry chefs serve one course, while a chef has to worry about a progression of courses. I think the stress is different. The hours can be just as long, but they are more controllable. You work with your hands a lot more than a regular chef does. A good pastry chef acquires a natural rhythm, a coexistence with the ingredients."

Miller points to another important difference between chef and pastry chef. "The pastry chef's palate must be different than that of a regular chef. It has to be more subtle because the range is smaller. You have to differentiate with chocolate, sweetness, degrees of caramelization."

> Pastry deals more with refined sugars, fruits, honey, and flours. Pastry chefs serve one course, while a chef has to worry about a progression of courses.
> —Mark Miller

Very few pastry chefs have had no experience with savory food. Many started in the cooking world as line or prep cooks and found an affinity for dessert making. Jacques Torres tried both. "In the beginning, I tried both the kitchen and pastry to see what I liked. Perhaps if I stayed with the kitchen and I liked it, I would be a chef today. I don't really know. I just started doing pastry and fell in love with it."

Sebastien Canonne started as a cook. "I was trained to be a chef on the hot line in a three-star restaurant and I loved it. I still cook at home all the time and I love to do it. But I always liked a little more artistic work and a little more playing. You know, a rack of lamb is a rack of lamb. You have a vegetable that you can braise, blanch, or sauté. The pastry chef has raw ingredients and from there it is never-ending. In food I felt more limited." Like Canonne, most pastry chefs have a desire to transform things, to experience the rawness of the ingredients and to bring them together in harmony.

Dan Budd is optimistic about the differences. "I think we look at food and the steps of making food differently. We work with different ingredients in different ways, but I think it all has to be treated as one. We all have to work together. I tell my students, we need to look at all the steps. The preparation concept in pastry is entirely different from that of cooking. If you need to serve fish today, then you're going to get that fish into the kitchen, portion that fish, season that fish. You're going to prepare it and then get it ready to serve. In pastry, if you're making a napoleon, then you should have started that puff pastry three days ago, or maybe you did it a week ago and it's frozen. In pastry, the steps can be much longer. What's hard for some students to understand is that the stress of pastry, like the stress of service, is in the morning. We have to get in early in the morning and we have to move. We have to make it happen. When you're working hard on the hot line, prepping, the stress of service is when the food is going out, but in pastry, that production in the morning is really important. You have to touch on everything in the morning, every piece of what you do—this sorbet running [in the ice cream machine], that sorbet running, this base is done, that pastry cream is done, these cakes are baking. Then you're ready for anything. If you don't do that, then something can put you days behind. You have to examine and taste everything to be ready."

The nature of the work of creating pastries and desserts often attracts a specific type of individual. The measuring, weighing of formulas, and exacting techniques draws people who are detail oriented and scientific. Torres makes an interesting comparison. "I think the mind of a chef and of a pastry chef are structured differently. I think a pastry chef is someone who loves to plan, organize, and not be rushed. A chef is someone who is going to deal with the rush and do their very best work in that situation. I have a mathematical mind and I like to organize. I like to do things step by step. I don't like to be rushed. That part of being a pastry chef is very important for me and it is related to the structure of my mind."

> I think the mind of a chef and of a pastry chef are structured differently. I think a pastry chef is someone who loves to plan, organize, and not be rushed. A chef is someone who is going to deal with the rush and do their very best work in that situation.
> —Jacques Torres

Gale Gand has experience in both pastry and cooking. "I have been cooking for about twenty years now and I spent eight years doing savory food. I used to go back and forth. When I first started, I was working at this vegetarian restaurant making salads and I was sort of this miniature hot line person. I think a chef doesn't have to be as exacting."

Lindsey Shere says, "It's a discipline in which you usually have to get it right the first time. You can't always add a little bit of this or that, like you can with potatoes to make them creamier. I think that you either have a feel for it or you don't."

Jacquy Pfeiffer loves the science of pastry. "There is always a reason why something happens. Also, on the creative side, there's always so much you can do. This work requires a certain mindset; not everyone can do it. The discipline that's required to scale everything correctly is not something everyone has. I think the savory kitchen is a little more vague. A little more or less of onion in the stew may not really make a difference."

Discipline is the appeal for Mary Bergin. "I like the preciseness of it. I like to be exact. I am a very organized person. I have a list for everything." Judy Contino started in the business as a restaurant manager and felt she was ready to take on more responsibility. "I thought that going in the kitchen would round me out." The question of pursuing work in the pastry or savory area of the kitchen was on her mind right away. "I think pastry takes a different kind of patience and a different concentration. When I was at Ambria, in Chicago, I was able to learn some of the savory cooking, but I just felt that pastry was more my forte. But I love cooking too. I remember asking if I could learn to make consommé. It was something I just loved to eat. They allowed me to learn and then to do what I could do."

Nancy Silverton recalls the reasons she began to gravitate toward pastry. "When I began at Michael's, it was the only position available, so I thought I'd try it out. My eyes were opened to the craziness of the restaurant business, but I began to notice that the pastry area is a much smaller department in a restaurant. In other areas of a restaurant, you don't do everything yourself. In other departments, your lettuce is washed for you and handed to you. Maybe your onions are chopped for you (at least this is the way it was in the kitchens I worked in) and your sauce is made, and then, when you go to put your dish together, you realize that nothing on the plate was made by you. Then suddenly you realize, 'Oh my gosh! The lettuce isn't washed thoroughly and the sauce is terrible, and the onions are chopped too big, and they didn't choose the best tomatoes.' This difference is not as obvious in some hotels because they have huge pastry staffs. As a pastry chef in a small restaurant, everything you do, you do for yourself. So you can make it as perfect as you want to. I liked that there was this little corner of the kitchen that I had total control over."

> As a pastry chef in a small restaurant, everything you do, you do for yourself. So you can make it as perfect as you want to. I liked that there was this little corner of the kitchen that I had total control over.
>
> —Nancy Silverton

Within the world of pastry and dessert, some pastry chefs specialize even more narrowly. Jim Graham is one example. "Different personalities definitely gravitate toward different areas of the food business," he says. "I would have made a lousy cook, in retrospect. Not that I ever tried it as a trade, but I would have gotten so bogged down in the details. My actions are very measured. I think I would have gotten completely slaughtered on my first night of service on a restaurant line. Even pastry is not as studied and meticulous and measured as the way I like to work. That is why I ended up doing chocolate, which is even less forgiving than pastry. I

Prep list at the Four Seasons

worked for five years doing pastry and any situation where I really had to produce, really crank out the pastry, was a problem for me. Every piece that was before me had to be just right before it left me and you can't be that way in a high-volume situation. That is why I thought chocolate was the place for me. Even though I had not worked with it much up to that point, I was aware that it had this element of precision to an even greater degree than pastry. That's why what I do here is well suited for me, because I'm not having to crank out desserts for a Saturday evening service. I've done that but it's not where I'm at my best. Being able to design a dessert or come up with an occasional dessert for a party, which allows plenty of preparation time, that I'm okay with. I've found that making chocolates on a day-to-day basis is really what I do best."

The desire to work with food or in a restaurant can be the impulse that leads to more choices later on. That choice could be a broad one, like wanting to own your own restaurant or wanting to learn everything you can about food, cuisine, and running a kitchen so you can be the chef several years down the road. Then there are those who become so fascinated and attracted to the intricate operations of crafting delicious desserts and pastries that they focus on unlocking their potential as a pastry chef.

Richard Leach found his beginnings to be more of a testing ground rather than a clear-cut choice to be a pastry chef. "It was just by chance. As my desserts kept developing, people started to enjoy my work, and I began to do it very well."

In 1987, Emily Luchetti was cooking at Stars in San Francisco. After years of cooking savory food, she began searching within herself for something different. "Jeremiah [Tower] and I sat down one day and he said, 'You know, I can tell you don't like what you're doing.' We had a really heartfelt talk. It came to my attention that I didn't like what I was doing. Therefore, I wasn't doing as good a job as I could have been doing. Some people would have just said, 'Well, I'm just going to leave and find something else to do,' but I looked at the situation and said to myself, 'Find something you do like and make it work.' The pastry chef of Stars was pregnant at the time and was leaving. I said, 'I'm going for it. This is what I want.' Jeremiah knew I didn't have much pastry experience, but he knew me and knew we both believed in the same style of food. You can teach people recipes but you can't teach them style, feeling, and approach. So he said, 'Go for it. It's yours.' I think back then, a restaurant could take a big risk like that. Today Stars wouldn't hire someone without pastry experience because the stakes are too high."

Elizabeth Falkner saw her choice partly as a business decision. "I saw that there was a huge gap to be filled. That's why I opened a pastry shop. I couldn't understand why the San Francisco Bay area, such a food mecca, wouldn't have more pâtisseries or wild pastry making like in New York. There's a lot to be done here."

Choosing the Career of a Pastry Chef

Becoming a pastry chef may not be a clear-cut goal that one sets out to accomplish. When I was still in high school, I worked evenings and weekends washing dishes in a small, formal restaurant. I'll never forget mopping the floor at one or two in the morning after Saturday night service while I idealized the notion of working in the pastry area. After working at my first job for a few years, I knew I could fit in to the restaurant business. Over time, I became attracted to the seemingly autonomous nature of the work. As Nancy Silverton says, "I always liked having a small part of the kitchen that I could control myself."

> After working at my first job for a few years, I knew I could fit in to the restaurant business.
> —Andrew MacLauchlan

Claudia Fleming didn't set out to make herself into a pastry chef—rather, it began as a matter of circumstance. "The sweet food was an accident. It was the only position open in the kitchen at Union Square Café at the time. I said that I would try it and I wound up loving it." Fleming found dessert making similar to the immediate gratification of performance she sought in her previous career as a dancer. "In the morning, you come in and there is nothing, and by 11:30 A.M. that speedrack is just full of product. There is nothing better than realizing you have created all these desserts and you get to do it every day, over and over. I am not the most patient person in the world, so I appreciate that immediate gratification every day. I love that about this business."

> The sweet food was an accident. It was the only position open in the kitchen at Union Square Café at the time. I said that I would try it and I wound up loving it.
> —Claudia Fleming

Elizabeth Falkner remembers that her calling came through her perceptive palate. "It was an accident, really. I helped out at this café and I couldn't understand why the baked goods tasted a little strange, a little off, and all I could think of was, 'These people need help!' So I asked, 'Why do we buy these desserts from the outside when we could make them? It's not that hard.' So I just began to immerse myself in it."

One summer, during a break from school, Mary Bergin started working for her older sister, who opened a restaurant called Hugo's in West Hollywood in 1980. "We made pasta salads, rolled sandwiches, the take-out stuff that started in the eighties. I was a starving student. Every penny went to books and Santa Monica College. I was going to school to become a teacher. She opened her restaurant in June and offered me a job for the summer. We were about a month into it and the pastry chef she had hired quit. So I started making simple things from Maida Heatter's cookbooks. About two months later, I realized I was never going back to college. I became very interested in pastry and made friends with the pastry chef at a restaurant called La Toke. I was just fascinated by what she could whip up in the 30-quart mixer—a batch of chocolate chip cookies without a recipe. I would start in the afternoons and work for free all night long because I wanted to learn."

In my early days of observing pastry cooks at work, it became obvious to me that this was a well-respected area of the restaurant that operated in concert with the kitchen, but seemed to have an entirely different set of rules. Those who worked with breads and desserts were appreciated for their knowledge of a craft. As a dishwasher, even though I put forth my best effort, I longed to be creative and acknowledged for it. Later on, in the beginning of my career. I concentrated on the fundamentals that worked for me at the time—which desserts people enjoyed most, which recipes worked best. Then a certain momentum began to build for me as I realized that people really liked what I was doing.

First impressions of the professional kitchen can be exciting and inviting or they can seem insane and frightening. Jim Graham remembers a bad experience. "I was in France and had difficulty getting work papers. I took the first job I could get. They were desperate and you know that is always a bad sign. It was a terrible place, a high-volume pastry shop. The quality was terrible and the sanitation was bad. Sometimes, when I catch odors related to that time— margarine smells, that sort of thing—a rush of bad memories comes back. The whole while I knew there were better places."

A positive sign for anyone considering a life in the kitchen is summed up in Claudia Fleming's first impression. "I was filled with curiosity and excited by the frenetic energy in the kitchen. It's exhausting, but I thrive on that." Claudia Fleming's first job was perhaps a premonition of her attraction to fast-paced, high-pressure, demanding work environments. "You know my very first job—and to this day it is my favorite—was working at Friendly's. I loved that job so much, with all the different flavors of ice cream. It was in a mall, so there was always a line going. I couldn't go fast enough."

> I think to be successful in the world of food—and we're so lucky to be involved with food—you've got to be generous by nature. You've got to want to give and do things for people.
> —Charlie Trotter

An important part to remember about becoming any sort of chef and cooking for people is that you need to be moved by a spirit of generosity. The business of restaurants and food has grown out of caring for, providing for, and comforting other people. Charlie Trotter echoes this view. "I think to be successful in the world of food—and we're so lucky to be involved with food—you've got to be generous by nature. You've got to want to give and do things for people." What can begin as the need to find a job or develop a passion taps into your spirit of generosity and genuine giving of your creative self.

The action and movement that is generated in pastry and dessert making can be contagious. Jacques Torres thinks back to his first day on the job at age thirteen. "I remember the first day I arrived. I had to get up at five in the morning to start at six. I played rugby the day before and I was sore all over. So I got up early in the morning and I could barely move, but I arrived at work and my boss shook my hand and said, 'Welcome! Take that scraper and scrape all those black sheetpans.' They were piled so high that I could not even see the top one. So I was scraping and scraping, and it was around the holidays, a very busy season, and I was in the middle of all those people working, making holiday brioche with all the fruits and sugar around. My first day in pastry and at six o'clock in

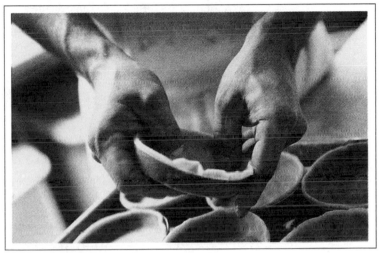

the morning I'm seeing all this action that I couldn't believe existed. Then I was allowed to decorate and put the fruits on top of the brioche. I loved it. I was happy. I licked my finger and I was in the action."

Trotter sums up his take on the requirements for becoming a successful pastry chef. "It's an attitude, a certain mindset, and a real love for being involved with the whole movement and scene of

Tucking short dough into the corners of a tart pan

it all. It's being willing to be part of a team of your pastry department *and* your entire kitchen. You're all part of the same mechanism that is trying to create a memorable experience in people's lives."

Many American pastry chefs started out in other areas of the restaurant business, or from line and pantry cooking. But some of us were attracted to the specialized and intricate processes of pastry and dessert making from the first. Perhaps it was an affinity for detailed work, an attraction to a seemingly peaceful work enviroment, or simply for the love of sweets. In the early part of his career in the kitchen as a line cook, Richard Leach was driven to learn as much as he could about all areas of the work. He used any extra time he had to extend his knowledge of pastry. "I had a six-month break between jobs, and I knew I wanted to learn the basics of pastry to better myself as a cook. I helped in the pastry kitchen of another restaurant and started to pull out some books and do a lot of reading. Then Aureole opened and I asked if I could start out in pastry. All the while I had been using my free time to experiment with recipes. The pastry chef who was there at the time,

Jerry Hayden, moved on about two months after I started, so I just fell into the job." Leach acknowledges his fascination with the craft was rather sudden. "When I had gotten out of cooking school a year earlier, I had no desire to be a pastry chef at all." The opportunity to work in pastry preceded his interest in becoming a pastry chef. Once he started, the world of pastry revealed itself to him.

Emily Luchetti gathered a variety of savory cooking experiences before she was drawn to pastry. After graduating from college, she moved to New York City and found a cooking job for an executive dining room near Wall Street. "I worked there for a couple of years and decided I really wanted to get into this. So I went to The New York Restaurant School and worked in a couple of restaurants in Manhattan. Then I went to work in Paris for a year. When I came back, I moved to San Francisco and worked at Stars on the savory side. I spent a total of seven years cooking in the main part of the kitchen before I switched to pastries when I found I was losing my love for the kitchen and for food because of the pressures and the stress. I would look over to the pastry station every day and think to myself, 'I know that's what I want to do.' I knew it was me. I thought it was just fabulous to get paid to make cakes and cookies every day. I just knew pastry was something I would like."

> I spent a total of seven years cooking in the main part of the kitchen before I switched to pastries because I found I was losing my love for the kitchen and for food because of the pressures and the stress.
> —Emily Luchetti

Judy Contino believes her desire to become a pastry chef stemmed from her efforts to broaden her horizons while she was working in the service end of the restaurant. "My experience in the kitchen was not focused on becoming a pastry chef but on getting a better understanding of the kitchen so I could become a better front-of-the-house manager. I went in not knowing anything, just trying to get that experience in the kitchen. I remember for months I didn't do anything except strain raspberries and peel apples. Ambria had just opened and we did apple galettes and raspberry soufflé cakes and that was my job for months. I was lucky to have the experience of being at Ambria, where I fell in love with the ingredients and seemed to have a great patience with the work, and I haven't left the kitchen since."

Dan Budd had no idea he would become a pastry chef when he attended The Culinary Institute of America. "When I went to culinary school and graduated, I wanted to cook. I wanted to someday be a chef. I went down to New

York City to cook. At one point I was a poissonier (fish cook) on the line. I worked six days a week, probably fifteen hours a day. I graduated high school at about 155 pounds, and I lost 15 pounds on the job. I was burned out. My life didn't feel rewarding to me anymore. I was rewarded by the food. I found inspiration in what I made. But I knew that pastry would make me happier. I had worked in pastry before, and I only worked the other stations because I wanted to know the rest of the kitchen and to be sure I was making the right decision. Then at that point I said, 'I like working in the morning and I really think that in making desserts and pastries, all the ingredients contribute to my personal creativity.'"

The calling to become a pastry chef can lead to a desire to travel in Europe. My eyes were opened on my first trip to France. Even now, as I think back on those travels of eleven years ago, I still can remember encountering regional desserts and specialties and using that as a source of inspiration.

Gale Gand speaks about her early groundwork in cooking and pastry with words usually reserved for the art world. "It was almost like a calling when it happened. When I was working in the kitchen for the first time, I felt that people were working with a medium that was very alive. It was a vegetarian restaurant, so we were working with a lot of vegetables, fruits, grains, and cheeses. It was very nurturing; there was a craft to it. The restaurant was called Light of Yoga and it had a really peaceful, Zenlike atmosphere. I used to eat there all the time and walk out on the check because I had no money. I thought, 'I've got to stop doing this. I'm going to get caught. I better work here and then I'll have some cash and I'll get a meal at least.' I noticed right away how people seemed to love what they were doing and their work had a creative side. We'd make different vegetable casseroles each day and there was room for personal input and personal creativity. I loved that."

For almost anyone, a career choice in pastry involves a process of eliminating many paths in the culinary arts and, eventually, leading to the field of pastry itself, which is historically derived from bread baking and further branches into areas of specialization such as chocolate work, candy and confectionery, and breakfast or Viennese pastry.

Jacquy Pfeiffer's decision to become a pastry chef was based on a desire to use a wide array of ingredients and products. "My father was a bread baker who made breads, cookies, and simple pastries. I wanted to do more than he did because to me, bread is kind of boring. You only work with a few ingredients and I wanted to work with more and also be more creative."

The reasons to become a pastry chef are as varied as the individuals who call this profession their own. For some, the detail of the work is an attraction. For others, the creativity, or the ability to have total control over one segment of the kitchen is the reason for the career choice. The small seed of attraction to cooking, baking, or the excitement of the professional kitchen grows into the passion that a pastry chef expresses through every creation.

Switching to a Career in Pastry

Choosing a career in pastry is not a decision you need to make early in life. If you are changing careers, you will want to consider many factors in aspiring to be a pastry chef. It is not easy to switch to a completely new career, but perhaps you have unexplored baking and dessert making talents that can be actualized. The intensity of a professional kitchen may not be for everyone, but those willing to work hard and who believe in their abilities may find their niche and be successful.

Dessert preparation at Park Avenue Café

People can be drawn to work in kitchens at different times in their lives and for an infinite number of reasons. Maury Rubin reminded me that his career change fit into specific factors of his life at the time. "My first job out of school became this 100 hour-a-week, very intense television network production job in New York," says Maury. "I loved it, but I wanted to pace myself. I came to pastry at just the right time in my life, with my maturity and my creative mind. I had been working in television, producing and directing for five years and had done high-quality work but not necessarily very original work. In pastry, I have been doing original work ever since, and I pride myself on the originality of the work I do at City Bakery."

$\mathcal{Z}$infandel Marinated
Cherry-Cocoa Tart

by Maury Rubin

Yield: 6 servings

For the cocoa tart shells:

½ cup unsalted butter cut into 8 pieces

1 cup minus 2 tablespoons unbleached all-purpose flour

2 tablespoons plus 2 teaspoons high-
quality, unsweetened, Dutch-process cocoa powder

½ cup plus 2 tablespoons confectioners' sugar

1 large egg yolk

For the finished tarts:

2 pints pitted dark cherries

2 cups red Zinfandel wine

3 tablespoons heavy cream

2 teaspoons granulated sugar

Cocoa powder for dusting

For the cocoa tart shells:

1. Let the butter sit at room temperature for 10 to 15 minutes. It should be malleable, but still cool.

2. Sift together the flour and the cocoa powder.

3. Place the sugar in the bowl of a mixer equipped with a paddle, or in a mixing bowl if using a hand-held mixer.

4. Add the butter and cream the mixture on medium speed until sugar is no longer visible. With a rubber spatula, scrape down the sides of the bowl, then add the egg yolk and beat until well blended.

5. Scrape down the sides of the bowl again, add half of the flour mixture, and mix until it becomes crumbly. Stop the machine, add the remaining flour mixture, and mix until a sticky dough forms.

Continued on next page

6. Flatten the dough into a disk shape, wrap in plastic, and refrigerate until firm (about 2 hours).

7. On a well-floured work surface, cut the dough into 1-inch pieces. With the hand, knead the pieces back together, using a dough scraper as necessary to free the dough from the work surface.

8. Roll the dough into a 10-inch long log and cut the log crossways into 6 equal pieces. Refrigerate the pieces for 5 minutes.

9. Line a baking sheet with parchment and place on it six 4-inch rolled-rim flan rings or six 4-inch fluted tart shells, spacing them 1 inch apart.

10. On a lightly floured work surface, place 1 piece of dough. Sprinkle it with flour and flatten it by hand to 2 to 3 inches in diameter, then roll it out to 5½ to 6 inches in diameter × ⅛ inch thick.

11. With a pastry docker or fork, prick holes all over the dough. Center the round of dough over a flan ring or tart tin. (If the dough is too soft to handle at this point, use a dough scraper to transfer it to a lightly floured baking sheet and refrigerate it for a few minutes before proceeding.)

12. Ease the dough into the ring gently, with your thumbs on the inside and your fingertips on the outside, pressing in the bottom corner to form a right angle between the bottom and side of the ring or tart tin.

13. Keeping your thumbs on the inside, pressing lightly against the sides, move in a circle around the ring or tin. There should be a ½-inch rim of excess dough extending above the rim.

14. With a paring knife tilted upward, trim the excess dough flush with the ring. Repeat the process with the remaining pieces of dough. The dough scraps may be kneaded together to make another tart shell.

15. Place the tart shells in the freezer for 30 minutes. Preheat the oven to 375° and position a rack in the center of the oven.

16. Bake for 8 to 10 minutes, until the interiors are dry and the pastry smells nicely of chocolate. If the bottom of the shells puff up, tap down lightly with your fingers as often as necessary.

For the finished tarts:

1. Place the cherries in a medium bowl and pour the wine over them. Cover with plastic wrap and let marinate for 1 hour.

2. Preheat oven to 350°. With a slotted spoon transfer the cherries to a plate, then pack them tightly into the tart shells with their smooth sides up.

3. Pour ½ cup of the Zinfandel marinade into a small nonreactive saucepan, stir in the cream and sugar, and place over medium heat. (You won't need the rest of the marinade.) Stir until the sugar dissolves, then remove from the heat.

4. Divide the Zinfandel cream among the tarts and bake for 20 to 25 minutes, until the juices are bubbling around the edges. Remove from the oven and let sit for 1 minute. Remove the rings with tongs or, if baked in tart pans, allow them to cool in the pans, then unmold.

5. Dust the tops very lightly with cocoa powder.

Maury's sage advice to career changers comes down to this. "If you make the change from another career, it may accord you a fresh perspective that can serve you well. The fact that you don't come up through traditional ranks I think can be used to a great advantage. I haven't been to a culinary school so I don't know exactly what they teach. But I think if you are ready to do this work and your mind is ready and your hands are ready, then the fact that you haven't been swayed by other people's styles of pastry can be a tremendous advantage. Years ago, my pastry was radical and, seven years later, by any conventional standards, my pastry is still radical. My pastry would never look or taste like what it does if I had learned what everyone else had learned or if I had gone to Lenôtre in Paris."

> I think if you are ready to do this work and your mind is ready and your hands are ready, then the fact that you haven't been swayed by other people's styles of pastry can be a tremendous advantage.
>
> —Maury Rubin

Chris Broberg, pastry chef at Lespinasse in New York, thinks it's important for career changers to know what they're getting into. "If someone is changing careers after having already dedicated their life to something else, people in the kitchen may be reluctant to take them seriously. I always give them a rundown of the job realities. Being a pastry chef is a lot of hard work. It's not a desk job. There's a lot of time on your feet. There's a lot of running. There's a lot of sweat involved. It's not glamorous. In this business, if you have a love for what you are doing and if you do it well, you will be rewarded, but I always emphasize that it's a lot of hard work. You are going to be up against people who are very young, have a lot of energy, and aren't concentrating on anything else in their lives. It can be a difficult transition, especially if a career changer has a family and is used to regular schedules."

Emily Luchetti has some advice for those contemplating a career change. "The first thing I would do is volunteer and spend some time in the kitchen. I have been cooking for twenty years and I haven't lost my passion for food. But I've seen people come into the kitchen, young and old, and from the stress of this business, they lose their love for it. If you're going to lose your love for it, then don't do it. It's hard enough to make eight dollars an hour when you're young and you haven't made anything else, but when you're a stockbroker and you've been making good money, going all the way back is difficult."

Nancy Silverton has inside experience with those considering a major career change in their lives. "There was a great deal of excitement when we opened La Brea Bakery and offered a certain style of bread. Right away it was a hit and I started getting these phone calls: 'Hi. I'm a surgeon and I want to give up my job and become a bread baker.' What I would say is before you change careers, before you give up your medical practice, hang out with me for a couple of nights. There wasn't one surgeon that ended up leaving his practice.

> Before you change careers, hang out with me for a couple of nights.
> —Nancy Silverton

First, I think that people have to understand that in the restaurant business, whether it's food or pastry, entry-level positions offer little money. Second, the hours can be demanding. It's not a nine-to-five job and if you look at it as a nine-to-five job, it's impossible to grow. I used to come in two hours before my shift to clean out my station, go through it and see what I had, and I would stay two hours after. If you're driven and you're passionate, then eight hours isn't enough time to do this work." Silverton's advice to people wanting to change to a career in pastry ends with on a note of optimism for those who may find pastry a true pathway for their lives. "Ask a chef, restaurant owner, or bakery owner to let you work in their kitchen for a week so you can see what really goes on. If you don't have that certain spark, it will just be a lot of hard work, but it truly can be romantic if you are inspired by it." She stresses doing this research to help you find out whether you really want to be a pastry chef.

Jacques Torres warns of the rigorous realities of the kitchen. "In France, we have a combination of school and apprenticeship—one day of school and five days of work. In the United States, we have a lot of people who decide to be chefs after six years in another profession. Unfortunately, some people don't realize that when you're a lawyer, when you're an accountant, when you are in another profession, you're someone who makes decisions and has some power in the company you work for. If you become a chef, you have to start at the bottom and learn to follow orders. You have to learn to have a chef push you for speed and push you for cleanliness. A lot of people don't realize that it's not always fun." The hard work of learning can be rewarding if you remain goal-oriented, focus on techniques and ingredients, and vow to do what it takes to go slowly and develop the required skills.

> If you become a chef, you have to start at the bottom and learn to follow orders. You have to learn to have a chef push you for speed and push you for cleanliness. A lot of people don't realize that it's not always fun.
> —Jacques Torres

Jim Graham's interest was piqued at age twenty-two, though at the time he was on a different path. "I was discontented with the work I was doing as a draftsman. I wanted to do something more manual, more concrete. In retrospect, I realize that several trades would have suited me quite well. It wasn't the food element that originally attracted me to pastry, it was the craft of it, the product. So I went back to France a couple of years later and took a few classes just to see if the work itself appealed to me, and it did. That is when I made a commitment to the trade." Mary Bergin was studying to be a teacher when she took a summer job working in her sister's restaurant. "I had every intention of being a teacher. I was into pastry for about two months when I realized I was never going back to college. Ironically, teaching is exactly what I do now. I teach people pastry all the time."

Many people who began a career in the arts have been attracted to a career in cooking and pastry. Some had day jobs or part-time jobs in restaurants to support themselves while they pursued other career goals. Gale Gand's dream was to be an artist; Claudia Fleming's first career was in dance. "I always worked in a restaurant because I was dancing and I wasn't making a living as a dancer," Fleming said. "I worked in the front of the house. I really always wanted to cook but wasn't willing to give up the money I was making in the front of the house. When I was working at Jonathan Waxman's former restaurant, Jams, he let me work in the kitchen. I left there and went to Union Square Café to work in the dining room while attending Peter Kump's New York Cooking School. Chef Michael Romano said to me, 'I hear you want to cook. You can start here as a prep cook.'" Fleming compares her work as a pastry chef to show business. "There is something very theatrical about cooking, about kitchens, about prep time. Then it's showtime—immediate gratification."

Elizabeth Falkner's path was art and film. "I was an abstract artist. I was doing installation pieces using film as my medium, but doing a lot of sculptural things too. I ran out of money at a certain point, so I started helping out with the baking at a café. I fell in love with it."

> First of all, I wouldn't discourage anyone from making a career out of what they love. No matter what age you are, go for it! There's no greater reward than doing well at something you really enjoy. And it's really nice to do something you enjoy doing and get paid for it.
>
> —Dan Budd

Dan Budd is optimistic for those with powerful belief in what they want to do. "First of all, I wouldn't discourage anyone from making a career out of what they love. No matter what age you are, go for it! There's no greater reward than excelling at something you really enjoy. And it's really nice to do something you enjoy doing and get paid for it." Budd has two pieces of solid advice for those who are thinking of leaving their current situations and careers for work in the pastry field. "In this day and age, definitely do some sort of schooling. Now that I'm an instructor at The Culinary Institute of America, I see that an incredible education is available for pastry. We are trying to set up the education so that we can give the most important things, the hands-on, the knowledge you can take and apply. The second piece of advice is to pick some of the restaurants, pastry shops, or hotels that inspire you and try to get work there. Get to know those chefs and give some of your time. Really feel it out and make sure you know that's what you want to do."

Nick Malgieri has instructed and advised many who have opted to switch careers. "You definitely have to give yourself some time. There's no substitute for starting at the bottom and paying your dues. That has to happen no matter what you pursue. A significant part of my first job in pastry was separating paper doilies and putting them onto platters. Every time the pastry chef walked by, he said, 'Are you putting the doilies on the platters or the platters on the doilies?' That was a joke someone had probably made to him when he was twenty-one and on his first job. You have to start at the bottom. You have to get through a couple of years of peeling apples and chopping walnuts because if you don't do that, then you've got no foundation. In our career pastry program at Peter Kump's New York Cooking School, we tell students about the career track options and salaries. We tell them specifically that it's not going to happen their first year out of school. One out of a thousand students is going to land a great job as a pastry chef right out of school because they just happen to be a genius. That doesn't happen to everybody; you have to have the skill and talent to back it up. Some people are talented, organized, intelligent, and could secure a major job within a year of getting out of school. The other 99 percent of people, myself included, have to spend time putting doilies on platters. I always use this analogy: If you go to music school and you learn how to play different instruments, you learn about theory and harmony, but when you graduate, the San Francisco Orchestra doesn't call you and say, 'We need a new director.' You start out literally playing second fiddle and you work your way up. It is exactly the same in our field. There is absolutely no replacement for starting at the bottom and the people I have seen who try to get away without it fall on their face. You have to learn to walk before you can run."

Dessert service at Coyote Café

People who have experience in other fields can be great sources of new viewpoints on and approaches to pastry. "They bring fresh air," says Markus Färbinger. "They look at things differently. An accountant looks at things differently than a marketing person or a political advisor. I think the people who come to pastry from other professions are important because other concepts can help develop what has been done for so long in the same way. They don't ever have to lose what they learned in other fields."

When looking at the origins of inspiration for these leading pastry chefs, perhaps you've discovered ideas for your own future in the business. No matter what your current situation is, look at your own food memories and experiences and take note of them. You can begin to understand the value of particular food and dessert experiences and formulate ideas based on all the influences that make you who you are—how you grew up, the flavors you prefer, the types of designs you like, the museums you go to, the types of cooking or chefs you admire. When you consider all these factors, you can take hold of your personal direction and set a course for becoming a pastry chef!

> I think the people who come to pastry from other professions are important because other concepts can help develop what has been done for so long in the same way.
>
> —Markus Färbinger

CHAPTER three

*F*OUNDATIONS OF LEARNING
AND HONING SKILLS

Developing as a Pastry Chef

The paths to becoming a pastry chef are as varied as the individuals who choose to travel them. Perhaps the most surprising assertion I make in this book is that there is no prescribed means for becoming a successful pastry chef. One adage in which I find much fortitude states, "Success is not a point to be arrived at, but is rather a manner of traveling." You carry success with you. It is an attitude that grows in you, one that no one can take away. In interviewing successful pastry chefs, I have found no consistent method of arriving at success. They do, however, seem to share a few common traits:

1. They are goal-oriented, self-confident people.
2. They work tirelessly to meet their goals.
3. They have developed specific skills.
4. They are generous teachers and mentors.
5. They are precise yet possess varying personal creative styles.

While these traits may or may not have influenced their career choices, they certainly have been cultivated and refined by the growing demands of their professional lives.

Considering Formal Training

There are now more opportunities for a formal pastry education in this country than at any other time in history. Not all successful pastry chefs started this way, but many recommend a culinary school's structured, less-pressured, more methodical way of acquiring the basic skills and rudimentary techniques. All pastry chefs stress the importance of learning classic techniques and styles as a foundation for a successful career. How you apply yourself in a school environment can make all the difference in what you receive from your investment in school and, ultimately, your investment in yourself.

> For me, it is important for pastry chefs to have a good basic foundation, knowledge, and skill, if for no other reason than to understand where they are going.
> —Markus Färbinger

Markus Färbinger delineates his view of what school is and what it is not. "It is different for every person. For me, it is important for pastry chefs to have a good basic foundation, knowledge, and skill, if for no other reason than to understand where they are going. Maybe you really like the retail aspect, the hotel aspect, the restaurant aspect, or maybe you want to be a chocolatier (chocolate maker). You won't know about these possibilities unless you go to school. The purpose of school is to give students a broad understanding about what is going on in the industry. It provides the hows and whys of what they are doing. Schools teach from the instructor's individual experiences and recipes. The learning comes from a well-structured curriculum—the steps, the methods, the skills, the options, the ingredients, the tools, the materials of the

trade. It should not be done in a generic way that is dry, cold, and institutional but should constantly focus on the methods and the skills. Style is less important at that point. Schools cannot be held responsible for giving students the industry experience of pastry making, meaning producing students with both skills and production speed. That's what the industry is for. That's what the student who becomes a professional will get from the industry. In the industry—in a shop, for example—pastry chefs have to do many things over and over from a limited menu of specialty items. They do not exploit the scope of their education. They say, 'I came in wanting to be the next Richard Leach, but now I've found that I'm more in love with bread—forget about pastry.' I think that is the school's job. There is no such thing as self-taught. You really can't teach yourself. You learn from books and from watching. I've seen

Cutting hundreds of fluted, round pastries

some students become really confident and strong, but other students are disillusioned. One instructor says one thing, and another, something else. The best instructors can effectively explain why they poached the apple differently from someone else. Pastry education has changed a lot from thirty or forty years ago. Then it was, 'Watch what I am doing. Repeat it. No! That's not how you do it! Do it like this!' If that still didn't work, they'd yell at them a little louder."

Nick Malgieri unravels the options for those considering this field. "I think school is important because it gives you a codified body of knowledge to work with. It gives you a set of terms and techniques that you need to be able to function in the field. If you start by working only in a particular place, you are going to be limited by what that particular place makes. Working in only one place makes for dogmatic professionals. They might make something and call it French buttercream, which it isn't at all. We've had people like this at Peter Kump's New York Cooking School. They finally broke down, decided they had to take classes, but they have this waterproof covering over them. When knowledge starts to trickle in, most of it rolls off them because they have all these preconceived notions. I think learning only on the job breeds the attitude whereby people think their way is the only way to do something. When you go to school, you are told that there are many ways to do something. School generally offers a coherent body of learning you can draw from."

> I think learning only on the job breeds the attitude whereby people think their way is the only way to do something.
>
> —Nick Malgieri

Emily Luchetti often fields questions regarding her opinion of culinary schools. "I equate it to an MBA," says Luchetti. "You can go out and get an MBA and get a job and still not have any practical experience. You can also work and become the owner of a company with barely a high school education. So it really depends on how you get the knowledge and information you need. I think school is a great place for giving you the fundamentals. If you don't go to school, you have to go out and get that information somewhere else. You can do it through school or by working, but your personality determines which way is best. A lot of people with culinary schools on their resumes didn't get anything out of it. Personality determines how individuals take their experiences and maximize them."

Luchetti was not formally trained. She started at the bottom and worked her way up cooking savory food as a line cook and, finally, giving in to a strong attraction to pastry and dessert making. "I read textbooks and figured things out for myself," she said. "Because of my experience as a line cook, I approach things differently, almost with the mentality of a cook—how flavors go together and how the components will work on the plate. Sometimes I wish I were a little more scientific with it, but other times I think, 'That's my mark, and if I change that, then everything else would change too.' "

Nancy Silverton thinks training is important. "You have to know the basics. You have to know the rules in order to break them. People who start off breaking the rules when they have no foundation are out there doing bizarre things. When I went to the Cordon Bleu Cooking School in Paris in 1977, I had never heard of The Culinary Institute of America. People from Los Angeles just weren't going to cooking school in New York, and there weren't all the culinary schools that there are now. Would I have chosen a cooking school in the United States? Maybe. But then it wasn't an option like it is now. A lot more chefs are available to work under or work with than when I was starting out. Formal training is important, but it is not always affordable. It also takes a lot of time, which must be considered."

Silverton stresses the importance of being ready for the responsibilities that lie ahead by having a broad foundation of skills. "In our restaurant, people might start with us who have never cooked before but show great potential—great line cooks. Eventually they move up to our head position, working the grill, then out the door they go to become a chef. Then I wonder if they've ever made a mayonnaise. Have they ever made a stock? I think many people now are missing important steps in their food education because they are moving up so quickly. They move on for more money, or someone opens a new restaurant and offers them a great deal, but there is so much that they missed."

> You have to know the basics.
> You have to know the rules
> in order to break them.
> —Nancy Silverton

Silverton also alludes to a phenomenon that could be the result of the perceived glamour of the cooking profession. "Now that cooking has become such a respected field," she continues, "many more people go through the programs. Maybe some of them go through because they didn't know what else they wanted to do. They come out of culinary school without the passion I like to see. Culinary students can be overconfident and inexperienced. The main thing you need to know when you enter this field is that you need to be patient. Try and learn as much as you can from the basics. I think that is what culinary school can provide."

Lindsey Shere's perspective takes into account the long-term career of the chef. "I think culinary school is great, but it is limited. It teaches people about how to behave in the kitchen so they have a start, some knife skills. They know how to clean up after themselves and all those basic things. Unfortunately, a lot of times, they think they know more than they do. Most people who come out of culinary school are still at the beginning rather than anywhere else. I think the best possible thing is just to have cooked all your life, to have significant experience in which you have seen what happens when you do certain things, to have done it over and over and perfected things, and to have paid attention to what happens in the saucepot, in the mixing bowl, and in the oven."

Teaching methods have certainly changed over the years to emphasize a wide variety of techniques. Curriculum is analyzed constantly to remain on the cutting edge of the latest food and industry needs and trends.

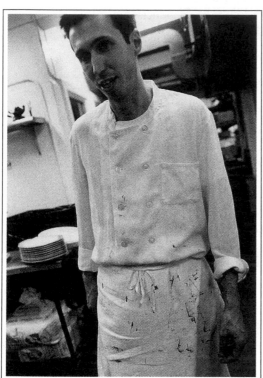

Richard Leach

Classroom learning can provide a foundation of basic ideas and formulas to which the student can refer in the professional world. Judy Contino reflects this view. "People ask me about culinary school and whether they should just go the way I did, right into the kitchen. They'll say 'Look at you! You are self-taught and look what you have been able to do.' I have created as I've gone along and learned from my mistakes, but I wonder what I would have been able to do if I could have gone to school, if I had had the time for training or working under a pastry chef with French training for a year. I could have been able to do so much more now. I tell people, 'If you can afford to go to culinary school, you should go because you can always get the work experience afterward.' "

Roland Mesnier agrees. "Of course you can't beat training on the job, but I think today you need both. I think you need to go to culinary school first. You can learn a lot in culinary school that is difficult to learn on the job. Then I think you should take approximately ten years and work for some really great chefs around the country and, if possible, abroad. I would really say that is the best training in the world."

Jackie Riley, of Tabla in New York, started at the Drake Hotel in Chicago before attending the pastry certificate program at The Culinary Institute of

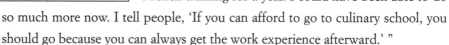

America. "In the hotel I had to make the same thing every day for a year. I was making tea scones, and I'm talking hundreds. When it was really busy, around Christmastime, it was one thousand. The Drake has a very busy kitchen with sixteen pastry cooks. I think it's important to attend culinary school, especially to prepare yourself for what's out there at any given moment. If someone tells you to make crème anglaise, you need a foundation, along with some understanding of what it is, and what can go wrong when making it. With an introduction to the products and techniques of pastry, you can at least discuss what it is you're trying to make."

Bill Yosses agrees. "A small percentage of people could go into a top-notch kitchen and start working there as a dishwasher or a potato peeler and become a great chef without formal training. The advantage of formal education is that it categorizes what is necessary and teaches you how to assimilate the information you are receiving. When you do that, you can retain a lot more. I would recommend culinary school to a lot of people, but some people have natural talent. They can go into a kitchen, after a certain amount of time, and go to it."

Richard Leach's first notion of his career-to-be came to him while studying at The Culinary Intitute of America. "As far as seeing pastry as a potential profession, culinary school was my introduction, because I never did any pastry work before that." He advises starting out with a good working knowledge of the basics. "You definitely need training before you can get creative. You need to develop a foundation—if not in culinary school, then in your early job experience."

> The advantage of formal education is that it categorizes what is necessary and teaches you how to assimilate the information you are receiving.
> —Bill Yosses

Michelle Gayer cites some of the benefits of culinary school. "I learned the basic techniques and some classic recipes, like ladyfingers and pear charlotte. It was an introduction, so I was taught only one way to do things. With respect to getting an entry-level job working in pastry, it seems important to have had at least a short course so you know how to hold and sharpen a knife, how a kitchen is run, and what a bain marie is."

When deciding how to go about your training, it is important to consider your stage in life. Jacques Torres emphasizes the importance of work experience. "I think it's good if you do an apprenticeship early. Of course, you can't go to culinary school for six months when you're sixteen. Ideally, I think it's best to have work experience before culinary school, so you know at least something about this business. With some hands-on work, you'll know many of the problems of the profession by the end of that experience." The decision to attend a culinary program depends entirely on the individual. Taking Torres's advice affords you the opportunity of knowing if you want to pursue a pastry career, and to then make an even greater investment in a culinary education.

> You definitely need training before you can get creative. You need to develop a foundation—if not in culinary school, then in your early job experience.
> —Richard Leach

You alone know what is best for you. Do you thrive in a methodical, academic, and hands-on environment? Are you a good student or do you find that you're at your best throwing yourself into a situation and learning in the moment? Entering the professional kitchen with a basic culinary education, with a knowledge of equipment and processes, can really get you off to the right start and help you progress in your career.

Desire and willingness to learn are what I look at when considering a person for an entry-level pastry position. The difference between a culinary school setting and a high-pressure restaurant kitchen situation can be equated to the difference between doing laps in a swimming pool and trying to swim in the ocean in a storm. One must understand that in an existing or brand-new business, whether it is a pastry shop, hotel, or restaurant, everything is on the line. Learning about food and labor cost in culinary school is vital because chefs and pastry chefs can be held accountable for these figures in the real-world setting of a multimillion-dollar business. In the working restaurant business, high food and labor costs can get a chef fired or drive a business under. The rules change quite a bit when money is involved. Ultimately, a restaurant's success or failure depends entirely on the focus, drive, and skill of its chef and crew.

Claudia Fleming doesn't mince words when it comes to the day-to-day pressures of running a top-notch pastry department in one of New York's finest restaurants. Claudia reminds would-be culinary school externs (students who spend time working in the field before returning to school) to take school seriously in order to be ready for the rigors of the professional pastry kitchen. "So few culinary school graduates come through here who understand the restaurant kitchen. They are shocked by the intensity when they get here. When people who work for me are talking while they work, I really have to say to them, 'When you can do this in your sleep, then you can talk. This takes 100 percent of your concentration right now, so please just think about what you are doing because you're not going to get more proficient any faster unless you concentrate.' It doesn't make me very popular to be on people for fifteen hours a day. I understand where culinary school education is lacking by having externs in my kitchen. I feel a class should be taught about etiquette in the kitchen, about what it's really like in a kitchen, and that when you work in a kitchen you're there to work and not there to socialize and daydream. I say to externs that the roles are reversed now. You are here to serve me. I am not here to teach you. You serve a function. You are getting paid. You must produce.

*Plating desserts at
Coyote Café*

Nancy Silverton is someone who has made the most of her training. When she started out, she was drawn to cooking and remembers feeling stifled and somewhat fearful of the perceived constraints of classic pastry making. "I was intimidated by desserts because I was told that unless you measure everything exactly, you're in big trouble. Before I started making pastries, which wasn't something I chose to do early on, I wanted to be a cook. I went to the Cordon Bleu Cooking School and there we would cook full-course meals all the time and, obviously, one of the courses was dessert. I couldn't stay in the limits or boundaries of what they wanted with respect to dessert. Everyone said dessert making is so exact. You have to do it in a certain way and everything has to be measured exactly. It's true. Scientific practices come into play in dessert making. If you bring eggs to a boil they will curdle, and if you add too much fat to a cake it will be heavy and greasy, but it seemed to me at the time that they tried to make it too exacting."

Becoming a chef or pastry chef requires an overwhelming desire and passion for food and cooking. Success depends, in large part, on a chef's passion, determination, and drive. Anyone attending cooking school with a mind for becoming a pastry chef must remember that simply attending school does not make one a pastry chef. Never. Period. Just like attending art school does not make one an artist. There is a clear parallel between the art world and the culinary world. Many people who attend art school never become artists. An art school graduate may practice physical arts, perhaps drawing or painting, just as a potential pastry chef who graduated from a pastry program may be a pastry cook, eventually an assistant, working in the field and continuing the growth and learning process. Artists develop themselves by experiencing the world and, by reidentifying themselves, they begin to develop a personal sense of their place in the arts and express that through the art form. This is nearly identical to the process of becoming a pastry chef. Pastry chefs are at once practitioners of a craft, leaders, visionaries, and philosophers. They reidentify themselves and can, at that point, in the larger scheme of things, understand their dessert- and pastry-making contribution as it relates not only to the specific style of cuisine, but also to the entire history of pastry and cuisine.

> Pastry chefs are at once practitioners of a craft, leaders, visionaries, and philosophers. They reidentify themselves and can, at that point, in the larger scheme of things, understand their dessert- and pastry-making contribution as it relates not only to the specific style of cuisine, but also to the entire history of pastry and cuisine.
> —Andrew MacLauchlan

Culinary school can be a tremendous introduction to the history and traditions of cooking and convey a sense of reverence for the discipline. Classes in cooking or pastry making may include hands-on cooking, one-time demonstrations by expert chefs, and accounting and business information. Programs differ in emphasis, length, location, and cost. These factors need to be carefully considered when seeking the right setting for your personal learning needs. Attending a cooking school for pastry exposes you to a large quantity of information in a relatively short period of time, including techniques, basic skills, and an introduction to the practical aspects of the field, as well as areas of specialization.

I spoke at length with Dan Budd on the topic of culinary school training. "The pastry school or culinary school is where you're exposed to as much as you can be in as short amount of time as possible. One thing I like to do is to bring a little business into the classroom so that you realize that to be successful with these desserts, you have to remember that customers are waiting every moment.

With my students in the pastry kitchen here at school, we need to be able to make realistic decisions that are going to work out in the pastry business world, in the pastry shop, or in the restaurant. That's where I can guide them. Any time they can put into school is incredibly valuable." Budd is candid with students and reminds them that one of the most important checkpoints of formal culinary education is the exposure to processes, methods, and techniques that they will receive. "At The Culinary Institute of America you receive a good foundation, but at the end of the program you are not going to be a pastry chef. I even tell my students that they are not even going to be pastry cooks because a pastry cook is a very efficient pastry worker, which they can be in time. But they are exposed to such a variety of desserts, pastries, techniques, equipment, ingredients, and flavors that when they are out there and see these methods, ingredients, and desserts, nothing will be unfamiliar to them and they will be comfortable with what they see. My biggest point is if you are comfortable with what you see when you're hired for your first job out of school, then you will easily get involved with it, do it, and learn more about it. But if you see something you've never seen before on your first day and you have an immediate sense of insecurity about it, or you have to say, 'I've never done that, so I don't know,' you can't act as quickly, get yourself involved, and learn more about it. That's what our education does here. It involves the student with learning the basics, seeing lots of things, getting their hands in it, and getting the confidence to go into the business and make it happen. That's why I support what we do here."

Pastry Degree Programs

Attending a pastry culinary program is one of the most immediate ways of getting yourself into the structured environment of a career in pastry. There is, perhaps, no faster way to expose yourself to the variety of techniques, methods, and supporting information than to attend one of these schools. There are also a multitude of smaller culinary schools in many major U.S. cities. For a more complete listing, consult Shaw's *The Guide to Cooking Schools* or *Peterson's Culinary Schools,* which are updated every year. The best way to determine which school is right for you is to consider time and money constraints. Attending school close to home may be more affordable than going out of town. Evaluate specific choices with regard to program content and the quality of instruction.

Obtain each school's literature, then visit the programs and schools that are attractive. Some culinary programs require applicants to have a specific amount of experience in the culinary field. For example, The Culinary Intitute of America requires six months of work in a professional kitchen, along with references from your employer.

When applying for a pastry program, it is always an advantage to have some job-related experience. You may accomplish this in a variety of ways. Culinary school can be comprehensive and challenging and you may decide to work full or part time while you attend so you can apply what you learn as you go. In addition, a period of work, also known as an *externship,* in an establishment of your choosing is required after introductory semesters, after which you return to school for more advanced classes. Whatever you decide to do, taking the first step and getting the hands-on and theoretical basis for a great start in the business of pastry could be the way to realize your dream.

The number and scope of programs of study in the culinary arts and, specifically, pastry have changed enormously in the past five years and continue to grow. The Culinary Institute of America in Hyde Park, New York, offers a two-year Associate in Occupational Studies (AOS) program and a four-year Bachelor of Professional Studies (BPS) program in baking and pastry arts, which includes advanced course study in such topics as supervising a staff, history and culture of Europe and Asia, foreign language, and business courses such as marketing and accounting. Johnson and Wales University in Providence, Rhode Island, offers a similar choice of associate and bachelor degrees in baking and pastry arts. The New England Culinary Institute in Montpelier, Vermont, offers no separate pastry program but features an associate's degree in culinary arts and bachelor studies in management and service, which includes baking and pastry courses. Western Culinary Institute in Portland, Oregon, and The California Culinary Acadamy in San Francisco have similar offerings without separate pastry programs. For complete and detailed information about courses and degree programs in the fast-changing world of formal pastry education, contact schools directly.

To give you an idea of the course choices in baking and pastry arts, here is the list of course requirements for the BPS at The Culinary Institute of America.

FRESHMAN YEAR (first semester—15 weeks)

BLOCK A	BLOCK B	BLOCK C	BLOCK D	BLOCK E
Introduction to Gastronomy Culinary Math	Food Safety Nutrition Product Identification and Food Purchasing	Baking Ingredients and Equipment Technology Writing Skills	Culinary Skills for Bakers	Baking Techniques

FRESHMAN YEAR (second semester—15 weeks)

BLOCK F	BLOCK G	BLOCK H	BLOCK I	BLOCK J
Hearth Breads and Rolls Supervisory Development	Pastry Techniques	Basic Cakes Cookies and Mignardises (Costing Examination)	Classical Cakes and Tarts (Baking Practical Examination)	Individual and Production Pastries

EXTERNSHIP—21 weeks

BLOCK K

Externship (18 weeks required)

SOPHOMORE YEAR (first semester—15 weeks)

BLOCK L	BLOCK M	BLOCK N	BLOCK O	BLOCK P
Business Principles and Facility Design Marketing Techniques	Budgeting and Cost Control Principles of Design	Confectionery Art Decorated and Wedding Cakes Restaurant Law	Advanced Baking Principles Modern Desserts	Chocolates and Confections

SOPHOMORE YEAR (second semester—15 weeks)

BLOCK Q	BLOCK R	BLOCK S	BLOCK T	BLOCK U
Specialty Breads	Nutritional Baking and Pastry (Baking Practical Examination)	Restaurant and Production Desserts (Costing Examination)	Beverages and Beverage Service	Café Operations

JUNIOR YEAR (first semester—15 weeks)

Composition and Communication	History and Cultures of Europe
Computers in the Food Business 1	Interpersonal Communication
Economics	Personal Fitness (non-credit)
French, German, Italian, or Spanish 1	Restaurant Assessment 1 (non-credit)

JUNIOR YEAR (second semester—15 weeks)

Accounting and Budget Management	Marketing and Promoting Food
Computers in the Food Business 2	Psychology of Human Behavior
French, German, Italian, or Spanish 2	Beverage Management (non-credit)
History and Cultures of the Americas	Personal Fitness Workshop (non-credit)

INTERSESSION—6 weeks

Wine and Food Seminar
(4 weeks at the Culinary Institute of America
at Greystone in St. Helena, California)

SENIOR YEAR (first semester—15 weeks)

Advanced Pastry	Human Resource Management
Financial Management	Personal Stress Management (non-credit)
French, German, Italian, or Spanish 3	
History and Cultures of Asia	Restaurant Assessment 2 (non-credit)

SENIOR YEAR (second semester—15 weeks)

Challenges of Managing a Pastry Shop	French, German, Italian, or Spanish 4
	Managing Quality for the Future
Ethics	Senior Thesis: Baking and Pastry Arts

Courtesy of the Culinary Institute of America.

THE MAKING *of a* PASTRY CHEF

Professional Development Programs

Professional development programs are vital to the growth and eventual success of many pastry chefs. Time and experience in the field are fantastic teachers, but for growth and new challenges, and for restaurant pastry chefs who want to go into business and open their own shops, or for pastry chefs who want to work in a restaurant with an unfamiliar style of cuisine, or for pastry chefs who want to continue to learn and add to their skills and, ultimately, to their value to their employer and their customers, professional development programs review classic techniques and address emerging ones. The Culinary Institute of America at Greystone in St. Helena, California, is devoted solely to career development and enhancement. In addition to their excellent team of pastry chef instructors, Greystone has created the Great American Pastry Chefs Series, which offers students hands-on classes with some of America's best pastry chefs as well as courses for those chefs and pastry chefs wanting to add to their base of knowledge in breads, plated desserts, or centerpieces.

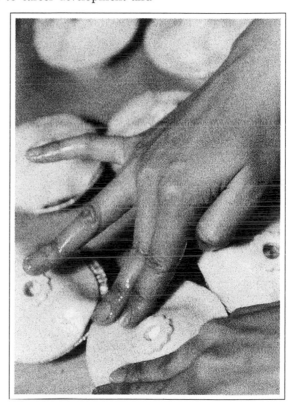

Sealing the dough of mini-pies together

Sherry Yard is a passionate believer in ongoing training and education. "I still go back to school. I spend time with Jacquy (Pfeiffer) and Sebastien (Canonne) at The French Pastry School in Chicago just to stay current." The French Pastry School offers three- and five-day courses in chocolate and sugar decoration, candy making, plated desserts, wedding cakes, and ice cream and sorbet.

What you go and learn should be directly related to what you want to do with the information. Chris Broberg notes, "Some people might want to be in charge of a factory that makes cakes for the supermarkets across half a state; others might want to own a bunch of cinnamon roll franchises and want to have enough comprehension of yeast doughs to inspect their shops and see how well things are going."

Judy Contino sees the need for periodic revitalization for both her staff and herself. "The shop offers me opportunities to do a lot of different things. Some of the members of my staff deserve to be sent to classes, so I send them to The French Pastry School. I myself have signed up for a cake decorating class. We've been here for five years and the whole time I've been doing the wedding cakes. I've developed my own very simple style, but I think it's time for me to go out and bring something back to all my staff." The French Pastry School's mission is to share knowledge and a vision of the pastry arts as well as to promote the art form. Jacquy Pfeiffer and Sebastien Canonne believe that the pastry arts are emerging tremendously in North America and that, in a few years, American pastry chefs will obtain well-deserved worldwide recognition. I spoke with them at The French Pastry School. Pfeiffer says, "We wanted to pass on the knowledge and that is our main goal. In all our classes we take a scientific approach—how and why things happen—and then we explain how to put a recipe together and not waste time. We created an eighteen- to twenty-week pastry program because we wanted a school that is structured as close as possible to an apprenticeship, like in Europe."

> We want our students to understand why things work so, if something doesn't work, they can go back and fix it themselves. We teach them the classics and what is going to work for them.
> —Sebastien Canonne

Canonne adds, "We want our students to understand why things work so, if something doesn't work, they can go back and fix it themselves. We teach them the classics and what is going to work for them."

Pfeiffer makes an important point about the old way of recipe and technique secrecy versus today's custom of sharing and passing on knowledge. "We are competing against those who keep secrets," he said. "We grew up with that in Europe; we weren't allowed to ask why. Now we are just the opposite. Anyone can ask us why something happened. We aren't keeping any secrets." That is certainly a good custom and good news for people wanting to enhance their range of knowledge and ability in the craft.

A chef's body of knowledge is never complete. There are always things to learn. Pastry chefs are constantly brushing up skills or exploring brand-new territory. This is true for beginning professionals and accomplished pastry chefs alike. The focus of the pastry chef depends on the specific branch of the business in which they work and the product variety for which they are responsible.

In a hotel, the pastry chef is responsible for the widest variety of products, usually with a focus on volume production. Breakfast pastry, whole desserts like cakes, tortes, and tarts, and buffet items like individual pastries, petit fours, cookies, and brownies are produced from the hotel pastry kitchen, as are plated dessert preparations for the hotel restaurant, room service, and banquet functions. Hotel pastry chefs, depending on the traditions of the particular establishment and the quality of the hotel, must also be adept at centerpiece work, elaborate structures of pastillage, marzipan, chocolate, and pulled, poured, and blown sugar, or any combination of these. Not all pastry chefs feel at ease with all of the skills required for creating these items. Continuing education is available to round out these skills.

For restaurant pastry chefs, plated desserts are the area of concentration. Their department may also produce the restaurant's bread and items for other areas of the kitchen—doughs, toast points, croutons, and tart shells for savory preparations, for example.

The pastry shop owner has yet another set of goals and educational needs. Business knowledge is especially important but, depending on the type of establishment, a chef may also need to know how to create breads and other products such as sandwiches, pizzas, and salads. Fortunately for today's pastry chef, the development programs that are available offer education in any techniques and knowledge they may feel are missing in their professional lives.

European Apprenticing Tradition

The European apprenticing tradition is a formal model of pastry chef training. It is important to understand this tradition, as it is the original way of learning both cooking and pastry. Though largely unavailable to Americans, apprenticeship is a rigorous approach to which culinary schools originally looked when developing their programs. I have a great respect for this method of training and feel that aspiring pastry chefs can benefit from understanding the process of apprenticeship and from witnessing the respect accorded the craft of pastry making in Europe.

Jim Graham shares his knowledge of this tradition, which he learned from his stint in France. "In French culture, pastry is considered a trade along with cabinet making, fine metalcraft, jewelry making, that sort of thing. It is treated that way in both the educational, formative process and in its social status. The training traditions established in the pastry trade are similar to those that exist in other manual trades, particularly the highly skilled trades."

Baked Apple-Hazelnut Tart with Chocolate Chantilly

by François Payard

Yield: One 8- to 10-inch tart

For the sweet dough:
⅔ cup butter, cold
½ vanilla bean
2½ cups flour
1⅓ cups confectioners' sugar
1 egg

For the apple filling:
1 apple
2 tablespoons clarified butter
1 tablespoon sugar

For the hazelnut filling:
½ cup sugar
3 tablespoons corn syrup
½ cup heavy cream
salt
1½ tablespoons honey
2 ounces milk chocolate, chopped
1 cup hazelnuts, roasted

For the chocolate chantilly cream:
½ cup heavy cream
4½ ounces milk chocolate, melted and hot

For garnish:
Chocolate spirals
Roasted hazelnuts

1. For the sweet dough, cut the butter into small cubes. Scrape the seeds from the vanilla bean and place them in a mixing bowl with the butter cubes. Add the flour and sugar. Using the paddle on low speed, add the egg and mix until all ingredients are well combined. Wrap the dough in plastic and let it rest in the refrigerator for 15 minutes.

2. On a well-floured surface, roll the dough to ⅛-inch thick. Place a tart ring or pan on the dough and cut around it ½-inch larger in diameter. Lift the dough circle into the tart pan and press the dough into the corners of the pan. Trim the top flush and chill the tart shell for 1 hour. Bake at 350° for 10 to 12 minutes or until brown. Remove the shell from the oven and set aside to cool.

3. Increase oven temperature to 400°. For the apple filling, peel and core the apple. Cut it cross-wise into three pieces of roughly equal thickness. Place the rings on a nonstick sheet tray or on a pan brushed with butter. Brush the rings with the butter and sprinkle with the sugar. Bake the apple rings for 12 to 14 minutes or until soft. Remove them from the oven and let them cool.

4. For the hazelnut filling, combine the sugar and corn syrup in a saucepot over medium heat. Bring the mixture to a deep golden caramel color. Carefully whisk in the cream. Add a dash of salt and the honey. Reserve 2 tablespoons of this caramel mixture for final assembly of the dessert. Combine the chocolate and hazelnuts in a bowl and pour the remaining warm caramel mixture over it. Stir until chocolate is melted. Set aside for final assembly of the dessert.

5. For the chocolate chantilly cream, whip the cream stiff. Pour the melted chocolate into the cream all at once and fold together quickly. Fill a pastry bag, fitted with a plain, round tip, with the chocolate mixture.

6. Place the cooled apples into the tart shell. Spread the hazelnut-caramel mixture over the apple rings. Pipe the chocolate chantilly cream onto the nut mixture and garnish with chocolate spirals. Cut the tart into pieces, place in the centers of plates and drizzle some of the reserved sugar and corn syrup mixture around each. Cut some roasted hazelnuts in half and place around each serving.

The training system in France is based largely on the guild system of medieval times. The modern apprenticing system was set up in the 1940s and is a rebirth of this guild system. A young person typically begins an intensive apprenticeship that involves many aspects of their lives at the age of fourteen or fifteen. A young man (it is almost entirely a male pursuit) goes to a special house run by the compagnon, and he basically eats, drinks, and lives the trade. Each day includes a certain amount of classwork and a certain amount of externship in the business. This continues for several years. After this intensive education, the apprentice does what is called the *Tour de France,* in which he goes from shop to shop, each run by a different compagnon, and does a stint at each place until he has traveled all over France. When he returns, he shares what he has learned with the other apprentices. It is only then, at the age of twenty or twenty-two, that he is allowed to go into business for himself.

François Payard, one such former apprentice and proprietor of Payard Pâtisserie and Bistro in Manhattan, recalls his start. "When I was thirteen, I started working for a pastry chef who was sixty-five years old and had been doing it all his life. He taught me everything the old-fashioned way. He was very tough."

Jacques Torres speaks of his compagnon experience with reverence and has the utmost respect for his mentor, who was most influential in those hard training days. "Mr. Louis Franchin was the one who helped me when I passed the *Meilleur Ouvrier de France.*" (The *Meilleur Ouvrier de France* is France's most prestigious professional trades competition, in which participants are assigned and judged for a specific centerpiece, a dessert, and chocolate themes that they must create. In France, the award entitles the holder to teach the craft at the highest technical level.) "I was twenty-six at the time and it was a very hard time, a lot of stress—stress to the point where people would collapse during the competition and fall apart. Mr. Franchin took me and a friend every weekend to train us. He was a teacher at the local culinary school and he just said, 'Come to the school and you will do just like it's your competition.' I think we did that for a whole month. Every weekend we spent two days like it was the competition. I could see at the end of the weekend that Mr. Franchin was tired himself. He was not that young, even at that time, but he worked with us from his core, not just from his mind. He shared the pain we suffered to do it. Then, the very next day, Monday morning, he would come back to teach his students for the week. The following weekend he'd do it again. Why did he do it? He was so good to us and what did we do to deserve that attention? Well, that is just the way he is. He is a compagnon. He belongs to a group of people who share knowledge and a philosophy about creation, about things you do with your hands. Later, when you go around France and experience different positions with other compagnons, you return and are required to help other people—not for money, just to help them with the knowledge you uncovered. I am not a compagnon, but I do have that same mind of being helpful. A compagnon is a truly giving person. He is not a *Meilleur Ouvrier de France*. He doesn't make a lot of money, but he's very talented. He's a true chef. He is the kind of person who takes somebody young and brings them through a stage and says, 'Now it's yours.' Quite a few of those Mr. Franchin trained have become well known. He helped them to get there. It's very rewarding as a chef, when you reach a certain level, to take people and give them that philosophy and knowledge, to tell them, 'Now you have to do it.' Mr. Franchin was the one who told me, 'Jacques, you should go to the United States.' That was sixteen or eighteen years ago. I had no idea at that time that I would one day come to this country. He said, 'Perhaps you should go to America, because I think you will do well for yourself there.' I have the ability to arrive in a new working

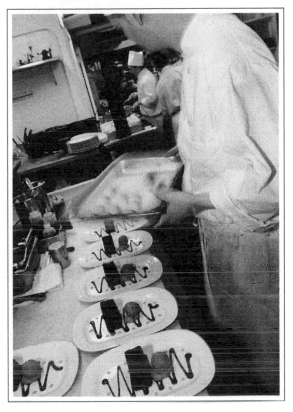

Dessert service at Park Avenue Café

environment and, two hours later, I know people around me and I can work anywhere. He saw that ability in me and thought I could be a success here. I know he was sad to see me go, but with his encouragement I was able to come here and make a great career. I respect him a lot."

Pastry Training Experience

I use the term *training* to describe any way of getting yourself in the position of learning about pastry from an experience or an individual. This differs from apprenticing in that an apprentice works in a single position for the same person or establishment for a longer period of time, usually a year or more.

American pastry chefs generally receive less training than do European pastry chefs. I feel that this is largely a cultural phenomenon. In European countries, sweets and desserts remain a more important part of everyday life and celebration, much more so than in the United States. Therefore, training for the craft was always available and quite thorough. American opportunities for pastry school basic and advanced classes, until recently, were fairly limited geographically.

> I'm wary of the term *pastry chef*. In my mind, it's so huge, so all-encompassing.
> —Claudia Fleming

American pastry chefs, to some extent, have had to create their own ways of educating themselves by reading, trial and error, and on-the-job training. In Europe, the pastry profession is a long-respected historical and culturally entwined career choice. In America, however, it is still a story unfolding. Some self-effacing American pastry chefs tend to downplay their own titles. Claudia Fleming, pastry chef at Gramercy Tavern, says, "I don't really think of myself as a pastry chef. I think of myself as a cook and someone who makes desserts. To me, a pastry chef is that very strict, very formal, from-age-fifteen-on European pastry chef. I think of François Payard and other people who can blow sugar and do all this crazy stuff that I have no interest in doing. I'm not inclined to decorate. I like to cook, and I find lots of inspiration from chefs. I'm wary of the term *pastry chef*. In my mind, it's so huge, so all-encompassing. It's so knowledgeable."

Ann Amernick started in this business catering in the early 1970s and then decided to focus on desserts. "In 1975, *Washingtonian* magazine named me best pastry chef and I was so humiliated. I said 'I'm not a pastry chef.' Pastry chefs start when they're fourteen years old. I am a housewife. I felt it was a slap in the face of every real pastry chef that there was. So I had to make a decision to either become what they were calling me or find another way."

Maury Rubin was afforded the opportunity to learn the craft of classic French pastry in France. "I learned at a six-day pastry course that had been set up in a town about a half-hour southwest of Lyons. The school had been set up because there was this collective thought that the craft of French pastry was very quickly going away. The Confederation of French Pastry Chefs, which is basically a union, decided that in order to save the craft, they had to adopt a one-for-all mentality. They organized this course at a château where, among four thousand members, they would teach themselves. Whoever was the best at croissants would teach the rest. This way, they would have someone in every town that could fight the fast-food croissant-and-brioche place. It was continuing adult education among great pastry chefs. When they had down time at the château, they decided to bring in Americans, and I learned in one of those classes. They just borrowed from their ranks to teach those classes. So the person who taught me that week was Denis Ruffel of Café Millet. He discussed the background and purpose of the château, which was to preserve the craft. So right there, before we even put our hands to flour, butter, and water, there was already this sense of pride for what we were about to do. I have been conscious of that ever since."

Rubin was able to make the right connections after his six-day course and found the training he needed to round out his knowledge of the craft. He set up several stages or short apprenticeships (a minimum of two months of working for free). "After that school, I spent eight months in Paris, five months as an apprentice in a bakery, two months in a chocolate shop, and three weeks in a restaurant. That was really my formative educational experience. I settled into this pastry shop where there were four men. It was an above-average neighborhood shop, but it was not one of the great shops in Paris nor a place you read about in a tour book. By landing there, I got to do everything; I worked every station. The owner of the shop took great interest in teaching me what he had learned as a child. He had grown up in his family's business. The experience taught me to respect the tradition. He felt it was his obligation to pass it on."

Gale Gand describes her approach to acquiring the training for her career. "My formal training was at La Varenne in Paris for two summers. At the time, I needed to work and couldn't afford the two-year program. So I got one month off from my job and went to school for two weeks and worked for two weeks in France. I did that for two summers. Mostly I just learned on the job. I would go up to the door at Le Pyramid and say, 'Hi, I'm here. Is there any way I can spend a couple of days in your kitchen?' They would say, 'Well, you're a woman. I don't know,' and I would say, 'I'll do dishes. I'll do anything.' Finally, they would let me in. So I spent as much time as I could doing that and I still do. I was just at Payard in New York and I said, 'So can I come and stage?' and François said, 'I'll always take free help.' So I always work in other kitchens and with other pastry chefs as much as possible." Gand has also racked up stages at Parisian pastry shops and French restaurants, including Troisgros and Gagnière.

 Tomatillo Sorbet

by Andrew MacLauchlan

Although tomatillos are often called Mexican green tomatoes, they're actually more closely related to Cape gooseberries. When I first learned this, I thought tomatillos would make a good sorbet and I began experimenting. The result is pleasantly surprising and is reminiscent of a crisp, tart, green apple. When choosing tomatillos for this recipe, look for dark green, rather than light green, fruit.

Yield: 1 quart

1 pound (approximately 1 quart) whole tomatillos
½ cup water
½ cup plus 2 tablespoons sugar
½ cup light corn syrup

1. Soak the tomatillos in water to loosen the husks, then remove the husks carefully by peeling them back from the fruit. Try to keep the husks intact, and reserve.
2. Combine the tomatillos, water, sugar, and corn syrup in a blender and puree for 30 to 40 seconds. Pass the mixture through a fine strainer to remove any seeds or lumps of fruit.
3. Spin the mixture in an ice cream machine and place in the freezer.
4. Place two husks in small bowls and open them to as close as possible to their natural shape. Scoop a round scoop of tomatillo sorbet to fit inside each husk.

Nancy Silverton had an intense desire to learn how to cook after college and she proceeded to create her own training experience. "I thought to myself, 'I'm going to get a job in the best restaurant—well, at least what I thought was the best restaurant in the area—and work for free.' It was a restaurant called 464 Magnolia in Los Angeles; it was *the* place to eat. It opened around the same time Chez Panisse opened. No one in there was a trained professional. We cooked out of cookbooks. At that time, my mother was a writer and my father was a lawyer and, coming from a professional family, my choice to be a chef could have been looked down upon. But my parents supported me while I interned at this restaurant because I knew I was going to see all aspects of the kitchen if I was not paid. I wouldn't get stuck making spinach salads. I took it very seriously. I worked five or six days a week. I read stories about people doing apprenticeships in France where they peeled carrots for a year and then they moved on to asparagus. That's how serious I saw training to be. It's so different now. People come in for a month and they are ready to move on and be a chef."

Professional cooking was once a trade totally dominated by men. In the United States, that is changing dramatically. Discrimination is something that many women have had to deal with, but barriers to women in the professional kitchen continue to fall. In the 1970s, many professional kitchens would not hire a woman. For a long time, the professional pastry kitchen was the only accepted place for women in the culinary field. Ann Amernick recalls the climate of the kitchen job market of the time. "When I decided that I would love to work in a restaurant, I tried to get a job and could not for about ten months. They told me they didn't hire women, that I didn't look like a baker, that I needed to gain fifty pounds and put my hair in a bun. One place said, 'Honey, stay at home and take care of your kids.' Another place said, 'The cooks will pick on you.' The fine dining restaurants hung up on me, but these were the good restaurants of the time."

Attitudes in Europe are slower to change. In the 1980s, Gale Gand sent twenty letters to prominent restaurants in France to try to get a stage. She got nineteen rejections and one letter that said, 'We'd love to welcome you in our kitchen, Mr. Gand.' "When I showed up, they were shocked that I was not Mr. Gand but Mrs. Gand. They really didn't allow women in their kitchen. It was quite awkward for the first half hour, when they slammed the door in my face and went away

> When I decided that I would love to work in a restaurant, I tried to get a job and could not for about ten months. They told me they didn't hire women, that I didn't look like a baker, that I needed to gain fifty pounds and put my hair in a bun.
>
> —Ann Amernick

to talk about whether or not to allow me in the kitchen. I'd come all the way from the States and I was going to be there for a good amount of time. They came back and said they would allow me in the kitchen, but they were very suspicious of me. They asked, 'Are you sure you're not an American journalist?' I really had to prove myself."

It might be tough to get a foot in the door in some restaurants, but it is a worthwhile experience and a good way to see how you like the action and pace of a working establishment. Many times, the idea to attend culinary school or seriously pursue a career in cooking or pastry comes after experiencing an entry-level job in the restaurant business. As a teenager, Richard Leach worked in an Armenian restaurant near his family's home on Long Island. "It was a real family-run restaurant. The man who owned it did it all. He was a waiter, a bartender, and a cook. Any time there was some spare time, he showed me something new, and I kept stepping up from there. I was there for almost five years. I started washing dishes and was cooking after one year. I was only sixteen when I did 110 covers. During the same time I was working there, I also worked at another restaurant, where I met a man who baked. He taught me some things and gave me some books. He had gone to Johnson and Wales University in Providence, Rhode Island. He got me interested in cooking school." Having had a taste of the restaurant business, Leach was intrigued enough to pursue his formal culinary training at The Culinary Institute of America, then returned to New York to start his career in some of the finest restaurants in the city.

> The first three to five years out of culinary school, students should repeat what happened in school, this time in real life.
>
> —Markus Färbinger

Markus Färbinger feels that early professional training experience is a great opportunity to find a place in pastry with which you are satisfied. "The first three to five years out of culinary school, students should repeat what happened in school, this time in real life. If they want production desserts, they should go to a large hotel or catering company. If they want to concentrate on chocolates and candies, they should go work for a chocolatier. If they have an interest in frozen desserts, they should try to get into an ice-cream–making facility. Recreating these aspects in the working world can give the person more insight into each area. No matter what they choose later on, they will be able to bring all these experiences to their area of specialization."

Jim Graham structured his early training with several trips to Europe. "I did a few months of pastry classes at the Cordon Bleu Cooking School in Paris, which gave me an idea of what it was like. The rest of my education was on the job. My first break was a restaurant in Houston, Texas, which closed within a year, but I was there long enough to really work in the trade. After that, I went back to France and really did it right. I was able to get working papers and get some serious jobs."

Graham divides his training experience into two stages. "I separate it into the pastry phase and the chocolate phase because, even though they both have to do with sweets, the work itself is different. I felt like I knew enough about the pastry trade to be fairly competent after about three years on the job. I define that crucial level of competence as being the point at which I could start drawing from different elements of my training and be creative. As long as you are just repeating recipes, your training is not complete, but as soon as you can start synthesizing from disparate elements of your training, that is a milestone! Chocolate has a much less clearly defined training period. With chocolate, for me, there wasn't a point when I felt accomplished. It has been much more a continuous learning curve. I went to Maison du Chocolat in Paris as soon as I decided to try chocolate. I wanted to do it in the best way possible. It was a very big break for me. I was there in the mid-eighties for almost four years."

Pastry cook focusing on a task

At the advice of guidance counselors, Michelle Gayer attended the culinary program at Kendall College in Evanston, Illinois, right after high school because she knew she wanted to be a chef. But she describes what can happen when you want to move up too fast in this profession. "After my externship in the middle of my education at Kendall College, I decided to focus on pastry. Right out of school, I went to a restaurant in St. Louis and got a job as the pastry chef, which I was not ready for. I should have been an assistant first, but I was out of my mind. My first day, the chef said, 'We want eight different desserts and three different breads and breadsticks.' I had no clue about breads. I thought different breads only meant flavoring them with a spice or an herb. I had no idea about the balance of flavors, textures, or flavor combinations."

I have found, from speaking with many American pastry chefs, that training in the past has largely been unstructured, more an individual collection of influential work experiences than anything formal. To some degree, it is true that pastry chefs get out of their later careers only as much as they put into their training and early working life in the field. Richard Leach, who attended The Culinary Institute of America before they introduced the associate's and bachelor's degree programs in baking and pastry arts, recalls that his interest in pastry wasn't really sparked until after his training at the school, when he could see clearly the potential for pastry work in the restaurant. "In school, the introduction was so quick and I can remember, in pastry class, all I wanted to do was leave and go back to work. I really didn't want to be there. Later, what I saw at the River Café, where I used to see things going on out of the corner of my eye, helped me make a connection to pastry. Desserts struck my interest because the restaurant business was all new to me and I was just beginning to experiment." As a natural development following culinary school, he seemed to need to experience the practical relationship of restaurant, food, and desserts to allow his cooking forte to unfold. "I never had training under a pastry chef. I've based myself more on cooking chefs," says Leach, who recommends spending at least a year with a good pastry chef. "You may not be able to expect to move up until you have several different job experiences." Leach also advises: "If you need to move on, that's okay, but at least move on to something different—different cuisine, different style of service, different volume. Don't go from banquets to banquets. Learn all different aspects of the business."

Passing a cooked custard through a fine strainer

Glazed Ricotta Cheese with Figs and Port

by Richard Leach

Yield: Six 4-ounce ramekins

For the cheese base:

1½ cups (12 ounces) cream cheese

½ cup plus 2 tablespoons (6 ounces) ricotta cheese

¼ cup plus 2 tablespoons granulated sugar

1 vanilla bean, split and scraped

2 whole eggs

1 egg white

¾ cup heavy cream

For the fig-port sauce:

2 cups port

4 ripe black Mission figs, stem removed, cut into ¼-inch dice

½ cup granulated sugar

For assembly:

3 tablespoons turbinado (coarsely ground sugar) or granulated sugar

For the cheese base:

1. In a mixing bowl equipped with a paddle, add the cream cheese and mix on low until creamy. Srape the sides of the bowl and continue to mix until smooth.

2. Add the ricotta, sugar, and vanilla bean scrapings and pod and beat the mixture on medium speed until smooth.

3. Add the eggs, egg white, and heavy cream and mix on medium until totally incorporated. Remove the vanilla bean pod and place the mixture in the refrigerator.

For the fig-port sauce:

1. Combine all ingredients in a saucepot over medium heat and reduce the mixture to half of its volume. Let cool.

Continued on next page

Assembly:

1. Preheat the oven to 275°. Divide the fig-port sauce evenly among six 4-ounce ramekins and place them in the freezer to firm the mixture, about 1 hour.

2. Remove the ramekins from the freezer and pour the cheese base over the fig-port sauce, filling each to the top.

3. Place the ramekins on a baking tray that has a 1-inch rim and pour a ½-inch-deep water bath into the tray to ensure gentle baking.

4. Bake for 30 minutes or until set. Test by gently tapping the side of a ramekin to see if the liquid ripples or if it has set. Remove from oven and cool.

5. Sprinkle the turbinado or granulated sugar evenly over the tops of the cheese. Melt and caramelize with a blow torch or, watching closely, place them under an oven broiler until the sugar melts and browns.

Claudia Fleming had limited training initially, but once she knew she wanted to pursue a pastry career, she made the connections she needed. Some resulted from stages in France. "I went to the cooking program at Peter Kump's New York Cooking School for a couple of weeks," said Fleming. "Then I was at Union Square Café, briefly. Then I went to Tribeca Grill and was in way over my head. I was pretty much doing it all, and it wasn't my menu. After that experience, I knew I wanted more training. I talked to Maury Rubin of City Bakery and he offered to introduce me to one of the people he trained with in France. I worked in France for nine months, first at Fauchon, then at Mondrian in Biarritz."

Opportunities always exist for creating an ongoing educational experience for yourself. That's part of life's challenge—to get yourself into places that give you the chance to learn and grow. Those places aren't necessarily the best-known restaurants or pastry shops; then again, they may be. Wherever you go, you need to get the utmost from your experiences because all of it can help you later on.

Pastry Chefs' Learning Experiences

A successful career as a pastry chef requires an innate ability to continually learn, grow, and adapt. Foresight and humility are necessary to staying open to learning and always applying that knowledge on the job. A new management skill may come to your attention, or a faster technique or better tool may become available. In the formative years, as well as at a time in the future when you are more established in your career, the learning never ends. There's much we can learn from our mistakes, and sometimes it is these turning points and memorized experiences that leave lasting impressions on us.

Judy Contino relates her learning experiences working for Michael Foley at Printer's Row. "I learned to push myself unbelievably. He would come in and leave a note for me with at least a dozen things. They weren't recipes or even ideas. They were just a combination of flavors. By the end of the week, he expected me to have created something with each of the things on the list. Whether it turned out to be a cake, a tart, or a soufflé didn't matter, but he pushed me and it was a great learning experience."

Emily Luchetti cites her transition from savory cooking to the pastry department at Stars as a point of growth in her career. Jeremiah Tower questioned Luchetti, a valued employee, about what could be bothering her. "Having someone come to me and say, 'Listen, I know you're not happy working on the line. You're not doing a great job here.' I had to step back and look at the situation myself. I had to have enough humility to look at myself objectively. I said to myself, 'You're not doing that great of a job because you don't like it, so what do you want to do?' That situation made me realize that what I wanted to do was pastry. When you're in this business for a long time, you're going to have failures and you're going to have successes. You can't win every award. You can't make the best desserts every single day. Successes, you say 'Great!' Then you're on to your next one, but what really makes you stop and think are the failures, the hard spots."

> When you're in this business for a long time, you're going to have failures and you're going to have successes. You can't win every award. You can't make the best desserts every single day. Successes, you say "Great!" Then you're on to your next one, but what really makes you stop and think are the failures, the hard spots.
>
> —Emily Luchetti

Errors in judgment can be situations to learn and grow from, but often a pastry chef must be ready for absolutely any calamity. Dan Budd recalled a few memorable hard spots. "One Fourth of July, I was working on the Trump Princess in New York. We had desserts going from the kitchen, which is at the base of the vessel, to the back deck. There were amazing, famous people there. I was very young and didn't have a lot of experience. Eric Gouteyron, pastry chef of the Plaza Hotel in New York, and I had made all these unbelievable desserts for this event, all while our restaurants back at the hotel were still running, and we put these desserts on large mirror platters and put them in an elevator with a waiter. The elevator was open on every level and the mirror caught on the second level of the boat and flipped the desserts straight up in the elevator shaft and the mirror slid down between the elevator and the floor and it traveled all the way down, smashing at the bottom of the ship. Donald Trump himself turned and said, 'What was that?'"

Budd had not one but two classic catastrophes. I think it's important to realize that even with the magnitude of these situations, all you can do, as Budd and Gouteyron did, is go back to the drawing board. Always be ready to do something that can serve to replace your masterpiece in case of disasters. Budd continues, "One time I was working with Eric Badusha and we finished a six-tier wedding cake. It was on a room service table and we had to bring it up to the banquet floor. We were pushing the table out of the elevator and the wheels turned sideways and got stuck in the space between the elevator and the floor. The cake started to tilt forward; it was happening in slow motion. The table was in our way and the cake was just leaning forward. Both of us knew what was going to happen and there was nothing we could do about it. The cake smashed all over the floor. We couldn't believe it. We went down to the pastry shop and were scratching everywhere to see what we could do. We ended up building a cake in an hour and a half from some things we had around and it looked okay. I guess it taught me that a pastry chef always has to be ready. It also taught me that if you think positively you can always make something happen. In the restaurant and food business, lots of things can happen. Any given minute, something can go wrong. You only need to know how to be aware and think positively."

> If you think positively you can always make something happen. In the restaurant and food business, lots of things can happen. Any given minute, something goes wrong. You only need to know how to be aware and think positively.
>
> —Dan Budd

Richard Leach remembers his most difficult transition in the first few days as the pastry chef at Aureole. "All of a sudden, I was given the responsibility of creating my own menu items *and* responsibility for the four or five people it took to produce the desserts. I can remember being held back, reserved, and kind of quiet. I didn't really want to say my piece with the people who worked in pastry, but eventually that piece just came out, and I've had no problem since then." Leach had to adjust his work approach to include leading and guiding his crew to success.

Claudia Fleming remembers an embarrassing experience. "It happened when I was at Fauchon in Paris and I had to make these tuiles (thin cookies). I thought they came out nicely, but the guy who worked the oven came back into the kitchen and said, 'Who made these?' Everyone turned and looked at me and I said, 'I did,' and he said, 'Oh, they're fine.' I knew they were horrible, so of course I did them over. I really felt terrible, but that experience gave me the standard for that place. I thought they looked good, but they had to look better."

Jim Graham points to an incident with the ovens at Lenôtre's pâtisserie in Houston. "The first thing that comes to mind is not necessarily a learning experience—more of an attitude adjustment. For a while, I was stuck running these huge closet-sized rotating ovens that you wheeled a whole rack of prepared pastries into. I was in charge of these monsters, but I had very little experience. We were struggling to keep up with production and I loaded an oven with a whole batch of pâte à choux (cream puff batter) piped onto trays, which was virtually a whole day's work. I went on my lunch break and forgot about it and burned all of it. I was devastated and, more than anything else, hated to confront my chef about it. Not because I was afraid of getting yelled at but because it was a violation of trust. Of course, the inevitable happened, and he saw how crestfallen I was. I said in French, 'I'm crushed.' He said, 'Jim, it's only pastry. It's only cakes.' For some reason I've carried that with me for a long time. I don't think I've reproduced a disaster of quite that scale since. That experience helped me in working with people under me. Chef Gerald was able to bring in the human element and remind me that it is the people who are important, despite the fact that my mistake was a major setback for his department."

Jacques Torres makes an interesting comparison that points out a challenging fact of this profession. "My father is a carpenter and I've heard him say, 'Your table is going to be ready on Monday.' Sometimes the table will be ready on Wednesday instead. The customer is not always happy, but he has their table and that's okay. Now, say you have a big wedding cake to do. Try to finish the wedding cake two days later than the wedding and you'll see what happens.

So to me, one of the worst and most difficult things in this profession is the stress of being ready. Sometimes you have so much to do that there is no time to eat, no time to sleep. It's just rush, rush, rush to get things done. That's the business. The Christmas season is especially difficult for all of us. That is when we put in the most hours. It's when the muscles in your legs hurt, your back hurts, you're exhausted, and you're cranky. This is not average work. It's out of balance sometimes."

Mary Bergin learned the hard way to ask for help when it is needed. "It was 1987, the first year that I was pastry chef, and I was out to impress the whole world, including Wolfgang Puck. For New Year's Eve, I was to make vacherin (meringue cups filled with ice cream or sorbet). Well, at Spago in Los Angeles, in the old kitchen, we had an old home freezer because we never froze anything except ice cream. So for 350 people, I had to make vacherin for tables of two, four, six, and ten. I had sheet pans of meringues, I put rings around them, and I piped in vanilla ice cream. Then I put the sheet pans in the freezer, but this freezer had no shelves, so Wolfgang said to stack them with cans in the corners. I was really nervous because I was under a lot of pressure and had never made this dessert before. There were 350 people coming for dinner and I was the new head pastry chef. I was stacking the pans like he said and working on my fourth sheet pan. I brought it over to the freezer and Wolfgang was standing right there cutting up fish. I opened the door and one of the cans had slipped and all the pans were at an angle. My ice cream was over here, meringue layers over there. I closed the freezer quickly then opened it, looked, and closed it again. Wolfgang looked at me and said, 'If you need some help, just ask for it.' I opened the freezer one more time, shut it, and said, 'I need some help,' and started crying. Well, Wolfgang has a hard time seeing a woman cry. He told a manager to take everything out of one of the walk-ins and turn the temperature down. 'We'll turn it into a freezer to make her stop crying.' Before that, I never asked for help. I used to be too proud to ask for help."

Gale Gand's advice to pastry chefs involves the up-and-down nature of restaurant reservation numbers. "Parties always go up. They can go down by ten then up by twenty, so you always have to be flexible and always make extra.

Don't be possessive with your desserts and preparations because someone is going to eat them. The nighttime butcher guy is going to find your cooler and raid it, so just have enough around for everybody."

Learning from negative experiences in your career is sometimes just part of the process. It goes with the territory of putting yourself in the vulnerable position of taking on more and more responsibility. No one's perfect and human error is part of the equation. The other side of learning can be ideas you glean from performing repetitive processes or working with particular techniques or foodstuffs.

Jim Graham reports, "Working with chocolate is not cerebral—it's instinctive. You have to have been around chocolate long enough, and in enough different circumstances, that you anticipate instictively how it's going to act. No one can tell you that. I have worked for some very knowledgeable people, but I can honestly say that it's the chocolate that teaches you. You're not going to get it from anyone else."

Humility is an important quality for a pastry chef at any stage of the game, whether you're at the beginning of your career or in charge of a crew. Nancy Silverton discovered this early in her burgeoning career. "I was at Michael's since the very beginning. I think I came in after it had been open three or four months, and it was the hot restaurant of the time. It was getting a lot of press. Everyone

Filling a container with chocolate cake batter

was raving about the food. I had done the desserts there for over a year when I went to Lenôtre Cooking School in Paris. I knew what we did at Michael's was terrific and I thought it was really innovative. I thought I was going to be able to go to Lenôtre and say, 'Well, this is what we do at Michael's,' and then maybe I would learn something from them too. The first day of class we introduced ourselves, telling how long we had been in the business and what we were doing. In France, educational programs are available to workers where they are allowed six weeks off a year, and the business gives them money for education. Here I was with pastry chefs who were working in the business for twenty years and taking brush-up courses. I'd been doing this for a year, and it was eye-opening for me that after twenty years they still felt the need to do a brush-up course. Here I am, this rich American, and I was going to sign up for four to six classes. These people had specific duties like making ice cream or chocolates or pastries, because in France you either make cakes or chocolates or ice cream, but you don't do all of them. Then we went to work and I watched these people work. I watched myself, how I hold a pastry bag and pipe sheet pan after sheet pan of perfect meringue. Then I watched them and thought, 'I need a few more years.' I watched them write on cakes. Here at Michael's we had to do our happy birthday writing on top of cakes and it looked like something you got at a local supermarket. Watching these Frenchmen write on cakes, I said, 'How do you do it?' They told me that part of their exercises when they were in school was to fill notebook after notebook with writing. If you can't write with a pen, you can't write with a pastry bag. So at that time, the experience of being exposed to the perfectionism of those pastry chefs made me realize what it takes is pure dedication. It really made sense to me at that moment that you never stop learning."

Dining, Traveling, and Developing as a Pastry Chef

A pastry chef continues to forge his or her vision throughout a career. It is part of this profession to continue to survey and acknowledge the shifting sands of public taste and the changing business world of restaurants and food. To remain in step and responsive, a pastry chef must see what's out there by taking in and devouring information whenever and however possible.

Emily Luchetti expounds the value of stepping out. "It is important that we all go out and experience other chefs' food because it reminds you of why you strive for the quality of food you do. It says to you, 'Don't lose sight of that in the back of the kitchen, in the heat of the battle, when you're trying to put out all this food and when you do all this production. Remember what you're there for.' "

Bruno Feldeisen gets inspiration from dining out on occasion. "I'm a believer that we don't create anything new. It's been done before in one way or another. We do, however, transfer things. We do get inspired by other people's styles and desserts. I don't go out to copy, but I do go out to be influenced."

One of the most eye-opening things a chef can do is to travel. When you travel internationally or regionally, you gain insight into the ways different people and cultures treat food. Finding yourself in a strange place without the reference points and comfort level of your home can push you to look at everything in a different light—your language and all of your notions of what is "normal" about food. Dining out locally on nights off from work can be an educational experience as well. This way you can see and taste the food and desserts of fellow chefs and hone and develop your sensibilities and attitudes for your own approach. A good chef or pastry chef never stops learning about food.

Lindsey Shere thinks travel is important for inspiration. "I think that it's very easy to forget all the possibilities that are out there. Traveling and eating helps to remind you of what is available and helps to stimulate you by showing all the incredible things that can be made. It's really an experience to eat Asian desserts, for example, because they are so completely different from what we know about, but I think they are a great resevoir of ideas. I think that's true wherever you go." Feldeisen agrees. "I travel maybe once or twice a month on small trips. Even if you go to someplace like Mississippi, you're always going to pick up something. It's a way to open up your mind."

Satisfied customer enjoying dessert

I traveled to France in the late 1980s and was moved by the reverence people have for food in Europe, particularly in France. It's an astonishing cultural difference. Good food seems much more central to everyday life there. I must have taken hundreds of photographs in outdoor markets and through the windows of pâtisseries and boulangeries. Travel can be a source of inspiration early in a career, but it can also be an important revitalization later on.

Jim Graham took a bicycle trip with a friend through France at the age of twenty-two. "We had a budget of five dollars per day for food. We were ravenous from our physical exertion during the day and from sleeping out in the fields at night and burning all kinds of calories just trying to keep warm. In every little town, we would stop and look into the pastry shop windows with all these pastries beckoning, and we had just a few coins to spend every day. It became a really big deal to go to these pastry shops and try to decide what we wanted. In fact, I remember once it led to an argument between my friend and myself. I said, 'Forget this! Here we are traveling through France and looking at all this beautiful food and we are not enjoying it. This might be a once-in-a-lifetime opportunity. Let's blow all of our money.' He stuck to his guns and wouldn't do it, so we stuck it out."

Gale Gand continually travels and works for a brief period in restaurants or bakeries wherever she goes. "I've learned so much from traveling, like the first time I went to Fauchon in Paris and looked through the windows and thought, 'How do they do that?' I found out that the chocolate wood-grain design is actually done with a tool you can find at a hardware store, but no one could tell me the name of it. When I worked at Harrod's in London, it was the first time I saw marbleized chocolate. Finally, I saw some guy open up a cooler and I saw sheets of acetate (thin, plastic sheets) stacked in there. I said, 'Okay, what is that stuff? Where do they get it?' I found out it was sold at art supply stores. So the journey of seeing something and trying to replicate it really stands out for me."

> I've learned so much from traveling, like the first time I went to Fauchon in Paris and looked through the windows and thought, "How do they do that?" I found out that the chocolate wood-grain design is actually done with a tool you can find at a hardware store.
> —Gale Gand

Travel experiences, dining out, or stints of training in Europe can be transformational for someone interested in becoming a pastry chef. Graham is glad to have learned in France. "Not only for the training," he says, "but for the cultural respect for food, right down to the way it is presented in the market. Just walking through the street market in France is inspirational. The way, for instance, if you go to buy a pear in the market, you don't go rummaging through the pile to pick them out. The person behind the counter asks, 'On what day are you going to be eating it?' Then he or she goes through and finds the pear that will be just right for when you'll be having it. That was always amazing to me."

Sometimes the simplest food experiences can set important standards in your mind for years to come. Dan Budd calls it "the library of inspiration." He goes on to say, "In a way, you formulate your inspiration from related food experiences and you're constantly building up your own library of inspiration. Sometimes you don't realize it when you read or travel and experience something you can use later on. I think the gift of a great chef is to have the memories of those food experiences just come back to you as you need them. Whether it's writing a new menu or coming up with a special dessert, travel can be a big part of it. I know that my travels in France inspire me every day. Maybe it was just the feeling of professionalism, the way that people treat food there. Those things have become a big part of what I do."

Emily Luchetti remembers her early experiences in France. "When I was in Paris eating my first croissants and breads, simple chocolate soufflés, and desserts, what really struck me then was the quality."

When you are out of your own culture, you can see and experience foods and flavors that you are familiar with prepared differently or at another level. Traveling and dining in another country can really help educate you about flavors and how they are used in different cuisines. Nancy Silverton comments on her travels. "I think eating food in another country is what really inspires me. I don't feel comfortable just mixing the flavors of the moment without really understanding them."

The multi-ethnic nature of the United States makes it possible to experience other cultures and authentic ethnic food without leaving the country. If and when you travel to a large city, be sure to include an adventure into an ethnic neighborhood and visit a market or a restaurant. When I lived in Chicago and worked at Charlie Trotter's, I took trips to Indian and Middle Eastern markets and restaurants to experience new foods. I also went to a particular Greek bakery to buy rolls of freshly made phyllo sheets to construct my napoleons and other desserts for the restaurant.

Richard Leach has traveled in Europe but finds much ethnic inspiration in and around New York City. "In New York, you see many things from different countries. I enjoy going to the different neighborhoods and checking things out, even just talking to people. I used to live in Queens and I'd see things in stores there that I'd never see in Manhattan. There are Thai stores and Mexican stores. Then there's Chinatown."

Sebastien Canonne had a strong desire to travel and see new places and enjoy new opportunities. "I wanted possibilities for learning outside the close circles in Europe where sometimes they don't let you see the whole recipe. They tell you only what you need to know and you've got to go for it and hope you don't make a mistake."

Claudia Fleming sees the value of traveling for her work. "I would like to do more exotic trips to understand ethnic cuisine and how people use ingredients and how I can adapt those ingredients to what I do."

Maury Rubin definitely did his homework. "For me, there was a very solid year of what I call 'homework,' basically eating pastry. I have never walked by a pastry shop in France and not gone in. For that matter, not in America, either. That investigative urge comes from my first love, journalism, which led to my career in producing and directing. I believe in doing your homework. I believe in reference points for quality. I eat pastry like a fiend. My girlfriend, when she was with me in France, would say, 'Come on, you know you don't need to go in that place, you know it's not going to be good.' I feel like I know what's out there and I have a very strong feel for the range of quality that exists. That always informs me of what we can do here at City Bakery."

> I have never walked by a pastry shop in France and not gone in. For that matter, not in America, either...I believe in doing your homework. I believe in reference points for quality. I eat pastry like a fiend.
> —Maury Rubin

I had an extraordinary opportunity to travel and live in West Africa in 1993 and 1994. I managed to take a leave of absence from Charlie Trotter's to work on the manuscript for *New Classic Desserts* and pursue my interest in landscape painting. While living in Benin, which borders Nigeria, I had incredible tropical fruit experiences, picking plantains and bananas in the field, tasting cashewfruit, (a rare fruit outside of the tropics because it is highly perishable), feasting on papayas and the juiciest pineapples and oranges. I left Africa inspired to do more with tropical fruits in my cooking and wound up using those experiences as the source for writing my third cookbook, *Tropical Desserts.* That travel experience still serves as a place I visit in my mind to conjure up new tropical desserts for my menus.

I think it's a mistake to underestimate the value travel can have on you. Inspiration can come from many sources outside the kitchen—traveling, visiting markets and restaurants, experiencing ethnic cuisine. These forays are limited only by your interests, the opportunities you create, and the particular cuisine(s) you intend to focus on.

Nancy Silverton comments, "Let's suppose that all you want to make is shortcake and angel food cake. Do you need to be on a street corner in Singapore? Not really. But if you want to do foods that have Asian influences, then yes, you have to be on that street corner in Singapore. That's something you can't only read about; that's something you really have to taste and experience."

In February 1997, I had the privilege of traveling with Mark Miller to Japan to cook a rice dinner for Japanese senators and businesspeople as part of a consulting project he was working on. We then spent three days in Shanghai, China, visiting markets, shopping for antique furniture for his new Asian restaurant, and sampling street food and restaurants. Freshly inspired from the trip, which immersed me in some of the culture and cuisine of Asia, I later developed the opening dessert menu for Miller's new restaurant. The trip gave me reference points with respect to the boldness of flavors and aesthetics of design. I learned a great deal from that trip that I was able to apply immediately.

The Value of Reading

If you love what you do, you have a voracious appetite for information and ideas that you can apply to your everyday work. I was inspired by *Mastering the Art of French Pastry* by Bruce Healy and Paul Bugat. To me, that book was seminal. The clear instructions, drawings, and photographs and the intelligence with which the material was presented were a revelation. When that book came out, I thought I had found the ancient secret to pastry and, armed with it, could undertake any challenge. I remember, when I was a pastry assistant at a large hotel, the executive chef collected cookbooks. He was in a book club that sent two or three books a month. When a pastry or baking book came, he loaned it to me as soon as it arrived. I remember poring over Nancy Silverton's first book and carrying Bo Friberg's *The Professional Pastry Chef* around wherever I went to read through the classical European recipes. Then *The Roux Brothers on Pâtisserie* came out and I was entranced. They seemed to pull so many classical recipes together in one book that said to me, "This is what you can do when you are a pastry chef." That book really touched on all of it, from breads and whole desserts, pâtisserie style, to plated restaurant desserts, petit fours, and pulled sugar. That was another book that never left my side until the binding became loose.

Richard Leach stresses the importance of self-teaching. "You can't teach yourself enough in your free time through reading. A lot of kitchens do not allow you to experiment and many processes aren't adaptable for experimentation at home. The best thing you can do is read."

Mary Bergin was inspired by Maida Heatter's books. "I think it is mostly because of the way she wrote her books. I could relate to them because I had no formal training. So I went out and got every Maida Heatter book I could possibly afford."

Claudia Fleming cites magazines as a significant resource for ideas. "Australian *Vogue* is an unbelievable resource and inspiration. I go to it constantly. Nancy Silverton's *Desserts* book, Lindsey Shere's *Chez Panisse Desserts*, and *New Classic Desserts*. Those are the three books I look at all the time."

François Payard says, "Sometimes I use books. Every idea you get is from someone else. The person who says they don't use other people's ideas is a liar."

A pastry chef's focus, whether in a restaurant, hotel, or pastry shop, can be forced in a single direction for a period of time. He or she may be concentrating on training new staff members, purchasing or sourcing a new product or piece of equipment, performing food and labor costing, or developing a menu. Looking to the world at large to reignite the flame of inspiration is a valuble practice for nearly every pastry chef. The best pastry chefs continue to grow and evolve. Reading cookbooks or books on food history is vital to understanding the directions you're taking as you develop your personal style as a pastry chef. Cooking from a good pastry cookbook from cover to cover is a good exercise and reemphasizes the fundamentals. When you start as a pastry cook, you carry out the chef's vision, you follow orders and do things that particular chef's way, but that's not the only way to do things. There are many techniques for some processes and several ways of visualizing certain fundamental recipes or finished desserts. From reading, you can expose yourself to different procedures and methods and begin to clarify areas of the craft that are still new territory.

Gale Gand learned a tremendous amount from reading. "I cooked every page of *Lenôtre*. That's how I learned a lot of things. I always keep *The Joy of Cooking* around. I was making peanut brittle last week and I needed a fundamental book. I have a library of about two thousand books, not all pastry.

The pastry portion is probably at about three hundred. When I start to develop an idea, I look it up in six different books and read whatever is integral to that recipe and then decide for myself what parts to keep."

The constant barrage of cooking periodicals also provides a multitude of ideas and flavor combinations as well as basic and more advanced recipes. Mary Bergin says, "I buy every cooking magazine and go straight to the back and look up the dessert section because to me it's like the sports page—it's always there."

Emily Luchetti refers to books on an ongoing basis. "I have lots of cookbooks. I go to certain cookbooks for certain things. I flip through some for inspiration and then there's some I go to for technique, like Flo Braker's *Art of Perfect Baking.* Her descriptions of choux paste and puff pastry are really well done. Other books, like Nancy Silverton's, are inspirational. Books like *Mastering the Art of French Cooking* I go to for technique."

Nancy Silverton herself reads cookbooks. "Reading is educational. I love to read cookbooks. I don't cook out of them because I don't follow recipes well, but I love to read them. Whenever I try, I leave out half of the ingredients. There is always something to learn, whether it's a food combination or that little technique that you didn't know about that will make something just a little bit better, like, 'So *that's* why my angel food cake is

Pastry cook labeling wrapped pastries

never light, because I'm overfolding, or I'm using granulated sugar instead of powdered.' There's so much to learn from reading."

Growing as a pastry chef involves looking to any possible source of inspiration. Finding a recipe in an old cookbook with unusual ingredients or a book on traditional regional foods can open up worlds of unexplored dessert and pastry avenues. Chris Broberg developed an unusually early interest in cookbook reading. "I think I was thirteen when I read Escoffier. I was fascinated by the sculptural aspects of pastry. Then there was the *American Heritage Cookbook,* which has history and recipes. I continue to be fascinated by older cookbooks. As a pastry chef, it is very important to read. Besides direct contact with someone, it is the way you learn. Our generation is lucky to have a lot of people sharing their information. Sometimes it's the best inspiration. You cannot live in a vacuum and if you think you are the focal point of all creation, you are wrong, because creativity is bouncing off other people in one form or another."

Dan Budd also promotes reading as an investment in yourself. "I think it is very important to read, to expose yourself to what other people have learned. Reading can expose you to ideas you've never heard of or seen before and it gives you the option of expanding and building them into your own repertoire."

When it comes to reading and traveling as ways of learning, the two may be inseparable, as Mark Miller believes. "The value of reading comes before traveling. If you go and see something before you know about it, it doesn't do any good. I used to teach art and culture, and if I showed my students an Indian rug before they knew the complexity of the mythology of the culture, then they were only looking at it from their own perspective. I think it really helps to read a lot." Miller owns over four thousand cookbooks or books on cookery and food lore. He suggests spending a lot of time with books, not just thumbing through casually for the look of the desserts. "If you are at home and you want to become a pastry chef, you should pick one pastry book and cook all the way through it, and take notes along the way on how you would change each recipe. You need to learn how your view of pastry will eventually be different, to learn to think about pastry rather than just eat it. If someone just picks out certain desserts—for example, all chocolate ones, because they are interested in chocolate—well, then they are not going to understand one philosophy of a particular pastry chef."

> If you are at home and you want to become a pastry chef, you should pick one pastry book and cook all the way through it, and take notes along the way on how you would change each recipe. You need to learn how your view of pastry will eventually be different, to learn to think about pastry rather than just eat it.
>
> —Mark Miller

Moving to New Positions

As your career as a pastry chef develops and unfolds, moving to new positions within the pastry department and to different establishments can be a vital way to learn all the facets of the business that, later on, you will use to create more value for your employer and, ultimately, yourself. Nancy Silverton feels you should question your motives and make sure you are moving for the right reasons. "First of all, whatever you do, you have to do because you love it, not for the money. You have to be patient with what you want to do. You also have to be in a place that you can make the kind of desserts you love to make. So, if you are moving to work for a different restaurant or pastry chef, make sure his or her work is something you really like. I know that a lot of people would be dissapointed if they worked with me. They would probably look at it and think, 'Where's the flash? Where's the gimmick?' and for those people, I'm not the

right person to work for. I suggest tasting what the chef is doing or that place is doing to make sure you like the desserts. I think that's the most important thing to do."

Claudia Fleming recommends getting as much out of every employment opportunity as possible. "I think it depends on the place and how much there is to learn in that place. Here at Gramercy Tavern, I advise people to stay until they have worked through every station in the pastry department. I think they should stay until they can do something with their eyes closed, until they know it backwards and forwards."

Understanding all the facets of the world of pastry can also give you an edge as a business owner in whatever path you may later choose, whether it's running a pâtisserie, catering, doing wedding cakes, developing new products, or consulting.

Jacques Torres believes in the learning process

Handing over finished desserts to a pick-up area

of switching jobs but he advises not to switch jobs too often. "You could stay two days if it's a lousy place and you're not happy with it, or you can stay for five years. To me, it's very important not to lose your time and it's not lost as long as you are learning. I have had people come to me and say, 'I'm not learning enough,' but I always think, 'Perhaps if you don't learn enough, it's because you don't want to learn enough.' Some places, like here at Le Cirque 2000, if you don't push to see different things, you're going to fall into a routine where it's easy for you and it's easy for me. But if you want to learn, you can come to me every day and say, 'I want to see how you do this.' You have to get that from people. Don't wait until people give you your profession. Go and take it. You're never going to make it otherwise.

"When I was thirteen, at my first apprenticeship, I told the owner I was going to switch from restaurant work to pastry. He said, 'Jacques, hundred profession, hundred misery. Take a profession you like and stick with it.' I remember that lesson to not switch jobs too often, to push people to help me grow where I am. You cannot switch jobs every month because you will not have time to learn anything."

Roland Mesnier believes in moving to new positions to learn how to be the very best at what you do. "When you work in different kitchens, you need to choose places where you're going to learn the missing links in your chain of knowledge. You must have a plan for who you want to be and every time you make a move from one job to another, you go to a job that will give you a missing link."

Maury Rubin advises budding pastry chefs to slow down. "You should work at a station for a much longer period of time than you ever thought was necessary. Work at a station to the point where you can say to yourself, 'There is nobody in this city that can do this better than I can do this now.' "

Nick Malgieri offers similar advice. "The reason to move around when you are young is to do a major part of the learning for your career. You have to develop a good balance between knowing when it is time to move on and not having your resume look like a jigsaw puzzle, because that can also be detrimental. You have to strike a balance so that you can learn as much as possible from many people without giving yourself the kind of employment history that makes you look like a butterfly going around and around. The up side of making a commitment to a job is exploring the possibility of moving around with the help of the chef. At the right point, when chefs feel that you have given them as much as they have given you, nine times out of ten they will get involved in getting you a better position, not just a lateral move. Jacques Torres does that. He gets

> I remember that lesson to not switch jobs too often, to push people to help me grow where I am. You cannot switch jobs every month because you will not have time to learn anything.
>
> —Jacques Torres

behind people who really give the most and finds them a job in another place. He gets them a paying job after they have paid their dues with him. It's not a myth; it happens. It's the best side of having a good relationship with your chef."

Mesnier has some good advice for those changing jobs. "When you go to a new job, you should stay a good length of time even if you don't care for it too much. You should never leave that job after six months; it always looks bad on a resume. A good year, year and a half, two years makes for a better resume. When people say they didn't learn anything, then they are not remembering that you can learn from the negative as well as the positive. I have never had a bad job and I think the reason is the way I handled those jobs. When you're the pastry chef and you're starting a new job, my philosophy is that you don't come in firing everybody and bullying everybody and changing everybody

> You don't make a big deal of who you are and what you do and you start working. You put yourself right in there with your staff and you do what they have been doing and then after a while you say, "You know, maybe tonight I thought we'd change that a little bit," and I guarantee that in a year or so you will have changed the whole pastry shop without them even noticing.
>
> Roland Mesnier

overnight. The smart attitude is to come in and instead of telling your staff how great you are and where you've worked and what you've done, you lower yourself and you don't mention those things unless they ask you. You don't make a big deal of who you are and what you do and you start working. You put yourself right in there with your staff and you do what they have been doing and then after a while you say, 'You know, maybe tonight I thought we'd change that a little bit,' and I guarantee that in a year or so you will have changed the whole pastry shop without them even noticing. This is how you're really going to make that job work. If you turn your staff against you right away when you come in, it will be a disaster because they will be working against you and they are not going to make you look good. Talk to them and make them understand that you care."

Every work experience is a unique road map that aspiring pastry chefs must plot on their own. This collection of viewpoints from the twisting and turning careers of great pastry chefs makes at least one thing clear. Each and every one of them took hold of their own direction at some point in their career and steered themselves through transformational learning experiences to arrive at new plateaus of responsibility and creativity. Your goals are your own and you must have them to achieve anything at all. You can set your course and step by step, job by job, meet the challenges, practice, learn, and attain the desired levels in an unfolding, developing career.

What do chefs and restaurateurs want in a pastry chef? I asked Charlie Trotter what qualities, experience, or education he looks for when hiring a pastry chef for his restaurant. "I don't know that formal education or culinary school is the most important thing. It certainly doesn't hurt that someone has been to a major program or has worked under a major pastry chef. That training is going to indicate a certain level of seriousness, but that is not the only prerequisite. Personally, if I am going to hire someone at Charlie Trotter's, I look for energy, sincerity, someone who is really self-motivated, who is very excited just to be around food, who almost becomes emotional when they are working with certain foodstuffs, touching certain things, smelling certain things. As a pastry chef, you have to have that kind of mental, sensual, and emotional relationship with your food. That's something that I don't think you can teach people. People can learn how to make a brown sauce. They can learn how to filet a salmon or how to make a pâte brisée (simple pie dough). They can learn how to make a pastry cream at a cooking school. Whether you gain that information and understand that technique through working under someone for a while or going to a cooking program, this natural love of food and flavors is either with you or not with you. I also look for people who are willing to do anything for the customer, for the guest. No request, whether it comes from the chef, sous chef, or waiter, is considered too big."

> Personally, if I am going to hire someone at Charlie Trotter's, I look for energy, sincerity, someone who is really self-motivated, who is very excited just to be around food, who almost becomes emotional when they are working with certain foodstuffs, touching certain things, smelling certain things. As a pastry chef, you have to have that kind of mental, sensual, and emotional relationship with your food.
>
> —Charlie Trotter

Gray Kunz, former executive chef of Lespinasse in New York, has a similar focus when it comes to hiring for the pastry chef position. "As with any person who wants to come and work for me, I look first at the personality, the heart and soul of a person. I don't look only at their technical skills, but also at how they perform with and manage others. Can they work with the chef? Can they be part of the kitchen? Can they keep their food cost low? Those are factors I look into."

Dan Budd knows what executive chefs look for when hiring a pastry chef. "They want someone who is energetic, who's willing to learn, who's willing to go that extra distance to do what it takes to help the operation, and any schooling that can help to back that up. Then you are ready for anything."

When considering people for a starting position in pastry at the White House, Roland Mesnier envisions someone with devotion. "I'm not necessarily looking for someone who is already highly trained, but I *am* looking for someone who is still willing to learn, somebody who is flexible and who is truly dedicated to food. I'm talking about not only beautiful decoration but also flavor, taste—everything. Someone must have a passion for what they are doing, regardless of the level that person is at. Possibly, the lower the level, the easier it will be to shape that person. That's what I look for."

Unmolding a delicate flan onto a plate

Jacques Torres, with all he has achieved, still seems to approach his work with the vigor and exuberance of someone going to their first day on the job. "What I tried to do is pick a profession and go as far as I can. I feel like I am not done yet. This is my focus. You have to have objectives. Money is perhaps an objective, but it should not be the only one. When students ask for my advice, I tell them to take a piece of paper and draw me a five-year plan. At the top, put where you are today and at the bottom put what you want to be in five years. Now every year in between, break that down, and make your plan. Now that you have a plan, review that sheet of paper on the same date every year. Every year you can look at it and ask yourself, 'Did I reach the first level? Did I do everything I could to reach that first level?' If you didn't, you have to step back and do everything you can to reach that first level, but you have to do it. You have to follow your plan. That's important."

The question of when to make your move for your own career advancement and learning is a crucial one for a pastry chef. I think it must be thought out with maturity and clarity, and with direct focus on the ramifications of the potential move on your future.

Jim Graham treads carefully here. "I wouldn't presume to give any sort of deadline. It depends so much on the interpersonal relationships. That is a key. If you can find somebody more experienced in the trade that you can latch on to and really click with on a personal level, that's an invaluable resource. When should you move on? There comes this point of inertia that's deadly. You don't want to push it beyond that—when the excitement and the interest in trying new things is no longer there, and when you don't feel the impetus to do things differently, it's time to make a change."

> When you work in different kitchens, you need to choose places where you're going to learn the missing links in your chain of knowledge. You must have a plan for who you want to be and every time you make a move from one job to another, you go to a job that will give you a missing link.
> —Roland Mesnier

Gale Gand has another view. "I don't think it's good for someone to be in a kitchen where they don't want to be. So I'm not one of those people who says that if someone doesn't spend two years at every job they've had, then I'm not hiring them. I don't look at people's resumes that much. I've had people who've worked in great restaurants, but they can't concentrate."

Moving to new positions is part of the process but the main thing to remember is to build relationships in each new position. You can always learn from work experiences, even if the lesson is how not to do something. When you are able to look back, you will be thankful for the opportunities that have shaped you into a pastry chef inspired by a solid and educational work history.

CHAPTER four

NSIDE THE WORLD OF
THE PASTRY CHEF

Restaurants

The restaurant has emerged as an opportunity for pastry chefs in America only within the past twenty years. Many restaurants did not have a pastry chef and it was not seen as a priority for a free-standing restaurant to spend the money or the labor and expertise in this area. Often, the chef, responsible for all food of the restaurant, would oversee the production of desserts. Prior to the 1980s, only French restaurants had pastry chefs. For restaurants owned and operated by American-born and -trained chefs to compete effectively, especially at the fine dining level, it became more important to have some concentrated knowledge for this highly detailed, specialized work. From this need, the pastry chef emerged. Richard Leach, who started in the restaurant business as a line cook, notes the relationship between making savory "plates," entrées, and appetizers, and creating plated desserts. "Creating a plate of food is what I started with in the restaurant business when I was fifteen. It was lamb or other foods, but it was plates. It's how my theme developed. There's always a plate in front of me that's a small framework within which to do different small things. To me, people can see more and taste more of my work if they have a nice selection of plated desserts. It's more interesting and challenging than being a bakery person. I couldn't bake pies all day."

For Sherry Yard, being a restaurant pastry chef seems to be the best expression of her personality. "I am so accustomed to the à la minute (at the last minute). Wolfgang [Puck] said he never met a last-minute person worse than himself until he met me. When they're putting out the entrée for a wine dinner, I know what I'm going to do but there are many times that I say to him, 'What do you think I should do?' I love that last-minute rush! Sometimes, with people who are new to working with me, it drives them crazy, but that's when I thrive."

> I'm allowed to do things à la minute so I don't have to prep a lot of things ahead of time and freeze a lot of things. It gives me a lot of freedom.
> —Claudia Fleming

Claudia Fleming feels that the restaurant setting takes advantage of her strongest skills. "I'm allowed to do things à la minute so I don't have to prep a lot of things ahead of time and freeze a lot of things. It gives me a lot of freedom." Mary Bergin feels tied to the restaurant environment. "I think starting with Barbara [Lazaroff] and Wolfgang

[Puck] was great for me because it was like being part of a family. When Spago opened in 1982, it was very family oriented, and we have stayed close over the years. I am also not that interested in the business part of it. I am much more interested in working fifteen hours a day to create desserts. I have the best of everything to work with and a beautiful restaurant to work in. I would rather not worry that at the end of the year, I'm going to make x amount of dollars because of the revenue of the restaurant."

Jackie Riley likes the single purpose of the restaurant setting. "Restaurants are intriguing to me because the focus is just the food. It's not the banquets. It's not the confectionery work. The restaurant is there strictly for the food."

Emily Luchetti notes her attraction to the restaurant arena of baking and pastry. "I like the fact that people come in to us to have dessert and we have control over it. We serve it to them the way we want it to be served. In a bakery, people come in and take their cake or dessert home and at this point the pastry chef has no control. They may leave it on the counter for two days or put it back into the oven for too long. I also like the fact that it's all part of a whole dining experience."

Pastry kitchen at the Four Seasons

Bill Yosses discusses why he chose the restaurant path. "I find people who are devoted to fine cuisine in restaurants. In hotels, even if they value their food, even with support from a general manager, it isn't the same as the support you'd get from the owner of a restaurant, where his restaurant is his livelihood. I like the everyday life of a restaurant."

Michelle Gayer of Charlie Trotter's speaks of the restaurant pastry chef experience as requiring a wide use of her talents. "At this restaurant, I get to do everything. I get to make the bread, the desserts, the ice creams. I am part of a larger dining experience."

Rhubarb Napoleon
with Preserved Ginger,
Vanilla Mascarpone, and Rhubarb Sauce

by Charlie Trotter and Michelle Gayer

Charlie Trotter says that braised rhubarb has to be one of his favorite desserts. "Its flavor is clear and straightforward but sophisticated. We had a little fun with the presentation by layering the lightly cooked rhubarb with vanilla-flavored mascarpone and crispy phyllo pieces to create a wonderfully textured napoleon. Oven-dried rhubarb strips augment the rhubarb flavor and add a further textural element. Finally, the mint syrup provides a touch of sweetness to counterbalance the slightly tart rhubarb sauce."

Yield: 4 servings

For the mint syrup:
2 cups fresh mint leaves
1 cup sugar
½ cup water

For the rhubarb napoleon:
1½ cups granulated sugar
2 cups water
6 stalks rhubarb
6 sheets whole-wheat phyllo
3 tablespoons butter, melted
2 tablespoons confectioners' sugar
1 cup fresh rhubarb juice
½ cup fresh strawberry juice
½ cup heavy cream
2 tablespoons julienned ginger root
1 vanilla bean, split lengthwise, with pulp scraped out
and reserved
4 tablespoons mascarpone

For the preserved ginger:

½ cup julienned ginger root

½ cup sugar

1 cup water

To make the mint syrup:

1. Start two days before serving. Blanch the mint in boiling salted water, then shock in ice water. Strain, squeeze out excess water, and coarsely chop the mint.

2. In a small saucepan, combine the sugar and the water and simmer for 15 minutes or until the mixture reaches a thick, syrupy consistency. Remove from the heat and cool completely.

3. Place the mint and the sugar syrup in a blender and puree for 3 to 5 minutes or until smooth. Place in a container and store in the refrigerator overnight. Strain through a fine-mesh strainer, then refrigerate one more day before decanting.

To make the rhubarb napoleon:

1. Preheat the oven to 250°. Place 1 cup of the granulated sugar and the water in a medium saucepan. Simmer for 3 to 4 minutes or until the sugar is dissolved.

2. Cut 2 stalks of rhubarb in half. The remaining stalks will be used later. Using a vegetable peeler, peel long strips of rhubarb the length of the stalk. Add the rhubarb strips to the saucepan and simmer for 2 minutes or until they just begin to soften.

3. Remove the strips from the saucepan and reserve the cooking liquid. Lay the strips flat on a nonstick sheet pan, making sure they don't overlap. Bake for 20 to 30 minutes or until strips are lightly golden and appear dry to the touch. Watch them carefully, as they can burn very quickly.

4. Shortly after removing strips from the oven, loosen them from the pan. They should become crisp as they cool.

5. Increase oven temperature to 350°. Lay one sheet of phyllo flat on a work surface. Brush with melted butter and sprinkle lightly with granulated sugar. Lay another piece of phyllo on top and repeat with the melted butter and sugar. Top with one more piece of phyllo and set aside.

Continued on next page

6. Repeat this process to complete another set of 3 layers. Cut eight 2-inch squares from both sets of phyllo sheets for a total of 16 squares. Place a piece of parchment paper on the back of a sheet pan. Lay the phyllo squares on the parchment paper and cover with another piece of parchment and another sheet pan.

7. Bake for 10 to 12 minutes or until golden brown. Sprinkle the top of the phyllo squares with confectioners' sugar and, using a blowtorch, gently caramelize the sugar, watching closely so it doesn't burn.

8. Place the rhubarb and strawberry juices in a small saucepan with ¼ cup of the granulated sugar. Bring to a simmer and reduce for 20 to 30 minutes or until you have about ½ cup of juice. Strain through a fine-mesh sieve covered with three layers of cheesecloth.

9. Place the heavy cream and ginger in a small saucepan. Bring to a simmer, let sit for 15 minutes, then strain and cool.

10. Place the cool cream in a mixing bowl with the pulp from the vanilla bean. Using a whisk, whip until soft peaks begin to form. Add 2 tablespoons of the granulated sugar and continue to whip until firm. Add the mascarpone and whip until incorporated. Refrigerate until ready to use.

11. Cut the remaining 4 stalks of rhubarb into ½-inch-thick pieces on the bias. Place the cooking liquid from the rhubarb strips in a medium sauté pan and add the rhubarb. Bring to a simmer and cook for about 3 to 5 minutes or until the rhubarb is tender.

To make the preserved ginger:

1. Blanch the ginger in boiling water for 10 seconds; drain. Blanch in boiling water 2 more times. Bring the sugar and 1 cup of water to a boil, add the ginger, and simmer for 20 minutes. Refrigerate the syrup until ready for use.

Assembly:

1. Place a teaspoon of the mascarpone cream, 2 pieces of rhubarb, and a piece of preserved rhubarb in the center of each plate.

2. Place a phyllo square on top and layer with the mascarpone cream, rhubarb, and preserved ginger.

3. Continue until you have 4 layers of the napoleon. Top the final layer with some of the mascarpone cream and a piece of rhubarb.

4. Lay a piece of preserved ginger at the base of each side of the napoleon and, using this as your anchor, lay a strip of dried rhubarb against each side, pointing upright. Spoon some of the rhubarb sauce, mint syrup, and a dash of the preserved ginger syrup around the napoleon. Serve.

Bruno Feldeisen, who has worked in both restaurants and hotels, looks at the value of each. "I think that you need to experience both sides. It's two different working environments. You should start in a restaurant. It's rough and it's tough, but that gives you a good view of the business."

The restaurant pastry chef must work very closely with the executive chef, probably more intensely in this environment than pastry chefs in other arenas, in order to create a cohesive, seamless dining experience. Gray Kunz says, "I cannot emphasize enough that I do not need a dessert resembling the Chrysler Building on my plate, but I do emphasize extracting the best flavors and tastes out of the ingredients. There is no question in my mind that this is lacking in many, many desserts, and it's detrimental to the whole menu. If you have very strong flavors on a menu, it's a challenge to match those flavors, to see that dessert doesn't fall short."

> If you have very strong flavors on a menu, it's a challenge to match those flavors, to see that dessert doesn't fall short.
>
> —Gray Kunz

Charlie Trotter agrees. "What we do at Charlie Trotter's with our degustation menus (each guest has six, seven, or ten plates of food prepared for them) makes it even more important that desserts fit with the structure of the menu to give the right balance and build of flavors. We make sure we are not repeating ingredients. If we use hazelnuts in one savory preparation, then we do not use them in any other savory preparation or in dessert. If we use ginger in a savory preparation, we do not use it in dessert. We want to make sure that everything has a purpose. It is not just the stacking up of courses. Every course needs to make sense vis-à-vis the preceding and the following course. There has to be a strand, a piece of thread that you could weave from the little starter course all the way through to the very last chocolate or mignardise (petit-fours) that you take off the plate. The whole progression has to make sense."

Hotels

Working in a hotel is something I would advise all aspiring pastry chefs to do, no matter what their ultimate destination job or career might be. The reasons are many. The hotel pastry shop is a world of its own. Its chefs are often responsible for the production needs of many of the hotels outlets simultaneously. The hotel pastry shop, at different times of the day and night, may produce breakfast pastries, cakes, tarts and pies, petit fours, and chocolates, and prepare items for a fine dining restaurant's dessert menu. Hotels and their food and beverage operations all have varying standards of quality and respect for their food, just as restaurants or pastry shops do. Some hotels purchase premade food and pastry products, or have some other shortcut, to help alleviate the demands of the enormous volume, while other hotels make nearly everything themselves. Working in this environment, depending on the hotel, can expose you to a multitude of standard pastry techniques, volume production of such items as viennoiserie or breakfast pastry, and service applications such as buffet display, centerpiece work, and wedding cakes, as well as plated desserts for banquets and cuisine-specific restaurants within the hotel.

From the perspective of Chris Broberg, hotel experience can teach you about volume and different means of production. "Hotel food sometimes has to be pop-up food or food that can be ready in minutes. Hotel kitchens have larger staffs and a lot of management is needed, so more delegation is involved. The advantage of working in hotels is that they often have more equipment and you get to see a wide variety of production and technique." Jackie Riley recalls working in many hotels. "It was great for making me aware of the possibilities. Hotels have a lot of different areas. There's a large support team and you can do a lot of artistic showpieces—sugar, chocolate—and there's time for that."

Nick Malgieri notes the tremendous learning environment a hotel provides. "The first thing you have to realize is the bigger the establishment, the more there is to learn, because there are different departments within the pastry department. A hotel with room service, outside catering, breads, and breakfast pastry provides

> The bigger the establishment, the more there is to learn.... A hotel with room service, outside catering, breads, and breakfast pastry provides an opportunity to learn not only the system as a coherent whole but also to move around from one station to another.
> —Nick Malgieri

an opportunity to learn not only the system as a coherent whole but also to move around from one station to another. Working at a big hotel gives you the quantity baking and organizational skills that working in a smaller place doesn't. Working in a big hotel affects your organizational skills in a smaller place. That is part of your experience and backround that shouldn't be neglected. The quality may not be the same as what you might achieve in a smaller place, but the techniques and organization you learn are irreplaceable."

Bruno Feldeisen remarks, "Hotels are a beautiful world where you probably won't hear any screaming. Working in restaurants is like crossing the ocean in a very small boat, while working in hotels is like crossing the ocean in a cruise liner."

> Hotels are a beautiful world where you probably won't hear any screaming. Working in restaurants is like crossing the ocean in a very small boat, while working in hotels is like crossing the ocean in a cruise liner.
> —Bruno Feldeisen

Sebastien Canonne says flatly, "I wanted them all, bake shops, restaurants, and banquets. In a hotel, you have it all. You have everything you can imagine. I learned in pastry shops and restaurants, but I wanted to travel and working in hotels offers more opportunities to travel."

Pastry Shops

For a pastry chef, the pastry shop can be a leap of entrepreneurship and a challenging opportunity to create a wide array of pastries, cakes, tortes and tarts, chocolates, cookies, and many other products. François Payard opened Payard Pâtisserie and Bistro in New York City in partnership with Daniel Boulud of the restaurant Daniel, where François was the pastry chef. "This is my life and I always like challenges," says Payard. "When I left Daniel, it was an even bigger challenge to open my own shop."

Gale Gand, who has experience in a wide range of cooking, baking, and dessert making in fine hotels and restaurants, opened a pastry shop in partnership with her chef-husband, Rick Tramonto. Gale not only oversees production of breads, desserts, and other products for Brasserie T and Tru but also promotes their new cookbook, *American Brasserie,* sells her own line of root beer, runs mail order, retail, and wholesale operations, tends to profit and loss statements, and makes key financial decisions. She has become extremely successful by incorporating a wide range of skills into her daily routine. About her decision to open a bakery, Gand says, "I've been waking up for twelve years now and going to bakeries. Obviously, I don't do it every day, but when we're on vacation, I like to visit bakeries, get up at three in the morning and watch them bake bread. Last year, I decided to stop gathering information and do something with all this great experience I've had and all this knowledge I've gathered. I've gotten to work with some of the greatest bakers in the world. It seemed like I should do something with it, or share it, so that was part of why we conceived the Vanilla Bean Bakery. At Trio, I made five different breads each day. I was accustomed to making breads for my restaurant. Then, at Brasserie T, we didn't have the room to make bread and it felt very weird for me to buy bread from someone else. It was like having someone else nurse my baby for me. It just didn't make sense. So I really wanted someplace else where I could make bread for Brasserie T and other restaurants as well. It made sense."

A dessert of sorbets and raspberries ready to be served

Elizabeth Falkner opened her own pastry shop after working as a hotel pastry chef and fine dining restaurant pastry chef at Masa's and Rubicon. "It's not so much that I wanted to be famous, but I did want the pastry chef to get more credit. It's slowly happening these days. What I've experienced is that pastry chefs can be sort of tucked under the carpet by the executive chef. I strongly believe in the grand finale of a dining experience, but I still hardly ever see the pastry chef coming out to the table; it's always the chef. To an extent, the chef is in control of the whole thing, but not entirely. There are a lot of hard-working pastry chefs back in that kitchen. I'm just trying to define what I do even more. I've decided to do my own thing, just like a chef or sous chef would break out on their own."

For Judy Contino, breaking out on her own seemed a logical progression for her career. "To tell you the truth, I think it just happened. I had wonderful opportunities and great jobs, but after I was corporate pastry chef for Lettuce

Entertain You Enterprises, I wondered, 'Where will I go?' I didn't feel that a hotel would be right for me. Having the bakery just evolved. I worked very hard. People often asked me, 'When are you going to work for yourself?' But it didn't happen just because I wanted to be my own boss. It seemed like a place where I could take all of my eclectic ideas and bring them together."

S'more Brownies

by Elizabeth Falkner

Yield: 14–16 brownies,
10 x 14-inch pan

1 cup granulated sugar
1 cup brown sugar
1¼ cups butter
10 ounces bittersweet chocolate, chopped
5 eggs
1 cup plus 2 tablespoons flour
½ teaspoon salt
1¼ teaspoon baking powder
½ cup graham crackers, broken
1 cup mini marshmallows
3 ounces milk chocolate, chopped

1. Preheat oven to 325°. In a thick-bottomed saucepot, combine the sugars, butter, and bittersweet chocolate over medium heat. Stir until melted and smooth. Add eggs and whisk until smooth.

2. In a separate bowl, sift together the flour, salt, and baking powder. Whisk this dry mixture into the chocolate mixture.

3. Stir in the graham crackers, marshmallows, and milk chocolate pieces. Pour mixture into a greased pan.

4. Bake for 25 to 30 minutes, until the top begins to crack. Cool and cut.

Maury Rubin's City Bakery in Manhattan sets a standard for the new American bakery. Rubin is contagiously optimistic. "I see bakeries as a creative project in the same way that I saw my work in TV production and direction. I thought I could produce and direct a bakery. I think that this was waiting inside me to come out. I just have an affinity for bakeries. I absolutely never stopped producing and directing. I see it very much in those terms."

Rubin's core philosophy has remained true from the start. "One of my ambitions was to bring a Chez Panisse style of cooking to a bakery. When we started, no one in New York was doing that. We use only organic flour. Our eggs are from free-range chickens. We buy produce only from local farms when it is in season. We make strawberry tarts only when there are local strawberries. This is a radical approach for a bakery. It demands something from our customers. From my point of view, this is what we've always done and now it's starting to have an influence."

Influencing the greater culinary world is not impossible for pastry chefs who have their own shops, but the obligations involved, the required range of skills, and unanticipated challenges are enormous. Falkner realizes the responsibility of owning her own business. "The advantage is that it's my vision. It's been hard for me to realize that. I keep looking around like someone is going to tell me what to do, because I was trained for that. Having my own business is good because I get to make it up as I go, but it's hard because there aren't enough people doing what I'm doing. I wish more people would open up pastry shops so we could all talk and figure out what really works and what doesn't work. Display cases present a dramatically different challenge from the production of plated desserts. I look back at plated desserts and think, 'God, how simple.' Now once I put desserts together, I have to make them last in a display case."

> The advantage is that it's my vision. It's been hard for me to realize that. I keep looking around like someone is going to tell me what to do. . . .
> —Elizabeth Falkner

According to Contino, there are multiple activities in a pastry shop. "Around the holidays, business really picks up. We serve a soup and sandwich of the day. Today, at noon, people are coming in to pick up their special orders, and we have tables of customers and the kitchen needs help. Everything is happening at once. It's different than in my restaurant days, when there was preparation time, then sevice time. We don't have that in the pastry shop. We hit the floor running."

Catering

Yet another arena of employment for the pastry chef is catering. This is closely related to hotel pastry work in its range of service styles, from plated desserts to banquets. Depending on the event, catering may require any number of valuable skills, including a knowledge of breakfast pastry, whole desserts, petit fours, and chocolates, as well as expertise in wedding cakes and centerpiece work using sugar, chocolate, fruit, and ice carving. Assisting with desserts in a catering business may be a good way to get your foot in the door of the culinary and pastry arts, helping with a party or two on a part-time basis and learning the techniques, timing, and artistry of preparing for these events. Another possibility for the aspiring pastry chef is to work for a catering business owned by a pastry chef who provides desserts, pastries, and wedding cakes for smaller caterers as a subcontractor. These businesses provide a needed service by catering 'desserts only' to private parties.

Splitting vanilla beans with a paring knife

To try these ideas would require research for needs in specific markets, but it would be worth the effort if it allows you to use your specialized skills as a pastry chef. These markets could represent lucrative business opportunities for pastry chefs with self-determination and an attraction to creating their own enterprise.

Finding a Niche

Ultimately, you must go step by step to find your place in this business. The influences and impressions you gain from your work experiences and the inspiration you get from foods, colleagues, and your own attraction to pastry and dessert making can be defining guideposts for your career. Your own passions can fuel a career full of challenge, satisfaction, and success. Focus and concentration are the starting points. Dan Budd advises potential chefs and pastry chefs about their future. "I regularly talk to students about what they want to do. They know they love this work, but they have no idea about where they should start. My advice is, first of all, try to witness the specific areas and places that pastry chefs work. Get a cover letter and a resume done and send it out to these places and be forceful, because even if a place says, 'We don't have anything available now,' ask if you can just come in and see the operation or visit the kitchen. When I was working in the restaurant business, I always allowed that. I would say, 'If you would like to come by and meet me and see the place, I'd be happy to have you come by. I'm very busy, so it may only be ten or fifteen minutes.' Now I tell my students, when you get in there, talk to the chef, observe the operation, so you've already educated yourself and gotten something out of it. Then maybe you can ask if you can stick around and see how service works. I think if you get in there and see how the particular business works, whether it's a hotel, a restaurant, or a retail bakery, eventually you're going to say, 'This is what I'd like to do!' "

> Even if a place says, "We don't have anything available now," ask if you can just come in and see the operation or visit the kitchen.
>
> —Dan Budd

Typical Day of a Leading Pastry Chef

Pastry work is so varied that, typically, no two days are alike. The short-term daily goal, however, is to balance the work flow so that you and the pastry department accomplish goals and prep all the desserts and other items required for the restaurant, pastry shop, or hotel. In addition, pastry chefs must always know where they stand for the following day. Does a hastily booked party need special preparation? Is there enough puff pastry dough, ice cream base, and so on made to carry you through service the following day? The daily tasks of pastry chefs depend on the needs of the business they are involved with. For example, the pastry chef who works at a small restaurant has different hours and a more limited but faster-changing product range than a hotel pastry chef.

Jacques Torres recounts his typical workday. "Every day is different, but usually the first thing in the morning is inventory of the refrigerator and freezer. That's my first need—to see what we have left and to organize it. I want those two places, the refrigerator and the freezer, to be spotless every day. Then I make lists and go through the entire station. My assistants are at work and I find out if we have any problems or anything to review. Then I work on the special of the day, make a list for myself, and start my workday. During lunch service, I help if anyone needs help, keep production going through the afternoon, prepare for any banquets, and get ready for evening service—whatever is needed. The shortest day will be ten hours, the longest about fifteen hours, an average of twelve hours. Every day is like that, nonstop."

Claudia Fleming describes her day. "My schedule is not that strict. I get in at 7 A.M. I check the walk-ins, I check to see that what is coming in is what I ordered, and make sure that all my employees are here, of course, doing what they are supposed to be doing. Two days a week I do production until about 12:30 P.M. Then I put out desserts for lunch service. After that, I order produce and supplies for the next day. I might do some tasting and help everyone get ready for service, answer phone calls or letters. Some days I come in later and work evening service. In between all of this, I am always trying to think of new things to do. I am working on component parts of desserts. I may have ideas of flavors I want to bring together, so I'll prepare them. The next day, I'll put them all together. I rarely go into new desserts with preconceived ideas of exactly what I want them to be. It's more a theme and variation scenario."

Sherry Yard insists there is no typical day at Spago. "I go in at 7 A.M., 6 A.M., or 4 A.M.— not often, but I've had to. I guess a typical day at Spago is prescribed by what the customers want and desire. That could be someone calling and saying, 'We decided we would like to come for breakfast tomorrow morning.' Now, we don't do breakfast, but are we going to say no? No, because

Gingerbreads just out of the oven

we never say no. So I might be up at 4 A.M. that day. Then I might be at the end of my day, but so-and-so walks through the door. It might be Mr. and Mrs. White from Orange County who happen to stop by for dessert. Am I going home? No. I go out and say hi to the Whites and tell them I have some really great figs and they've got to try them and then go back into the kitchen and do my thing."

Pineapple Beignets

by Chris Broberg

Yield: 6 servings

1 whole pineapple

For the piña colada sauce:
4 egg yolks
¼ cup sugar
1 cup plus 2 tablespoons coconut milk
¾ cup pineapple juice
2 tablespoons dark rum

For the pineapple tarragon sorbet:
2 cups water
2 cups sugar
10 to 12 sprigs fresh tarragon
½ pineapple (from above)

For the pineapple chips:
1 vanilla bean
2 tablespoons canola oil
8 paper thin slices pineapple (from above)

For the pineapple jam:
Pineapple, rough chopped (from above)
½ cup granulated sugar
1 teaspoon fresh ginger, very finely chopped

For the beignets and assembly:
1 cup plus 2 tablespoons Duval beer
½ teaspoon dry active yeast
¾ cup all purpose flour

2 cups grapeseed or canola oil for frying
12 pineapple pieces, ¼ inch thick (from above)
granulated sugar for sprinkling

1. Peel and core the pineapple and cut in half crossways. Set aside one half for sorbet.

2. Cut four ¼-inch-thick slices, then cut each slice into 3 equal pieces. Reserve for beignets.

3. From the same pineapple half, on a slicing machine or with a good slicing knife, slice 8 very thin (⅟₁₆ inch thick) slices of pineapple and reserve for chips.

4. Chop remaining pineapple and reserve for jam.

For the piña colada sauce:

1. In a medium bowl, whisk together the egg yolks and the sugar.

2. In a saucepot, combine the coconut milk and the pineapple juice and bring to a boil over medium heat. Whisk the yolk and sugar mixture into the milk and juice. Stirring constantly, cook the mixture until it is thick enough to coat the back of a spoon. Do not boil.

3. Strain through a fine strainer, add the rum, and chill the mixture.

For the pineapple tarragon sorbet:

1. In a saucepot, combine the water and sugar and bring to a boil over medium heat. Remove from heat, add the tarragon, and let steep.

2. Juice the reserved pineapple half in a juicing machine or purée in a blender. Remove the tarragon from the water and sugar syrup. Combine equal parts of pineapple juice or purée and syrup.

3. Churn in an ice cream machine and reserve.

For the pineapple chips:

1. Preheat the oven to 200°. Scrape the seeds and pulp from the vanilla bean and stir with the canola oil in a small bowl.

2. On a parchment-lined baking tray or a nonstick pan, smear the vanilla oil to coat the entire surface, then lay the pineapple slices on the tray.

Continued on next page

3. Bake the pineapple slices for 45 minutes or until pineapple chips are dry and crisp.

For the pineapple jam:

1. Combine chopped pineapple, sugar, and ginger in a saucepot over medium heat.

2. Cook for 10 to 12 minutes, stirring periodically until mixture reduces and thickens. Remove from heat and reserve.

For the beignets and assembly:

1. In a medium bowl, combine the beer and the yeast, then whisk in the flour. Let sit for 5 minutes.

2. Meanwhile, in a saucepot, heat oil over a low heat to 340°.

3. Dip 6 pineapple pieces in the batter and carefully lower them into the oil. Turn them with a spoon and fry to a light brown color. Drain on paper towels and repeat with remaining pieces.

4. Sprinkle the beignets with granulated sugar and place them under a broiler, or use a blow torch in sweeping motions, to melt the sugar.

5. Spoon 2 tablespoons of the piña colada sauce onto the center of each plate and spread to a 5-inch circle.

6. Place a scoop of sorbet in the center of each circle.

7. Place three ½-teaspoon dollops of pineapple jam around each sorbet scoop and place 1 beignet between each dollop of jam (3 per plate).

8. On each plate, place a pineapple chip on top of the sorbet, add another scoop of sorbet, and top with a final pineapple chip.

Judy Contino describes her day. "I arrive a little bit later in the day, about 10 A.M., and usually work for ten to twelve hours. We do preparation at night. Last night, I got home at 4 A.M., so I almost met my morning baker coming in. During the holidays, I'm probably here, on average, until midnight. The night before, I leave a prep list and a delivery list. I leave the orders that have to go out and need to be boxed for my morning crew. I usually call by 8 A.M. to see if they have any questions. I talk to my front-of-the-house people and my back-of-the-house people to see if anything's been forgotten or anything has to be ordered. I can do that from home in the morning. When I arrive, I make sure that my crew is ready to serve lunch and that the display cases are full. I just check on everything. I answer the phones during lunch and serve lunch. It's nice for me to be able to spend a few minutes with some of my steady customers. Then I do whatever needs to be done in the kitchen so no one has to work a twelve-hour day. When the first shift finally does leave the kitchen, we have preparation to do. We build cakes and decorate cookies for the next day. We also make our own tart shells in the evening. I oversee all these jobs. A lot of evenings I have wedding cake appointments and tastings. People buying wedding cakes require a lot of attention. At 7 P.M., we close the shop. Everything is put away as neatly as possible and we fill a few orders and look at what we need for the next day."

Elizabeth Falkner finds no steady routine in her varied responsibilities. "We opened right before Thanksgiving and Christmas. We had a couple of weeks to recover before Valentine's Day, but when January came, everybody called me for wedding cake appointments. On a day-to-day basis, I come in and write up our savory menu, mostly sandwiches and pizzas. I see what I have in the walk-in to use, then I check on pastry production—kind of quality control. I check the case and say, 'This needs to be cleaned,' and 'I have to redo this.' So I go back and look at all the prep levels and then I usually start taking phone orders. I start baking, working on new items, or talking to my staff about ideas so we can come up with new items. Then I get bombarded with lunch. Sometimes I work the pizza oven. Then all of a sudden it's 3 P.M. I talk with my assistant manager, and get some office business done. My business partner might stop by and we may have to discuss some crisis or how much the architects want to charge for certain fixtures or 'Does the sign look good out there?' and how important that is to us because we're a new business."

The needs of a hotel pastry shop present many challenges. At the Four Seasons Hotel in New York, Bruno Feldeisen recalls what it took to start off his day right. "I liked to arrive early. If I came in at 9:30 or 10 A.M. I felt I might as well go back home because I didn't feel in control and things went too fast. I liked to come in between 7 and 8 A.M. This way I felt more in control because I could go over everything in my mind. The morning period was the most intense part of the day for us because most of the banquets that we did were in the afternoon. So our first goal was to get the food out on time with the quality required. We slowed down for lunch, but we did a small buffet that changed every day. Nighttime is a different story. We were a twenty-four-hour operation. I wouldn't leave until I felt comfortable and until I felt that my employees were okay. When I leave for the day, I have to feel that my staff is relaxed and happy. I stay until I'm not needed anymore."

> When I leave for the day,
> I have to feel that my
> staff is relaxed and happy.
> I stay until I'm not
> needed anymore.
>
> —Bruno Feldeisen

Caramel Fudge Brownies

by Janet Rikala

Yield: One 10 × 10 × 2-inch pan

1 cup butter
12 ounces bittersweet chocolate
4 eggs
2 cups sugar
1 teaspoon vanilla extract
1½ cup plus 2 tablespoons all-purpose flour
½ teaspoon salt
¾ cup semisweet chocolate chips

For the caramel:
⅓ cup corn syrup
½ cup plus 2 tablespoons sugar
2 tablespoons water
⅓ cup heavy cream
1 tablespoon butter

To make the brownie:

1. In a bowl set over a pot of hot water, melt the butter with the bittersweet chocolate. Remove the bowl and allow to cool for a few minutes.

2. In another bowl over the hot water, whip the eggs and sugar to soft peaks, about 10 minutes. Remove the bowl from the heat.

3. Fold in the chocolate mixture and stir in the flour and salt. Preheat oven to 350°.

To make the caramel:

1. In a saucepan over medium heat, combine the corn syrup, sugar, and water. Cook until the mixture caramelizes and turns a golden amber color.

2. Meanwhile, warm the cream and butter in another saucepan until the butter is melted.

3. Carefully and slowly stir the butter mixture into the caramel. Adding it too quickly will cause the caramel to bubble up. Cook over low heat for 5 minutes. Remove from heat and allow mixture to cool.

Assemble the brownies:

1. Pour half the brownie batter into a greased pan and bake for 10 minutes.

2. Remove the pan from the oven. Sprinkle the chocolate chips over the batter in the pan and pour ¾ cup of the caramel on top.

3. Spread the remaining brownie batter over the caramel. Return the pan to the oven and continue baking for 30 minutes. Remove pan from oven and let brownies cool.

Janet Rikala of Postrio in San Francisco comes in between 7 and 7:30 A.M "I always go through everything to see what sold. Then I go through the walk-in to see what product we have and what is coming in. I start baking and think of what I want to do for a lunch special. I'm usually inspired by the weather, a craving I'm having, or a product I have. In the afternoon, my pastry staff and I get everything ready for lunch and any lunch parties. Then, in the late afternoon, we prep for dinner, get menu changes together, and get ready for evening parties."

Mary Bergin walks us through her typical day at Spago, Las Vegas, where she also oversees dessert production at Chinois in Caesar's Palace. "A typical day starts at 7:30 or 8 a.m. I make sure production is coming along—ovens are on, and line cooks have their mise en place (prepared items). I write my production list for the day, what people have to do, then go over party sheets and check the books from the previous night. We keep log books where the night crew leaves notes about if we were really busy, or steady, any problems—anything like that. I check the mail and voice mail to see if people have called about cakes. Then we get set up and ready for lunch and any parties. I work until 10 or 11 p.m. seven days a week. I knew what I was getting myself into; what opening a new restaurant is like."

Michelle Gayer takes us into her pastry department at 8 A.M. as she prepares for another night of service at Charlie Trotter's in Chicago. "Start the ovens and bake the bread, which rose overnight. Activate the bread starter. Clean out the coolers so I know how much of everything I have. I start my prep list and bake the brûlées and other custards. I roll all the doughs before anyone gets here. When my assistant arrives, I go over everything with her and answer any questions she has. I activate the bread starter again at noon so I can make the bread doughs for the next day. I spin sorbets and ice creams in the ice cream machine from 11 A.M. to 1 P.M., then roll the bread into rolls, finish up dessert prep, help set up the dessert station with all prepared items and sauces, and then begin dinner service."

Chris Broberg's day at Lespinasse goes like this. "At 6 A.M., I check to see if there are any new parties booked from the night before. Then I check my list of every dessert and every individual component that goes with each that was checked off the night before. I do a production list for the day and start working on any mise en place for new desserts that aren't on the menu yet. Then I do my ordering list for the following day, work the dessert line for lunch, and finish off petit fours. In the afternoon, I do cakes or sugar work and check with the chef on how new items are selling. Then my assistant comes in and we finish up mise en place for the evening, have lunch, and set up for dinner service. I leave at 6 or 7 P.M., but some days I come in a little later and leave later, and that's six days a week during our busy season. It's definitely different than working in a hotel, where the pastry chef has a bigger staff, there's a lot more paperwork to do, and more time is spent making sure that things are in the computer. I also spend time on the phone throughout the day because here in New York City there are a lot of organic purveyors and small specialty food companies to deal with."

Gale Gand maintains no typical schedule, but this summary represents the range of her engagements and responsibilities. "There are days when I'm bakery- and restaurant-dedicated, but then there are days when I'm traveling and doing television. I get here by about 8:30 A.M.—not real early right now, because I'm a mother and I'm really enjoying my time with the baby. Probably the first half hour is spent on office business. An hour after I get here, I start baking. The staff may need me to work through regular mise en place or we may need to decorate cookies or make pie dough. I may need to work with a member of my staff who has never made scone dough. If everyone is all caught up, I have little specialty projects to do to enhance the bakery. So I'll work for four hours on whatever needs to be done. By this time, the world is knocking at my door too much. So I usually end up going over to the restaurant to help the pastry staff. Then I have to be a restaurateur for a while. I have to review the accounts payable and cash flow and remind the bookkeeper that she's supposed to get that midmonth profit and loss statement to me. I need to keep up with restaurant-related correspondence. Then I come back to the bakery for two to three hours. I might make a batch of my root beer, starting the infusion for it, which then has to be brought downtown for bottling."

Finishing a dessert with some powdered sugar

At City Bakery, Maury Rubin's commitments have evolved and changed over time. "For the first three years, I worked from 3:30 A.M. to 10 P.M. six days a week. Looking back, it will probably always be the accomplishment of my life, that I was physically capable of that. The energy for that came strictly from adrenaline. The pastry was phenomenal, so the business started to grow. It needed to be dealt with in a serious way. Then I started to evolve slightly out of the kitchen and more into the business. My hours changed to the point where I don't want to be in the kitchen that much, and I leave that work to my rock-solid staff."

At Park Avenue Café, Richard Leach is hard at work by 7:30 or 8 A.M. "First I see what's left from the night before and decide what quantities of items are needed for that day. I go through all my refrigerators and see if anyone has written me any notes, then I make a prep list for the day and start in on that. We have to reach certain goals by certain times of the day. As my crew gets here, I delegate jobs, have them set up for lunch, and check what they need for lunch. In the morning, I take the time to organize for the rest of the day. We hope to have the bulk of production done by lunch service. I have two people set up the dessert service area for lunch, then one breaks off and bakes all the phyllo, tuiles, cookies, and other things we need every day. That takes about four hours. After lunch is done, the service person from lunch makes all the sauces we need every day. I go in between them, helping with service and getting my own prep list done. By 5 P.M. we are all cleaned up with the mise en place ready to go. I have two kitchens, a production kitchen and a service kitchen. The production kitchen is scrubbed down and the service kitchen is reset for evening service. At 6:30 or 7 P.M., I start one of my service people at more production in the back for the next day. About half the week, I'm here until 6 or 7 P.M. The other half of the week, I stay until about 10 P.M., and I'm off on Sundays and Wednesdays."

> I have two people set up the dessert service area for lunch, then one breaks off and bakes all the phyllo, tuiles, cookies, and other things we need every day. That takes about four hours.
> —Richard Leach

Jim Graham approaches his days with the enduring patience and passion of a true craftsman. "The great thing about working with chocolate is that you have a tremendous amount of advance notice. There is very little time pressure. You can see everything from a mile away and you have plenty of time to prepare. So there are never surprises waiting for me when I come in in the morning. Typically we take advantage of the cool morning temperature and get the enrobing [coating] machine going. This involves tempering about twenty kilos of chocolate and loading the machine. The centers were made the previous day, when we made any final adjustments. That is a very demanding process.

Although the enrober is not a manual process, it takes a lot of fussing, a lot of skill, and a lot of knowledge of the chocolate to get the coating just right. Setting up the machine is a good two-hour process. After that, we enrobe the centers. A typical run takes another two hours to enrobe and decorate. Then we put the machine away and package the chocolates for storage. In the afternoon, we make ganache fillings and get them ready for enrobing. We work in a leapfrog fashion. We never start at point A and work all the way through to a finished product, because each step requires a certain waiting time afterwards. At any given time, we work on three or four different chocolates, leapfrogging the various stages of the operation. Most days we are finished by 6:30 P.M. That's the advantage of the chocolate business. We're not tied to the service hours of the restaurant. We can pretty much set our own time frame based on what we have to do that day. If we need to cut a day short for any reason, we can do that. If we need to extend a day, we can do that. We have a great deal of flexibility."

> We never start at point A and work all the way through to a finished product, because each step requires a certain waiting time afterwards. At any given time, we work on three or four different chocolates.
>
> —Jim Graham

The Hardest Part of the Job

Almost every pastry chef I've spoken with has described work situations that were practically intolerable. These experiences can be helpful in the larger scheme of things. They can help define what you want. Though areas of the job can be difficult, these situations give you a sense of your own standards and can serve to harden your resolve to better yourself, your surroundings, and your desserts. You must remember that you can learn something from every operation and every situation. Every day as a pastry chef, faced with the responsibility of being creative and maintaining high standards, is an opportunity to succeed.

Pastry chefs confront many obstacles, but challenges can be overcome. Given the wide variety of skills required of pastry chefs, it is natural that some aspects are easier to learn while others seem more difficult. François Payard speaks passionately on this subject in broad terms. "The hardest part is not the competitions or demonstrations. The hardest part is to be good every day because being good at what you do means being good at it every day."

Chris Broberg agrees. "The hardest thing is staying fresh every day when you're working as hard as you do in a restaurant that is taking everything out of you. You want to give your most every day and there's never a rest. There's always someone else coming in. There's always someone else you have to do something new for. You want to stay fresh to give them that 'pow' every night."

Bill Yosses is moved by continued challenge. "One of the hardest things is not being numbed by routine. I think that's a chef's greatest challenge. Luckily, that's one of the good things about the clientele being informed and demanding, because they are always asking for something new. That should be taken as a challenge and not a chore. It's a way of keeping yourself fresh and alive. When you have ten things going on and the chef comes up to you asking for something new, don't be afraid to stop and say, 'What can I do that's different?' Keeping ideas fresh is one of the hardest parts of the job."

Jacques Torres echoes this sentiment as well. "The hardest thing is to have everyone on your staff achieve high quality every day. As a pastry chef, you have to demand hard work and dedication all day long. It's not difficult to do a beautiful cake. It's not difficult to have one spark. Every chef can have a spark. To hold that position for a long time, to do quality work for years—that's a big commitment."

Champagne Strawberry Gratin, Pistachio Ice Cream, and Banana Crisp

by Jacquy Pfieffer

Yield: 8 servings

For the gratin base:
4 teaspoons unflavored powdered gelatin (or 4 gelatin sheets)
½ cup cream
½ cup lemon juice
½ cup sugar
10 egg yolks
⅓ cup water

¾ sugar

6 egg whites

**For the champagne-marinated
strawberries:**

2 pints ripe strawberries, washed

¼ cup sugar

¾ cup champagne

For the banana crisp:

4 ripe bananas

1 lemon, juiced

¼ cup sugar

For the pistachio ice cream:

2¾ cups milk

½ cup nonfat dry milk

2½ tablespoons butter

¾ cup sugar

4 egg yolks

¼ cup corn syrup

1 cup pistachios, roasted

1 teaspoon kirsch

Roasted pistachios, crushed mint sprigs

To make the gratin base:

1. Soak the gelatin sheets in cold water, or sprinkle the powdered gelatin over 1 tablespoon cold water.

2. Combine the cream and lemon juice in a saucepot over medium heat and bring to boil. Remove from the heat.

3. In a separate bowl, whisk the sugar into the egg yolks. Temper the hot cream mixture into the egg yolks. Return the mixture to the saucepot and cook over low heat, stirring until mixture thickens to coat the back of a spoon.

Continued on next page

4. Squeeze the excess water from the gelatin sheets and whisk into the hot lemon mixture.

5. Combine the water and sugar in a saucepot over medium heat and cook for about 8 minutes or to soft-ball stage.

6. In a separate bowl, whip the whites to soft peaks, then drizzle the hot sugar syrup over them and continue whipping to stiff peaks.

7. Fold the meringue into the cream. Divide the mixture among six 3½- to 4-inch diameter ring molds, place on a sheet pan and freeze.

To make the champagne-marinated strawberries:
Cut the strawberries into quarters. Mix in the sugar and champagne. Cover and refrigerate.

To make the banana crisp:
1. Preheat the oven to 250°. In a blender, purée the bananas with the lemon juice and sugar. With a spatula, spread the mixture very thin on a silpat or nonstick sheet pan.

2. Bake in the oven for 40 to 45 minutes or until completely dried. Cut the banana crisp while still warm into triangles or other desired shapes. Reserve the crisps in an airtight container until assembly.

To make the pistachio ice cream:
1. In a saucepot, combine the milk, dry milk, and butter over medium heat. Bring to a boil, then remove from the heat.

2. In a separate bowl, whisk the sugar into the egg yolks, then temper some of the hot cream mixture into the yolk mixture. Return the mixture to the saucepot and set aside.

3. In a food processor, pulverize the pistachios. Add the corn syrup and process until a paste forms.

4. Add the paste to the saucepot mixture and turn the heat to low. Cook the mixture, stirring, for 10 to 12 minutes or until the mixture is thick enough to coat the back of a spoon. Do not allow to boil. Remove from the heat and transfer to a container. Cool the ice cream base in the refrigerator.

5. Freeze in an ice cream machine and store in the freezer.

To assemble:

1. Preheat the oven to 350°. Drain the strawberries and place them in soup bowls. Run a knife around the inside of each ring mold to remove the frozen gratin. Place each round frozen lemon gratin mixture on top and place in the oven for 3 minutes.

2. Using a blowtorch or under a salamander, glaze the top to a rich golden-brown color.

3. Top each dessert with a quenelle of the ice cream and garnish with a sprinkle of crushed roasted pistachios, a mint sprig, and a banana crisp. Serve immediately.

"Maintaining my knees is the hardest part. That's the truth," says Maury Rubin. "Otherwise it is based right now on maintaining the quality and consistency of a young business that has a great reputation. It's about keeping the growth going, thinking about the future, thinking about new ideas, but at the same time keeping a close eye on every bit of food we make and making sure the quality is where it should be."

Emily Luchetti thinks the hardest part is balancing it all. "It's the most challenging thing, but it's also the most rewarding. When you've been in the business for so long, you can't do production all the time. You have other demands on you to create a menu, write books, write articles, so the balancing act becomes vital. How do you instill your vision for the people that work for you and keep your hands in it and keep control when you can't always be there? I get to the point where some days all I want to do is bake and be left alone with the flour and sugar. Other days, that's just not challenging enough. I know I can do production faster than everyone else and, after a while, I want a bigger challenge. Pastry is a very hands-on business and quality has to be reinforced every time

Scooping a quenelle
of ice cream

something goes in or out of the oven. So how do you maintain that, when you're not in the kitchen side by side with the staff all the time? It's really tough."

Nancy Silverton feels the pull to be at the ovens. "For me, the hardest part of the business is not being able to do what I started—the baking, creating, producing. It's the managerial part of it that's rough on me, being responsible for so many people. I long for the days when I worked for someone else. So I set up activities that bring back that spark. That might be doing an article where I'm forced to come up with recipes, which is really fun for me. That's also why I travel and do benefits, because I get to cook. I get to go into the kitchen and make something again."

Lindsey Shere explains her greatest challenges. "It's different things at different times. Sometimes it's just standing on my feet for twelve or fifteen hours. Sometimes it's inspiration, when I'm trying to come up with ideas for the menu and they just don't come. For the most part, I've found being a pastry chef very rewarding. I always feel lucky to be doing something I truly enjoy doing."

Buttermilk Panna Cotta with Lemon Jelly

by Claudia Fleming

Yield: 6 servings

For the buttermilk panna cotta:

2 cups buttermilk

1½ teaspoons unflavored powdered gelatin

⅔ cup heavy cream

¾ cup sugar

For the lemon jelly:

½ cup lemon juice

1¼ teaspoons unflavored powdered gelatin

¼ cup sugar

1 cup water

To make the panna cotta:

1. Pour 1 cup of the buttermilk into a metal bowl.

2. Sprinkle the gelatin over the buttermilk. Let it stand to soften, about 5 minutes.

3. Meanwhile, in a small saucepan, bring the cream and sugar to a boil. Add cream mixture to the gelatin mixture and place the metal bowl over simmering water, whisking until the gelatin dissolves, about 5 minutes.

4. Stir in the remaining cup of buttermilk and pass the mixture through a cheesecloth-lined strainer.

5. Divide the mixture among six 4-ounce ramekins. Cover and refrigerate until set, about 4 hours.

To make the lemon jelly:

1. Place ¼ cup lemon juice in a mixing bowl. Sprinkle the gelatin over the juice and let stand to soften, about 5 minutes.

2. In a small pan, bring the sugar and water to a boil over high heat.

3. Pour the syrup over the gelatin mixture. Whisk to dissolve.

4. Add the remaining ¼ cup lemon juice and allow the mixture to return to room temperature.

To assemble:

Once the panna cotta has set, pour a thin layer, about ¼-inch deep, of the room-temperature lemon jelly on top of each ramekin and refrigerate until set, about 30 minutes. The panna cotta ramekins can be prepared up to 24 hours in advance, covered, and refrigerated. Serve chilled and garnished with crispy tuile cookies.

At Charlie Trotter's, Michelle Gayer is the leading force of the dessert experience for guests. Her biggest obstacle is managing people. "I can cook. I can bake. I can do my job. But making sure that everyone else can do their job and do it right and in a timely fashion, using the right product, is the hardest part of my job."

Claudia Fleming agrees. "Being a manager is the hardest part. I started making desserts because I love to make desserts, not because I wanted to manage people. Because I work in such a large restaurant, I'm forced to manage people. Sometimes, in wanting to get my job done, I get frustrated enough that I begin to insult my staff. I realize I need to be inspiring instead."

According to Nick Malgieri, the hardest thing to master is whatever doesn't come naturally to you. "For me, the thing that was the hardest was developing the management and people skills to organize the baking and make desserts. Those are two completely different pursuits. The first time I had a big supervisory job was the hardest for me. I had to develop management techniques that were as effective as my dessert-making techniques."

Mary Bergin says her daily challenge is tasting everything. "I learned a long time ago from Wolfgang Puck that you have to taste everything. If your name is on the menu, you'd better taste it all. Sometimes you just don't feel like it. I had been making vanilla ice cream with the same recipe for seven years, and then one day I decided I wasn't going to taste it. I was standing there in the kitchen taking the ice cream out of the machine and Wolfgang was walking by. He took a scoop like he always does—his fingers are always in everything. He took a bite, then spit it out and said, "Where's the sugar?" I had forgotten to put the sugar in that batch. So from that point on, I taste everything."

> I had been making vanilla ice cream with the same recipe for seven years, and then one day I decided I wasn't going to taste it. Wolfgang. . . took a bite, then spit it out and said, "Where's the sugar?"
>
> —Mary Bergin

For Elizabeth Falkner, priorities changed as she grew into the demands of being self-employed. "Right now, it's the paperwork that's the biggest challenge. It's not so much managing the kitchen but managing everything from the business to the front, maintaining all these areas, trying to delegate without having a huge staff, and making sure people make espressos right. That's probably the hardest thing."

Like Falkner, Judy Contino has a strong backround as a restaurant pastry chef. She says the morning is the toughest. "A shop is different than a restaurant. In a restaurant, there is a preparation time and a serving time. In a pastry shop, we come in and everything has to go out right away. My hardest part of the day is the morning. Everything that could possibly be used from the previous day must be minutely looked over to make sure it is okay. Then we have orders going out by 7 A.M. We have a huge repertoire of products for a shop, so it's a huge rush in the morning."

Jackie Riley feels the most difficult thing is maintaining the enthusiasm of her staff for the important work they accomplish. "The hardest part is keeping everyone excited about what they are doing. Even though they are making this recipe for the fiftieth time, it still needs to be made. I have to keep everyone enthusiastic, consistently inspired, positive, and interested in what they are doing."

Dan Budd finds life balance to be the most difficult thing to create in the pastry profession. "I think the hardest part is the amount of time and energy we put into it. It's definitely hard on family and friends. I had a big struggle with that for a long time. I know that I worked at least six years, six days a week, with very limited time off. I'd do the laundry, barely get a good meal, and I was back into the week again. I ask my students in my classes, 'How many of you sat down every day to eat a meal in your regular workday?' The answer? One in eighteen of our students works in a restaurant where he or she can sit and eat a meal. I think

> If you work really hard, then you should play hard and do things that you enjoy outside of work. What does that do? It brings longevity to your career. It inspires more creativity.
>
> —Dan Budd

it's a tragedy that we work so hard to bring out the best in food, but we don't even sit down just to achieve basic nutrition, much less to enjoy food. That was the toughest thing for me and I'm trying to make a change now. I think we sacrifice something great in our professional lives and our personal lives if we don't change this. We tend to beat ourselves into the ground by working, working, working. We have to treat ourselves with respect. If you work really hard, then you should play hard and do things that you enjoy outside of work. What does that do? It brings longevity to your career. It inspires more creativity. It makes you a more positive, respectable human being."

Jim Graham relates his most difficult challenge. "Coming up with something that's really fresh is hard for me. I am a craftsman and I enjoy the work process itself. I enjoy the actions and motions of my work. Creation is a painful process for me. I can do it and I like my results, but it's painful and it hasn't become easier over the years." Tasting constantly and putting some time aside each day for creative recipe development can help to push you on to new creative heights. This way you can integrate the creative process into a production day and try new things.

Hiring, Training, and Maintaining Staff

The people who constitute a stable, productive pastry department are the living, breathing, and growing lifeblood of the pastry chef's world. How they are chosen, taught, and fostered is vital to success. The pastry crew can reflect the best skills and qualities of a good pastry chef, while poorly trained, badly managed employees may only get by with what is necessary for the day.

Bill Yosses comments, "I would say the first rule is to hire enthusiastic cooks and try to keep them that way, which is a great challenge. It's hard work and long hours, but I think it's the job of the chef or pastry chef to set the spirit and the tone. You have to work every day to create a team."

Adding the finishing touches

Sherry Yard tries several approaches to maintaining a close relationship with her staff. "I have to make them understand how important they are to the big picture, but it's hard to keep them happy and make them feel appreciated. For me, it's watch, supervise, and teach. One thing I've always done is give recent hires a binder. Each time they make a recipe, then they get that recipe to add to their binder. Three of my staff of eight have been with me for four years and they have full binders because we change the menu constantly. We have done all sorts of new things and built on them. I also give my staff written tests. It takes away the informality of just saying, 'How are you doing?' This way, I'm really going to see how they're doing because it will be right there in black and white. It's a little more clinical, but then I can always go around that and say, 'You're doing a great job today! Thanks so much.' The test really does seem to do something. They see that I care that they're on their toes. They are happy to be learning something new. They don't feel stagnant, even if they are in a plating or entry-level position. I always ask myself how to keep someone's attention when they've been here for six months plating. Sure, desserts change, but they're still just putting them on the plate, so I try to move them around to different stations. Then you also have to get upset now and then and say, 'Come on, we have to get in that walk-in! Did you bring your eggs out so they're at room temperature? Come on, we have to move! What are you thinking about?' "

Roland Mesnier believes the attitude the pastry chef demonstrates sets the example. "The number-one thing is that you care—you care for your employees, you care for the job. You didn't come here to be the big shot and make tons of money. You came here because this is a great place and you're going to make it work, and we're going to make it work together. I think this is the key to success." Ann Amernick, having recently hired someone for her pastry team, says, "I looked at her hands and I knew that she was going to work very hard. She wants to learn and that is the most important thing for me. Whether she can hold a knife or not, I don't know and, frankly, I don't care. I brought her in because I was told she was a quick study—and she is. She is very quiet and that's what I wanted. I don't want somebody who talks about all the things they have done and all the places they have worked. I won't hire them. I don't need those credentials. I want someone who wants to learn; then I'll show them whatever they want to know."

> This business is not a collaborative effort so much as it is employees latching on to my vision, executing it, and seeing it through. I don't pretend in any way that this is a collaboration. This is one person's vision and then a lot of other people's extremely dedicated, hard work.
>
> —Maury Rubin

Maury Rubin's approach is to find good people who are capable of hard work. "I prefer to hire people who know nothing. My staff has been with me for five or six years. I taught them everything. I trust them. I see them as the engine of City Bakery and myself as the driver. The only time I'm in the kitchen now is for quality control, if I'm not happy with something, or if I'm working on new products." Maury doesn't mince words when it comes to leadership, which he contrasts with his days in television. "The nature of television broadcasting requires collaboration. This business is not a collaborative effort so much as it is employees latching on to my vision, executing it, and seeing it through. I don't pretend in any way that this is a collaboration. This is one person's vision and then a lot of other people's extremely dedicated, hard work."

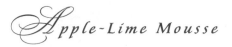

Apple-Lime Mousse

by Ann Amernick

"Many years ago, I came across a recipe using canned applesauce and lime Jello"
says Ann Amernick. "The result was an interesting meld of flavors. I decided
to create a recipe that would replicate the dessert but use fresh ingredients.
Here is my version of this simple, light, and tart dessert."

Yield: 8 servings

To start the mousse:
¼ cup cold water
2½ teaspoons unflavored powdered gelatin
8 McIntosh apples
¼ cup apricot jam
Zest of 2 limes
¾ cup lime juice (about 5 large limes)
2 cups crème anglaise (from below)

For the crème anglaise:
1 vanilla bean (split and scraped) or 1½ teaspoons vanilla extract
1½ cups milk
¼ cup sugar
6 egg yolks

To finish the mousse:
½ cup sugar
2 cups heavy cream
½ cup Beaumes-de-Venise (or other white dessert wine)

To start the mousse:

1. Pour the water into a small metal bowl and add the gelatin to soften it. Set aside.

2. Peel, core, and chop the apples into 1-inch chunks and place them in a heavy 3-quart saucepot. Cover and cook over low heat about 10 minutes, stirring often.

3. When the apples have softened and can be broken with a spoon, add the apricot jam. Raise the heat to medium high and cook, uncovered, stirring frequently, for about 5 minutes, or until the apples have lost a lot of moisture and form a mound on a spoon. Remove from the heat to cool slightly.

4. Purée the apple reduction in a food processor until smooth. Measure out 4 cups of purée and set aside any remaining purée for the sauce.

For the crème anglaise:

1. Combine the vanilla bean pod and scrapings with the milk in a saucepot over medium heat; bring to a simmer.

2. In a bowl, whisk together the sugar and egg yolks.

3. Temper one-half of the hot milk into the egg yolk mixture, then return entire mixture to the saucepot.

4. Reduce heat to low and stir the mixture until it thickens enough to coat the back of a spoon; do not boil.

To finish the mousse:

1. Place the bowl of gelatin over a larger bowl of very warm water to completely dissolve it, then stir the gelatin, zest, lime juice, crème anglaise, and sugar into the apple purée.

2. Transfer the mixture to a bowl and chill by placing the bowl in a larger bowl, half filled with ice water. Stir the mixture as it cools.

3. Whip the cream to soft peaks and fold it into the cooled mixture until well mixed and no streaks or lumps of cream remain.

4. Spoon the mixture into individual dessert or soufflé cups or mold in ring molds lined with acetate. Chill for several hours or overnight.

For the sauce:

Whisk together the remaining apple reduction with the Beaumes-de-Venise and any sugar needed to taste.

To serve:

Unmold the mousse onto plates and drizzle with the sauce. If serving in soufflé cups, simply drizzle the sauce onto the top of each before serving.

Nick Malgieri points to the first time he had to assess a potential employee's attitude and motives. "The best trait that people can show in an interview is a little nervousness, which means they really want to make a good impression. A little bit of fear is a good motivator. Sometimes when someone is slapping me on the back with a brag or their personal scrapbook as thick as a phone book, I don't care. I feel like saying, 'You are here to do what I want, not all those things you have already done.' I look for the more docile personalities rather than the enormous ones."

Chris Broberg's approach to hiring is to observe the subtleties of work habits

Glazing chocolate mousse

that potential pastry cooks demonstrate in a trial setting. "Their general attitude, when I talk to them, is important. It's good to have them come in. I can then see how dedicated they are and if they are more interested in the work. I like to find out how motivated they are. I think that in the beginning, people have to show that they do a job well over and over again, without complaining, and that they try to do it better every time. If there's a problem with it, they ask you, 'Is this turning out right?' and 'What could I do to change it?' Holding on to people for the long term is difficult. Successful people move on after they have learned all they can from you. Some learn quickly and you want to see them succeed. You might push them toward it and give them extra attention because you know they can do it.

Bruno Feldeisen maintains a responsibility-based management style with his staff. "I hold them each responsible for their own work. I give them the big picture and don't tell them every morning what to do. I try to empower them with decision making. I want them to figure things out for themselves without me there all the time. It's not always right, but sometimes it's okay to be wrong because it's part of learning. You make a mistake, then find a solution. I give them lots of freedom but responsibility at the same time. Some people don't like this. I've had pastry cooks quit because they need a prep list every morning. I guess they need more structure in their daily routine, but I still think that's the way to do it—force people to make decisions because maybe some day they will be a pastry chef and this will prepare them."

When it comes to hiring, Feldeisen focuses on the person rather than the resume. "I tell them to come to me and we'll sit down and talk. I think that personal connection is very important. The resume comes into it in part, but the personal connection is the most important."

François Payard takes the same approach. "I never look at resumes. I look at the person. I like people who work fast. I like people who understand that working in a tough kitchen is for their own good."

> I never look at resumés. I look at the person. I like people who work fast. I like people who understand that working in a tough kitchen is for their own good.
>
> —François Payard

Emily Luchetti tries to consider the diverse needs of each individual on her staff. "The longer you're in this business, the more you realize it's the management part that's really tricky. You want to instill values, you want to instill your system, you want people to learn and do what you want, but at the same time you have to realize that there are different types of people out there. Everyone has his or her own personality and opinions. So how do you teach them your way? How do you get them to do it your way without robbing them of their own creativity and desire to learn? If you squelch it too much, then you're only hurting yourself because they have things to add. It's important to have a balance between managing, creating, and leading. You need to be a really good leader to instill vision and direction, but at the same time you need to have a consensus. Where do you draw the line?"

Nancy Silverton makes specific efforts with her staff as she anticipates their needs for growth. "Even though I do a tremendous amount of management between the bakery, the retail shop, the kitchen, and my own products, I try to continually inspire, encourage, and make suggestions to help those I work with. I try to make available to them the inspirations that I have or the ingredients that I have just tasted. I'll bring them

> It's important to have a balance between managing, creating, and leading. You need to be a really good leader to instill vision and direction, but at the same time you need to have a consensus. Where do you draw the line?
>
> —Emily Luchetti

back a whole new energy with 'Look what I just got at the farmer's market today.' I try to be sensitive to their needs. I try to read them. I try to be appreciative and that's really hard, because sometimes I just forget to thank people. I try to create a comfortable workplace so they have what they need. When people show promise, I try to find places for them in the pastry department so they can continue to learn."

Pistachio-Rosewater Ice Cream Sandwich on Espresso Pizzelle with Chocolate Sauce

by Wayne Brachman

Yield: 8 servings

For the pizzelle:

2 large egg whites

¾ cup confectioners' sugar, sifted

⅛ teaspoon salt

1 tablespoon coffee extract

½ cup all-purpose flour, sifted

¼ cup butter, melted and cooled

For the pistachio-rosewater ice cream:

1½ cups milk

1½ cups heavy cream

¾ cup granulated sugar

8 large egg yolks

1 teaspoon vanilla extract

¼ teaspoon almond extract

1 tablespoon rosewater

1 cup pistachios, roasted, coarsely chopped

4 ounces semisweet chocolate, melted

For the chocolate sauce:

1½ cups heavy cream

4 ounces bittersweet chocolate, melted

To make the pizzelle:

1. Preheat the pizzelle iron and brush the cooking surface well with vegetable oil.

2. In a mixing bowl, whip the egg whites to stiff peaks. Gently fold in the confectioners' sugar, salt, and coffee extract. Fold in the flour until combined. Gently fold in the butter.

3. Place one heaping tablespoon of the mixture onto each pizzelle grid. Close the lid and bake until lightly browned and set, or about 1 minute. Remove from the iron and let cool. Make 16 pizzelle.

To make the pistachio-rosewater ice cream:

1. In a saucepot, combine the milk, heavy cream, and 1 tablespoon granulated sugar over medium heat. Bring to a boil. Remove from heat.

2. In a large mixing bowl, whisk the remaining sugar into the yolks.

3. Temper the hot cream mixture into the yolks. Return the mixture to the saucepot and cook until the mixture thickens slightly, enough to coat the back of a spoon.

4. Strain the custard through a fine-mesh strainer into a container that is nestled in an ice bath. Whisk in the extracts and rosewater and let cool.

5. Spin in an ice cream machine and fold in the pistachios. Drizzle in the chocolate into the ice cream through the holes of a slotted spoon while folding with a rubber spatula. Place in the freezer.

To make the chocolate sauce:

1. In a saucepot, heat the cream to a boil. Place the chocolate in a bowl and pour the cream over the chocolate. Let sit for 5 minutes.

2. Gently whisk until smooth.

To assemble:

1. Scoop or spread ¾ to 1 cup of the ice cream onto 8 pizzelle and top each with the remaining cookies to form 8 sandwiches.

2. Place each ice cream sandwich on a plate and drizzle chocolate sauce on top of and around each sandwich. Serve immediately.

Lindsey Shere has a mindful approach with new employees. "I think that you should hire very carefully. You need to have a good sense of what they are interested in. You also need to know what you need from them and be able to communicate that to them, what you expect from them and what they need to do to work in your restaurant. Try to be sensitive as time goes on. It was hard for people in pastry at Chez Panisse because they were thrown into a situation that was completely different from what they were used to or expected from other restaurants. They couldn't come and make desserts for a standardized menu and that was it. They had to be able to think about tomorrow and today knowing that they weren't sure what they had to work with at the beginning of the day and that they would have to respond to whatever they got from the market that day. Sometimes it was hard for people to deal with the work load. It usually took new people at least a year to really feel comfortable about the situation."

Dessert service action at Coyote Café

Nick Malgieri sums up what it takes to successfully manage a pastry crew. "You can't just let them loose; you have to monitor what is going on. Training is the time when communication has to be very, very accurate. A good chef has a lot of parental qualities in the sense that the personnel should feel that the chef is benevolent and not out to get them, but employees also need to follow direct orders. It's a hard balance to maintain."

Success as a manager and leader of a crew ultimately depends on your own confidence and ability to demonstrate by example. The pastry chef sets the tone and mood of the work day and must balance the needs of employees with the pressures of production. Communication is key to creating a benchmark of quality which the pastry crew must meet every day with every perfect ice cream, shortbread, or tuile cookie they produce.

The Importance of Knowing
the Customer

The source of success in the food business boils down to the customer. Do you know your customer? What do you know about them? Why do you show up for work every day? Why be in tune with the seasons? Why try so hard to make great desserts? It's all about the customer.

What it comes down to is that the most successful pastry chefs are humble and giving. A pastry chef genuinely and unpretentiously cares for the desires and sometimes simple tastes of his or her customers.

Nancy Silverton comments on customer perception. "I try to make food that tastes good. It's easier to make food to ooh and aah over visually because that's the first sense. Customers see the dessert and say, 'Oh, that's so gorgeous,' and then they go on talking and don't even taste what they are eating. The visual is what's remembered. When a pastry chef makes something that's simple, there's nothing to hide behind. That's why so few pastry chefs are known for that, because it's so much more challenging to make things simple."

Bill Yosses feels that knowing the customer is a two-way street. "It's important for them to communicate with you, and it's important for you to have some feeling for them so you're not just producing on an assembly line. Just think of how much more fun it is when you know that this plate you're working on is going to a friend, a family member, or a guest you know and like. You put a lot more heart and soul into it."

> Just think of how much more fun it is when you know that this plate you're working on is going to a friend, a family member, or a guest you know and like. You put a lot more heart and soul into it.
> —Bill Yosses

Mary Bergin looks at the importance of knowing the customer. "You need to know what people like and what they don't like. When they walk into a restaurant, customers want you to know who they are—whether they're famous or not. Guests want to feel welcome. They want to feel invited."

Judy Contino insists on knowing her customers. "We are in a small neighborhood, so that makes it even more important. We have people who come in here every day for soup and a sandwich. They are all supportive, but they can also be demanding because they are steady customers and they expect special treatment."

Jacques Torres is passionate on this topic. "I love to know customers and I love to have customers know me. I love to have a relationship with them. I love to know what they like; it helps me so much to please them. I mean, some people are going to like a fruit dessert, some people are going to like caramel, and some are going to like chocolate. It's very important to know them."

When I asked Jim Graham about the importance of knowing the whims and tastes of his customers, he replied by looking within himself in a measured, philosophical way. "You must be in tune with what you're doing. Certainly, I have my personal tastes, and I know that my tastes are not eccentric but that I'm very hard to please. I've always figured that if I'm working to the best of my ability and I'm pleased with my result, then enough people will be out there whose tastes align, more or less, with mine. I try to be true to my customers by being true to myself. It's not that it is not important for me to please people, but I feel that our customers have granted us a certain fidelity or trust. I owe them the best I can do. I gauge that by how it pleases me."

> You need to know what people like and what they don't like. When they walk into a restaurant, customers want you to know who they are—whether they're famous or not. Guests want to feel welcome. They want to feel invited.
>
> —Mary Bergin

One pastry chef with an enormous responsibility for customer satisfaction (it could be a national security issue) is White House pastry chef Roland Mesnier, who must take a behind-the-scenes approach to the desserts he creates for heads of state. "I have to remember, from the guests' point of view, this is not me doing this. It's the President and the First Lady. I'm there to serve them. I'm not the one who's supposed to shine. I'm just the man who's doing the job, but the desserts I make are a reflection on the President and the First Lady. I usually start with the embassy of a country or contact its cultural center and have them send me whatever literature they have about the president or prime minister that's coming in. I look at the people of the country, the landscape, the flavors, the customs. We also have to be very careful about what we do because of religion and beliefs. We don't want to insult anyone, so we have to be careful in what we make. We recently did an Italian dinner and I found out that the Prime Minister of Italy came from

Bologna and the main landmark there is a tower that was built in the twelfth century. So we reproduced in pastry the Tower of Bologna and the prime minister of Italy was touched by that. By doing things like that, the guest of honor is truly honored by having something from his country there, shared by everyone at the table."

Maury Rubin says, "Knowing what the customer wants could not be more important. On the one hand, making raspberry tarts only when the raspberries are good, four weeks out of the year, demands a lot from my customers, to appreciate what makes us unique. On the other hand, we didn't make cookies or muffins for the first year and a half. I had no interest in making them. I knew we could start by making a great croissant. I thought, 'This is going to thrill everybody as much as it thrills me.' Now we sell more muffins because that's what customers wanted."

Dan Budd emphasizes knowledge of the customer as well. "I think that it's really important to know them by being aware of your menu and your sales percentages. If you have lower sales of some items, then of course these must not be the kinds of things that your customers want. Then you look at the season, run specials, and change the menu. This way, you understand what your customers expect from you. You constantly have to look for those hot-selling things and see what's happening. This is how you have a dialogue with your customers, by seeing what they respond to. It's also important to talk to your waitstaff. You need to get their feedback on what people are happy about or what they aren't satisfied with. Then maybe you can make it better, but you have to pay attention to your menu and your sales."

> You constantly have to look for those hot-selling things and see what's happening. This is how you have a dialogue with your customers, by seeing what they respond to.
>
> —Dan Budd

Gale Gand emphasizes going out to the tables to talk to customers. "I'm not one of those people that hides in the kitchen. I spent years working in basement pastry kitchens. I won't go there anymore. I always like an open kitchen—a kitchen with windows, a kitchen that encourages guests to poke their noses in and ask what we're doing, so I can get some contact with them. I also get to know customers through teaching and demonstrations."

Apple Mousse on Walnut Crust
with Caramel Sauce and Apple Crisps

by Markus Färbinger

Yield: One 10 x 14 x 2-inch pan

For the walnut crust:

½ cup butter

1 cup confectioners' sugar

3 whole eggs

½ teaspoon vanilla extract

½ cup all-purpose flour

1½ cups roasted and ground walnuts

1 cup cake or cookie crumbs, finely ground

1½ teaspoons lemon zest

1 teaspoon cinnamon

For the apple mousse:

2½ teaspoons unflavored powdered gelatin

½ cup plus 2 tablespoons apple cider

½ cup sugar

2 egg whites

2 medium apples, peeled, cored, and chopped

1½ cups heavy cream, whipped to soft peaks

For the caramel sauce:

1 cup sugar

¾ cup apple cider

1 cup walnuts, chopped, toasted

½ vanilla bean, split and scraped

For the apple crisps:

2 Granny Smith apples

Sugar (for dredging)

To make the walnut crust:

1. Preheat oven to 350°. In a mixing bowl with a paddle attachment, cream the butter with the confectioners' sugar. Add the eggs slowly, then add the vanilla extract.

2. In a separate bowl, stir together the flour, nuts, crumbs, zest, and cinnamon.

3 Fold this dry mixture into the egg mixture until combined.

4. Spread into the bottom of a greased 10 × 14 × 2-inch baking pan and bake for 16 to 18 minutes.

To make the apple mousse:

1. Soften the gelatin by sprinkling it over ½ cup of the cider and letting it sit for 10 minutes.

2. In a mixing bowl, combine the sugar and egg whites and stir over low heat with a whisk until mixture is very warm.

3. Whip the warmed mixture to stiff peaks on high speed.

4. Heat the gelatin cider mixture in a small pan over low heat until gelatin is completely dissolved, then drizzle it into the whipped whites while whisking on medium speed.

5. In a saucepot, over medium heat, combine the chopped apple with the 2 tablespoons of cider. Cook for 10 to 12 minutes, stirring occasionally. Purée in a food processor.

6. Fold the egg whites into the apple purée. Fold in the whipped cream. Spread the mixture over the walnut crust and refrigerate until service.

To make the caramel sauce:

1. In a thick-bottomed saucepot set over medium heat, allow the sugar to melt and caramelize, stirring only occasionally.

2. When caramel is a deep amber color, but before it smokes significantly, stir in the cider in small increments until all of it is incorporated.

3. Add the walnuts and vanilla bean. Stir and simmer over low heat to reduce and thicken slightly. Remove the vanilla bean pod and reserve the sauce for final assembly.

Continued on next page

To make the apple crisps:

1. Preheat the oven to 300°. Peel and core the apples and slice crosswise to ¹⁄₁₆-inch thick with either a sharp knife or a mandoline (slicing tool) to make rounds.

2. Dredge slices on one side in the sugar and lie them sugar-side down on parchment paper or on a nonstick baking sheet.

3. Bake for 20 to 22 minutes, turning the tray a few times to ensure even browning. When slices are golden brown, remove from oven. While they are still warm, remove them from the tray. Reserve for final assembly.

To assemble:

1. Cut the mousse into 2 × 2-inch squares or other desired shapes.

2. Place each square on a plate and drizzle the caramel sauce around. Place a few apple crisps out the top of each. Serve.

Bruno Feldeisen goes out to a table only if requested by the guest. "You always have five or six customers who get the same dessert every time they come in, and if you take a dessert off the menu, you'll hear about it."

Elizabeth Falkner pays more attention to customers than to anything else. "If people ask you for fresh fruit and you don't have it on the menu and you complain because you have to cut it up every time, then you're not respecting the customer. You must pay attention and make something really snazzy. It doesn't have to be just a bowl of grapes and apples. You must take pride in every single thing that goes out of your kitchen."

Nancy Silverton stresses the importance of making what is going to sell. "We aren't baking for the trash can. There are certain things that I really love. I'll put them on the menu and I know we won't sell them, but it's something I would like my customers to experience. We'll make sure we have enough of the other things, but they're sometimes there for my own pleasure. Ninety percent of the menu is there for someone else's pleasure."

There are indirect ways of connecting to the customer. Many pastry chefs keep close tabs on customer likes, wants, and dislikes through the waitstaff and restaurant managers. Claudia Fleming takes this approach. "We get extraordinary feedback from our waitstaff. It's critical to listen to the customer. They are your business. They are why you have a job and, as much as you like to experiment, you must want them to like what you do. If they don't like something, either change it or get rid of it. The waitstaff is the mouthpiece of the guest. We also bring comment cards to the table with the check."

Richard Leach's approach is similar. "It is important to know the customer. I listen to customer reactions from waiters and managers. I pay extra attention to feedback for the first few days after I make a change to the menu, and pay attention to how items sell." Emily Luchetti stresses the importance of the relationship between the front and back of the house. "You get to know the customer through the waitstaff and managers. I think it's important to work together with the front of the house because they are your spokespeople."

> I pay extra attention to feedback for the first few days after I make a change to the menu, and pay attention to how items sell.
>
> —Richard Leach

François Payard is so adamant about knowing his customers that he splits his time. "I meet my guests every day. I normally work in the kitchen until 10 A.M. Then I work in the dining room all day and come back to the kitchen and work all evening."

Sherry Yard uses her experience in front-of-the-house management to know and care for the customers of Spago. "When Wolfgang and I first sat down and talked four years ago, that was the one thing we agreed on immediately. He said, 'We have a very unique clientele down here and they want things in a certain way,' and I said, 'You mean like Mrs. Roman who likes her orange juice squeezed and likes her caramel sauce on the side?' He stopped and looked at me and I said, 'I've been doing that for years at Campton Place in San Francisco,' and I started naming guests that I remembered were from Los Angeles. He was impressed because I always look at the books and the empty plates."

The Customer and the Wider Marketplace

A good chef has his or her finger on the pulse of popular culture and fashion. Food tastes change. Foodstuffs, styles, and restaurant concepts come into and go out of style and, to be successful, no matter what his or her style of cuisine is, a chef must be aware of the fluid nature of the marketplace. One of the greatest skills a chef or pastry chef—or any businessperson, for that matter—can possess is the ability to determine the needs or desires of the market, to define and predict what people are most willing to spend their money on as fashion, tastes, and time march on.

Mark Miller looks at statistics and market trends constantly. "Candy has been the largest- growing market increase in the 1990s in national retail food sales and it's also the most profitable. So people are eating candy daily and that changes their views on what dessert should be.

Strawberries decorated with white and dark chocolate

They go to a supermarket and see high-end chocolate bars like Valrhona being sold. Then they go to a restaurant and eat something made with Valrhona chocolate and it isn't special anymore because they also eat it as a snack at the office. The availability of specialty ingredients has put more pressure on pastry chefs to be creative, to create dessert ideas that have not yet been popularized. The flip side is that Ben and Jerry's and Häagen Dazs took ideas like the classic Eskimo Pie and produced an upscale product with dark Belgian chocolate. The presence of premium products has added pressure to restaurants to have a higher standard than what is available in the marketplace."

Nick Malgieri notes that the pastry chef must consider the demand for specific items. "You have to stay in business. What people will actually buy in a retail pastry shop can be very limiting sometimes. I think in a restaurant it is a little bit less so because people go there for a particular kind of experience."

Sherry Yard is sensitive to the preferences of customers in different geographic locales. "The more you communicate with people, the more you get a feel for what your average customer wants. Moving from coast to coast was a big transition for me. Some desserts work very well in New York but not in San Francisco."

It's amazing how tastes differ from city to city and region to region. "You can be doing the best desserts in the world," says Emily Luchetti, "but if it's not what the clientele wants, then it doesn't matter. The American public wants something new and exciting but, at the same time, they want to be able to trace it back to that cobbler or crisp. People grew up on crisps, cobblers, and pies, but I think you have to be careful when you put them on a menu because so many people can make these desserts at home. They don't neccessarily want to go out and get it in a restaurant—therefore you have to make it more interesting."

Bill Yosses agrees. "Customers are looking for something extraordinary, either because it looks new and they haven't had it before or because it's a traditional dessert done impeccably well."

> Customers are looking for something extraordinary, either because it looks new and they haven't had it before or because it's a traditional dessert done impeccably well.
> —Bill Yosses

Bruno Feldeisen received sage advice along these lines from a trusted mentor. "Joachim [Splichal] showed me how to adapt what I learned in Europe and apply it to the American market. He said, 'Don't be narrow-minded. You have great tools, but it is different here. You have to know how to give the American people what they want.' "

"For the first five years," notes Maury Rubin, "my products came purely from what was flowing through me creatively. It was all about the food and my imagination. Now it is about paying attention to the market and listening to customers. Now it is about strategic decisions for the bakery and the business. Part of my job is that I'm vice president of strategy, product development, and marketing of City Bakery all rolled into one."

> Joachim [Splichal] showed me how to adapt what I learned in Europe and apply it to the American market. He said, "Don't be narrow-minded. You have great tools, but it is different here." You have to know how to give the American people what they want.
> —Bruno Feldeisen

Paying attention to market trends can be accomplished through reading both food and fashion periodicals and newspapers, traveling, dining, and keeping in contact with, or knowing about, the work of other chefs. This can point you in the direction of success because it builds a sense for your place in the business, a sense of what desserts or products your customer wants and, if you strike out on your own, what type of pastry business will be embraced by the public.

Finding your place in the world of pastry is a step-by-step process. You may know exactly what you want from this profession, what type of business you wish to create, or what level of autonomy you seek as a leader. Or you may enter this profession without clear goals in mind but, through discipline and a variety of work situations, you may find your own style and area of specialization within the field. Your work experiences are the fertile training ground for success. Wherever your aspirations take you, whatever goals you formulate and realize, you must taste, experience, create, and constantly look for effective ways to improve your skills and draw upon the wisdom of these pastry chefs and the request of the customers .

> Part of my job is that I'm vice president of strategy, product development, and marketing...all rolled into one.
>
> —Maury Rubin

CHAPTER *five*

INGREDIENTS FOR SUCCESS
AS A PASTRY CHEF

Familiarity with Flavor, Foodstuff, and Method

The main ingredient for success as a pastry chef is experience. Nothing can replace the experience gained from performing many responsibilities in a variety of positions. Auguste Escoffier's advice is as valid now as it was a hundred years ago: "No theories, no formula, no recipe, no matter how well written, can take the place of experience." Your level of self-confidence, mastery of the craft, and knowledge of effective techniques are honed through the fires of will, determination, and fortitude.

According to Charlie Trotter, the success of the pastry department evolves in various ways. "It can be accomplished by a pastry chef working with a chef who has strong opinions and is able to convey those opinions, or it can be accomplished by an equal collaboration of a chef and a pastry chef. Or sometimes there is the rare pastry chef who is not even given direction by a chef and is smart enough and adept enough to work his style of dessert in different directions and sensitive enough to make those desserts fit with the savory food."

Charlie Trotter's assessment describes a developed, confident person with a true passion and love for food. Such people are not only talented technicians but also team players and individuals with an inherent deep concern that their contribution to the experience of the customer fits with the flow of the meal and effectively complements the preceding courses. It is precisely these individuals—open-minded and open-hearted, industrious, focused, strong-willed and even-tempered—who adjust to the rigorous, intense, and demanding surroundings of production and managerial sensibility. All your technical and communication skills will be needed. When you are ready for these demanding responsibilities, you are the person for the job. You can take your career at this point and mold it into what you want it to be. You are practiced, concise, experienced, and mature enough to make clear decisions about your career. You have finally got what it takes and the will to give more than is required. At this point, you are aligned with the forces that can make you a success. You have come into your own and can create a path that leads to your own highest potential as a pastry chef. Having achieved this attitude

> No theories, no formula, no recipe, no matter how well written, can take the place of experience.
> —Auguste Escoffier

of success through experience, your approach can focus more than ever on the specific tasks and goals required for your chosen arena of production.

As a pastry chef, you set the parameters for your daily work. This is a natural process of using what you have learned from your work and life experiences, the experiences that have shaped the creative person you have become. You employ your specific personal philosophy to create a climate in the kitchen that reflects all your sensibilities as a pastry chef. This is both your approach to foodstuffs and technique and your treatment of those you work with.

Richard Leach comments on his path. "I like basic rules. I keep fresh ingredients. I try to have a nice presentation that is surprising to people and pleasing to the eye. In an à la carte restaurant, this also becomes a selling point. I usually stick to one flavor per plate, plus a couple of accents—for example, a banana dessert with star anise, or raspberry with a little thyme. I don't combine chocolate with berries. To me, chocolate is better with nuts or spices. I also like to mix temperatures on a plate, warm components with cold components. I'm trying to get away from heavy anglaises, and to make my sauces thin and delicate."

Jacques Torres sums up his professional approach. "Good ingredients. Buy good ingredients. You cannot create good desserts without them. If you start with good chocolate and you don't make any mistakes and you have good technique, perhaps you're going to have a good dessert. If you start with something bad, you can be as good a pastry chef as you can be and still not have a good dessert."

> The integrity of the source of the ingredients is way up there on my list. More and more small farmers are producing really great products and I think it's the responsibility of a chef to seek them out and help get their product to the public.
>
> —Bill Yosses

Bill Yosses echoes this sentiment and looks at the creation process long before the basic ingredients arrive in the kitchen. "The integrity of the source of the ingredients is way up there on my list. More and more small farmers are producing really great products and I think it's the responsibility of a chef to seek them out and help get their product to the public. The second thing is to respect those ingredients. Sometimes a great chef is someone who does very little to ingredients and is very humble, preparing and presenting food in a way that is not only healthful but also pleasant to eat."

Dan Budd agrees with this philosophy. "You have to try to bring great things out of the food. Be inspired by the food in its natural state. In pastry, sometimes you see people running around for things. 'Do you have the rubber spatula? Can I borrow some scissors?' It's at this point that they've forgotten what they're doing. So not only are they not being efficient but they have lost track of the food. I can recall days at the River Café and Park Avenue Café when I saw line cooks sink. Why? In the long run, it was because they had no idea about the food. If you're a fish cook, for example, the most important thing to know is your fish. You know how many portions you have. You know the quality of that fish. You know everything from the date the fish came in to how you're going to season it. You know exactly what's going to happen with it. Food is your *life* and if you don't realize that, then you're in a dangerous place. I think we make mistakes in pastry because we tried to contrive a lot of things and forgot to bring out the best in that food. One of the things Ferdinand Metz [president of The Culinary Institute of America] says is that the hardest food to make is the simplest food. I've learned, as an instructor here, to look at that food, taste that food, and concentrate on making it the best it can be."

> Working with food means taking it back to its original point, unadorned pure flavor, because that particular flavor is what you want to taste, combined with an appropriate texture. I look for contrasts in simplicity by combining the simplest of things so that they say something together.
>
> —Claudia Fleming

Claudia Fleming thinks of her impact as a pastry chef in relation to her restaurant and from the customer's point of view. "I prepare the last course of dinner. It is a continuation of dinner. It is a derivative of the cuisine of the restaurant. It's simple, straightforward, refined, and pure. I like to have a contrast in the temperature and the texture. Often I go with the same flavor but different textures or temperatures; if that doesn't work, then I try contrasting flavors. I brainstorm and write down every possible thing I can associate with a certain component and see how I can make them fit together. Working with food means taking it back to its original point, unadorned pure flavor, because that particular flavor is what you want to taste, combined with an appropriate texture. I look for contrasts in simplicity by combining the simplest of things so that they say something together."

Gray Kunz views dessert as every bit as important as any other course of the entire dining experience. "What a wonderful canvas a pastry chef has. Think about the flavor extractions. I think there is a misconception about how important pastry should taste and not just look. I would say that keeping pastry on the simple side while featuring flavor is the most important thing. But the pastry chef must blend the finale and give closure to a well thought-out menu. It's important that the pastry chef and his work are not segregated but are part of the team, especially in creating the whole menu."

Charlie Trotter echoes these ideas about dessert. "Pastry chefs must make flavor their number-one priority. Only then can they respect ingredients so much that they can let the strawberries and the rhubarb have their moment with the ginger and explore the textures. Once that is done, everything else is a benefit. Presenting this in a nice way, a delicate way, is just a benefit, because flavor is the most important issue with all cooking."

Jackie Riley lists working with seasonal ingredients as one of her top priorities. "If you start with something that is fresh, tasty, and seasonal, then very little needs to be done with it. This way, its simplicity can be enjoyed. I don't like to overgarnish or mix too many flavor combinations together because that is confusing. Someone could

Blueberries on the stem

say, 'What is this? What is this supposed to be? What is it supposed to taste like?' So I think simple, straightforward pastry with flavor, texture, and temperatures all working together can make intense and wonderful desserts."

Elizabeth Falkner looks east and west for her influences. "I've tried to merge my respect for the pastry chefs here in California with what I learned from working with people in New York. California has such incredible produce, and there's no time to make architectual desserts with it. Elephant heart plums, for example, are only here for one or two weeks. It's the same with a lot of seasonal fruits. I could spend a lot of time finessing with tropical towers or something, but I would prefer to deal with the fruit as it comes in throughout the year."

Caramel-Coriander
Ice Cream

by Jackie Riley

Yield: 1½ quarts

2 tablespoons coriander seed

2 cups heavy cream

½ cup milk

1 cup sugar

1 teaspoon lemon juice

¼ cup plus 2 tablespoons water

10 egg yolks

1. In a small pan, toast the coriander seeds over medium heat, stirring often, for about 2 minutes. Remove from heat and cool.

2. Coarsely grind toasted seeds in a mortar and pestle or in a coffee grinder.

3. In a 2- or 3-quart saucepot, combine the cream, milk, and coriander over medium heat. Bring the mixture to a simmer to infuse the coriander flavor into the cream mixture.

4. In a 3-quart pot, combine the sugar, lemon juice, and water. Stir once to help dissolve the sugar. Then, over a medium heat, allow the mixture to caramelize, stirring occasionally.

5. Bring the mixture to an amber color, then remove from the heat.

6. With a ladle, carefully add some of the hot cream mixture to the caramel. Be cautious as the mixture will splatter a bit at first. Finish this step by adding the entire cream mixture.

7. In a medium-sized bowl, stir the egg yolks and slowly drizzle some of the cream mixture into the yolks to temper. Stir the yolk mixture back into the main cream mixture.

8. Over a medium flame, while stirring, bring the mixture to nappe, or thicken to the point where it coats the back of a spoon.

9. Strain through a fine strainer. Cool the ice cream base in a container set in ice or in the refrigerator. Spin in an ice cream machine. Serve immediately.

Janet Rikala follows similar reasoning. "I think the biggest thing I've learned here in San Francisco is not to try to take the food too much out of its element. If you take a perfectly ripe peach, it's great just the way it is. Don't cover it up too much or mask it with other components so that you don't know what it is anymore. I still think one of the hardest things in the whole wide world to make is a perfect peach pie. Dessert can be made to look really interesting and beautiful, yet the food needs to be respected for what it is."

"Flavor, flavor, flavor, flavor," emphasizes Emily Luchetti. "I take a traditional dessert and give it a makeover, trying to stay true to its regional roots. My primary concern is flavor and taste. Presentation is important, but it's secondary."

Gale Gand similarly critiques her approach. "My style is to draw from the classics but turn them inside out. I like to have a surprise or something unexpected on the plate. I think I view plated dessert differently than most pastry chefs because of my design and art training. I look at the plate as a canvas; I use shading and light and dark and highlighting and negative space and height, contrast in temperature, contrast in texture, complementary flavors, and cut richness with acid. I always want to make sure there is a sense of humor in my desserts. I think that is important in life in general. To do something like a banana split, which has all kinds of history for people, but do it 'upscale' is really fun for me."

Tasting your creations is vital in this work. I've never forgotten what Charlie Trotter taught me about tasting my desserts. It's not good enough to just taste the elements or components of a dessert individually, having a little taste of the ice cream or the sauce. You must eat and experience the whole dessert as though you are a customer in the restaurant. That's the only way to understand how all the details of that dessert work together. Bite after bite, is it too sweet, too rich, too light? Is the sauce effective with the dessert or bland in comparison to the main element? These concerns can only be addressed by the fundamental exercise of eating, tasting, and analyzing the whole dessert from start to finish.

> When it's all happening, when it's all synchronized and food is coming out as good as it can be, you're very silent, you're very concentrated physically, but mentally, in the back of your head, you're riding a bucking bronco and inside you're screaming, "Yee-haa!" and you're holding on for dear life. I have to say, that's my high.
>
> —Dan Budd

Tangerine Sorbet
with Pomegranate Sauce

by Janet Rikala

Yield: 4–6 servings

For the tangerine sorbet:

2½ cups tangerine juice

¼ cup sugar, to taste

For the pomegranate sauce:

4 cups pineapple juice

1 stalk lemongrass, inner white part only, smashed

½ cup sugar

1 tablespoon tamarind paste

2 whole star anise

½ tablespoon Szechuan peppercorns

¼ cup mint, chopped

¼ cup basil, chopped

1 cup pomegranate juice

To make the tangerine sorbet:

1. Whisk the tangerine juice with the sugar to taste.

2. Process in an ice cream machine.

To make the pomegranate sauce:

1. In a saucepot over low heat, simmer the pineapple juice, lemongrass, sugar, tamarind, star anise, and peppercorns for 45 minutes.

2. Remove from the heat and add the mint and basil. Let sit for 10 minutes.

3. Strain. Whisk in the pomegranate juice. Refrigerate to cool the sauce.

To serve:

1. Chill 4 to 6 bowls. Divide the sauce among them.

2. Scoop the tangerine sorbet into each bowl. Serve immediately.

Nancy Silverton takes a similar approach to evaluating her desserts. "I think one mistake pastry chefs make is to make something, take one bite, and then say it's perfect, it's done. What you have to do is not necessarily eat the whole thing but at least anticipate eating the whole thing and see if it will hold your interest. That's where I think people lack. One bite is fine, but after three bites, you're bored. The flavors have to be exciting to keep your interest. Another feeling I have about keeping interest is you need to make things one bite short, so that when the diner returns, he or she wants more. If you make it two bites short, however, the customer walks away and says, 'Well, that was a rip-off.' So it's that *little* bit of wanting more that brings the customer back."

Pumpkins

"There's not a thing at the White House, not a recipe that I don't taste," says Roland Mesnier. "If I make a batch of Danish pastry, I cut it into the number of people working in the shop that day. Everyone will have a piece and everybody will make a comment like, 'Oh, the Danish is particularly flaky today. Why? What did we do differently?' By analyzing our products and making these comments, this is how we all get better and better."

Successful pastry chefs distill their personal philosophies and ideas about their work from their many years of learning from others and their often high-pressure production environment. When your formula works and you know your food is pleasing people, this is perhaps the most unglorified yet secretly satisfying moment you will ever achieve in this business, to which Dan Budd's enthusiasm attests. "Being involved and enveloped in all the good food and the pastries makes me feel like I can do anything. When it's all happening, when it's all synchronized and food is coming out as good as it can be, you're very silent, you're very concentrated physically, but mentally, in the back of your head, you're riding a bucking bronco and inside you're screaming, 'Yee-haa!' and you're holding on for dear life. I have to say, that's my high."

Orange Brûlée with Julienne of Orange

by Roland Mesnier

Yield: 8 servings

8 large navel oranges, peeled with a potato peeler

4 cups water

1¼ cups sugar

12 egg yolks

1 cup sugar

¼ cup Grand Marnier liqueur

4 cups heavy cream

1 cup raspberries

For the julienned orange peel:

1. Slice the orange peel into ⅛-inch- to ¼-inch-wide strips and blanch in 2 cups of boiling water for 4 to 5 minutes. Rinse under cold water.

2. Combine the remaining 2 cups of water and the sugar in a saucepot over medium heat to bring to a boil. Add the zest strips and reduce the heat to low, simmering the strips for 20 to 25 minutes or until they appear translucent.

3. Remove from the syrup with a fork and cool on a lightly greased tray.

For the Grand Marnier sauce:

1. Cut the tops and bottoms off of the oranges, then remove all the white pith. Cut between each membrane and remove each section of orange. Refrigerate until ready to use.

2. In a mixing bowl, whip the yolks for 3 to 4 minutes or until the color lightens. Fold in the sugar.

3. Place the yolk mixture in a bowl set over a pot of gently simmering water. Whisk, gradually adding the Grand Marnier.

4. As the mixture begins to thicken, gradually add the cream. Continue to whisk. When the mixture has thickened enough to coat the back of a spoon, remove from the heat and reserve.

To serve:

1. Arrange the orange sections in the centers of ovenproof plates or on an ovenproof platter. Pour the sauce around the oranges, not over them.

2. Sprinkle the candied orange julienne over the top, then place under a broiler for about 15 seconds or long enough for the cream to lightly brown.

3. Remove from the broiler. Sprinkle with raspberries and serve.

Ingredients

A good pastry chef builds his reputation on a solid foundation by using high-quality essential ingredients. The ability to discern the quality of ingredients is attained through many seasons and years of working with a variety of flours, sugars, dairy products, fruits, nuts, and chocolate.

"I think the more confident I get with ingredients, the simpler I get, because I really believe in letting ingredients speak for themselves," says Claudia Fleming. "I choose ingredients based primarily on the season and then choose things that either complement or contrast with them. I think about ingredients constantly. It really consumes me."

Red currants

Great pastry begins at the farm, in the fields and orchards, and with the care given to the products along the way. In July, prime peach season, one of my purveyors sent me a box of peaches not yet ripe, which was fine because I had planned on some ripening time so the fruit would be at its peak. As time went on, I found the peaches would not ripen. They went from firm to the touch to spongy and then started rotting. I immediately called my produce company and let them know, pointing out that in the process of getting the fruit from the field to the restaurant, the company had ignored the fruit itself. They picked it too green and, though it looked great, the sugars in the fruit never got a chance to develop. The company credited me for the cost, picked up their rotting, unripe fruit, and became more aware of what they were selling. The next day they delivered luscious, juicy, bursting-with-flavor peaches and only now would I put my new peach dessert on the menu. If all pastry chefs did this, soon the quality of care given to such perishable product from farm to marketplace would have to improve because there would be no market for bad produce. If it costs more to have a better peach because it needs to be shipped faster after ripening in the field for a little longer, it's worth it.

> Every product that we use in pastry is alive. The flour is alive. The sugar is alive. It all has a life and a lifespan. That is how you have to treat it. Treat it with respect and you will get back that respect. This is a tremendous profession because of that.
>
> —Roland Mesnier

European produce companies have the utmost respect for the humble, perishable fruit and other produce, and they have an effective delivery system in place. The Japanese are even more extreme. In Japan, fruit trees are impeccably pruned and cared for to produce perfectly nurtured fruit. The produce sections of some markets are arranged like a boutique. This comes at great cost. In one Japanese market, the price of a particular melon, the most perfect and delicious one I have ever had in my life, was one hundred dollars. No matter where you are, what it comes down to is that, be it melon, peach, or strawberry, it needs not only to be in season but also the best it can be.

Roland Mesnier is passionate about his ingredients. "Every product that we use in pastry is alive. The flour is alive. The sugar is alive. It all has a life and a lifespan. That is how you have to treat it. Treat it with respect and you will get back that respect. This is a tremendous profession because of that."

Ingredient Flavor Combinations

I've created a general-use flavor combination chart that draws on the menus and recipes of many pastry chefs and chefs as well as my own. These combinations are used in both classic desserts and those that reflect many of the world's cuisines. These are not rules but rather reference guidelines for conceptualizing the flavors in a dessert.

ALMOND

apple
apricot
Asian pear
banana
caramel
cherry
coffee
fig
honey
nectarine
orange
peach
pear
plum
spices

ALLSPICE

apple
Asian pear
banana
carrot
mamey sapote
nuts
pear
pineapple
pumpkin
sweet potato

APPLE

allspice
caramel
cardamom
cheese
chestnut
cinnamon

clove
cranberry
crème fraîche
currant
date
ginger
hazelnut
mango
maple
nutmeg
pecan
raisin
rosemary
tamarind
walnut
yogurt

APRICOT

almond
black pepper
caramel
cardamom
ginger
hazelnut
honey
nectarine
orange
peach
pecan
pistachio
plum
Sauternes
vanilla

ASIAN PEAR

allspice
almond
apple
black pepper
cashew
cinnamon
ginger
honey
macadamia
nutmeg
raisin
vanilla

BANANA, RED BANANA, BABY BANANA

allspice
brandy
Brazil nut
brown sugar
caramel
cherry
chocolate
cinnamon
coffee
dark rum
ginger
hazelnut
honey
Madeira
mango
molasses
papaya
pecan

Vital Ingredients of Pastry Chefs

CLAUDIA FLEMING chocolate, salt, basil, lemon verbena, thyme, cilantro, peaches, apples, figs

GALE GAND butter, sugar, chocolate, cream

EMILY LUCHETTI fruit, chocolate, caramel, butter

JACQUES TORRES all of them

MARY BERGIN butter, chocolate, eggs, vanilla beans, lemons

MICHELLE GAYER fruit

SHERRY YARD salt, love

ELIZABETH FALKNER chocolate, cream, butter, flour, sugar

BILL YOSSES fruits, chocolate, flours

JIM GRAHAM chocolate, butter

RICHARD LEACH chocolate, spices, vanilla, citrus, cream, butter, eggs, flour, sugar

strawberry	**BLACKBERRY**	apricot
tamarind	apricot	banana
walnut	black pepper	berries
BASIL	champagne	cherries
apple	cinnamon	chestnut
berries	citrus	citrus
citrus	crème fraîche	fig
honey	hazelnut	hazelnut
mint	lemon	mango
pineapple	nectarine	melon
BAY LEAF	other berries	papaya
apple	peach	peach
chocolate	plum	plantain
nectarine	port	plum
peach	red wine	pumpkin
pear	**BLACK PEPPER**	red wine
plum	almond	squash
quince	apple	

BLOOD ORANGE

allspice
almond
cardamom
chocolate
cinnamon
clove
fig
ginger
honey
other citrus
pistachio

BLUEBERRY

almond
cardamom
cheese
citrus
crème fraîche
fig
ginger
hazelnut
lemon
mango
other berries
lemon verbena

BRAZIL NUTS

banana
caramel
chocolate
citrus
coconut
spices

CARDAMOM

apple
apricot
banana
berries
chocolate
citrus
ginger
nectarine
orange
peach
pear
plum

CARROT

allspice
brandy
brown sugar
cinnamon
dried currant
ginger
molasses
nutmeg
pecan
raisin
star anise
walnut

CASHEW

apple
banana
caramel
chocolate
citrus
pear
spices
tropical fruit

CHERRY, SWEET

apricot
black pepper
chocolate
citrus
fennel
nectarine
peach
plum
red wine
spices
vanilla

CHERRY, TART

apricot
chocolate
citrus
cream cheese
plum
port
red wine
ricotta
spices
vanilla

CHESTNUT

apple
caramel
chocolate
coffee
dried fruits
pear
spices
vanilla

CILANTRO
apricot
berries
cherries
citrus
corn
nectarine
peach
plum
tropical fruit

CINNAMON,
CASSIA,
CANELA
apple
apricot
cherries
chocolate
citrus
coffee
fig
ginger
mango
nectarine
papaya
peach
pear
plum
pumpkin
red wine
squash

CLEMENTINE,
MANDARIN,
TANGERINE
allspice

cardamom
cherry
chocolate
cinnamon
coffee
dried fruits
fig
ginger
nutmeg
star anise
tropical fruit
vanilla

CLOVE
apple
apricot
banana
citrus
coffee
date
nectarine
peach
pear
pineapple
plum
pumpkin
squash
sweet potato
tropical fruit
vanilla

COCONUT
banana
Brazil nut
cashew
chocolate

kaffir leaf
macadamia
pineapple
plantain
tropical fruit

CORN
allspice
blackberries
caramel
cilantro
molasses
nutmeg
raspberries
vanilla

CRANBERRY
apple
chocolate
cinnamon
citrus
clove
mango
mint
pear
red wine
spices

CURRANT,
BLACK AND
RED
berries
cassis
chocolate
citrus
port
red wine

Jim Graham Discusses His Vital Ingredient: Chocolate

As you work with any material over time, you develop a conceptual model of it. At first, in the beginning of your association with this material, your model may be handed to you in the form of instruction from somebody else. It may come from books. You may have read that to temper chocolate you have to do "this, this, and this." "Chocolate doesn't like that." "Never do this to chocolate." "Always do this to chocolate." That initial model is inevitably a crude one, but when we are confronted with chocolate that has to be transformed in some way, the only way we can do that is by referring to that model. Over a period of time, the model becomes more and more refined. You learn that some elements of the early model are completely off base. You learn that in other areas there is a flexibility that wasn't implied when you first acquired the model. You learn that in yet other areas the model is much too broad, that there is actually less room for adjustment than you initially thought. The refining process of this model goes on over a long period of time. Certainly, the most notable times when you pull up your model is when there is a problem, when something is not going according to plan. You pull up your model, you pull up all the data you know about chocolate, and compare it with what you perceive as the problem. You eventually get to a point where that model accords so well with the reality in front of you that the model almost disappears—you almost don't need it anymore. This doesn't happen immediately, but when it does, you begin to become aware that you are not treating the chocolate objectively—rather, you are simply "with the chocolate." You are responding to its nuances and changes naturally without having to think, "Okay, it's doing this, and that means I need to do this." A flow sets in that is not possible when you constantly have to cross-check with your model. Chocolate is so responsive to slight changes that often you don't have time to refer to notes or books. You often have to respond immediately to the circumstances. You need to know instinctively which stage the chocolate is in, what it's doing, where it's going. No one can communicate that to you. Once you have acquired that, you realize the futility of trying to teach this to anybody else.

spices
white chocolate
CURRY
banana
carrot
citrus
coconut
plantain
pumpkin
squash
sweet potato
DATE
banana
chocolate
citrus
coffee
fig
rum
vanilla
whiskey
ELDERBERRY
apricot
cheese
fig
honey
lemon
nectarine
other berries
peach
plum
red wine
FEIJOA
banana
berries

cinnamon
citrus
mango
tropical fruit
vanilla
FENNEL
apple
cherry
citrus
mint
orange
pear
pineapple
plum
strawberry
FIG
almond
black pepper
cinnamon
citrus
crème fraîche
goat cheese
hazelnut
pear
pine nut
port
red wine
spices
vanilla
GINGER
almond
apple
apricot
banana

berries
Brazil nut
caramel
chocolate
citrus
coconut
grape
hazelnut
macadamia
nectarine
passion fruit
peach
peanut
pear
pineapple
plum
tropical fruit
GOOSEBERRY
hazelnut
honey
other berries
white chocolate
GRAPE
brandy
cheese
chocolate
citrus
dried fruit
ginger
raisin
spices
wine
GRAPEFRUIT
basil

black pepper

caramel

citrus

mint

rosemary

spices

thyme

tropical fruit

vanilla

GUAVA

citrus

coconut

huckleberry

kaffir leaf

pineapple

strawberry

tropical fruit

HAZELNUT

apple

apricot

banana

berries

caramel

cherry

chocolate

citrus

fig

goat cheese

nectarine

peach

pear

plum

red wine

HUCKLEBERRY, BLACK AND RED

apple

citrus

crème fraîche

ginger

guava

mango

pear

spices

KAFFIR LEAF

banana

citrus

coconut

lemongrass

tropical fruit

watermelon

KIWI

apple

banana

berries

cherry

citrus

coconut

mango

tropical fruit

KUMQUAT

berries

cherry

chocolate

cinnamon

coffee

dried fruits

persimmon

plum

spices

LEMON

apricot

berries

black pepper

cardamom

cherry

citrus

ginger

nectarine

peach

plum

prickly pear

tropical fruit

LEMONGRASS

berries

cherry

citrus

coconut

ginger

guava

kaffir leaf

tropical fruit

vanilla

LEMON VERBENA

apple

apricot

berries

blueberry

cherry

melon

peach

plum

yogurt

LIME

apple

berries

cherry

ginger

papaya

plum

strawberry

tequila

tropical fruit

LONGAN,

LYCHEE,

LOQUAT

citrus

ginger

gooseberry

tropical fruit

vanilla

MACADAMIA

banana

caramel

chocolate

coconut

ginger

honey

spices

tropical fruit

MAMEY SAPOTE

allspice

cinnamon

citrus

lime

MANGO

apple

banana

berries

caramel

citrus

coconut

melon

muscat

Sauternes

spices

tropical fruit

vanilla

MELON

berries

champagne

citrus

lemongrass

lemon verbena

white wine

yogurt

MINT

apple

apricot

berries

chocolate

citrus

ginger

nectarine

peach

plum

vanilla

NECTARINE

almond

apricot

berries

caramel

citrus

fig

ginger

hazelnut

orange

peach

pear

pecan

pistachio

plum

pumpkin

spices

squash

vanilla

walnut

NUTMEG

almond

apple

apricot

chocolate

ORANGE

allspice

almond

basil

berries

brandy

cherry

chocolate

cilantro

cinnamon

clove

coffee

cranberry

fennel

fig

ginger

grape

hazelnut

mint

muscat

nutmeg

pecan

persimmon

pineapple

pine nut

pistachio

star anise

tamarind

tea

vanilla

PAPAYA

black pepper

citrus

lime

mango

spices

tropical fruit

PAWPAW

apple

black pepper

black walnut

lemon

orange

pear

pecan

pine nut

PEACH,
WHITE PEACH

allspice

almond

apricot

berries

black pepper

caramel

cardamom

cinnamon

clove

ginger

green tea

honey

nectarine

plum

vanilla

PEAR

allspice

almond

apple

brown sugar

caramel

chestnut

chocolate

cinnamon

citrus

clove

ginger

hazelnut

pecan

pine nut

pistachio

port

spices

vanilla

walnut

wine

PEANUT

banana

caramel

chocolate

coconut

dried fruit

ginger

grape

raisin

PECAN

apple

apricot

caramel

chocolate

cinnamon

honey

molasses

nectarine

peach

pear

plum

pumpkin

squash

PERSIMMON

apple

black pepper

brown sugar

cinnamon

citrus

dried fruit

kumquat

pear

PINEAPPLE

basil

caramel

cilantro

coconut

macadamia

muscat

rosemary

rum

tropical fruit

PINE NUT

apple

apricot

caramel

citrus

fig

goat cheese

honey

nectarine

peach

pear

plum

PISTACHIO

apple

apricot

banana

berries

caramel

chocolate

citrus

ginger

lemongrass

melon

mint

nectarine

peach

pear

plum

quince

lemon verbena

PLANTAIN

allspice

brown sugar

caramel

chocolate

cinnamon

dark rum

Madeira

tropical fruit

PLUM

allspice

almond

black pepper

chestnut

cinnamon

citrus

clove

dried fruits

hazelnut

honey

port

red wine

vanilla

POPPY SEED

cinnamon

citrus

honey

lemon

strawberry

POMEGRANATE

apple

citrus

mint

red wine

tropical fruit

PRICKLY PEAR

citrus

lime

tomatillo

tropical fruit

PUMPKIN

allspice

apple

brown sugar

caramel

cardamom

chocolate

cinnamon

clove

dried fruit

ginger

molasses

nutmeg

pear

pecan

pumpkin seed

quince

raisin

squash

vanilla

walnut

PUMPKIN SEED

apple

caramel

chocolate

pear

pumpkin

QUINCE

allspice

almond

apple

caramel

cardamom

chestnut

cinnamon

clove

cranberry

date

dried fruit

ginger

hazelnut

honey

maple

nutmeg

pear

pecan

pistachio

pumpkin

tamarind

walnut

RASPBERRY, BLACK, GOLDEN, AND RED

apricot

berries

cinnamon

citrus

crème fraîche

ginger

lemon

nectarine

peach

plum

rhubarb

thyme

vanilla

RHUBARB

apple

apricot

berries

black pepper

citrus

cream cheese

crème fraîche

ginger

nectarine

peach

plum

strawberry

SAPOTE

citrus

muscat

Sauternes

tropical fruit

vanilla

SESAME SEED

almond

apricot

caramel

cardamom

chocolate

cinnamon

citrus

honey

nectarine

peach

plum

vanilla

STAR FRUIT

citrus

tropical fruit

vanilla

TAMARILLO

apple

citrus

ginger

lemongrass

melon

tropical fruit

vanilla

TAMARIND

allspice

apple

banana

brown sugar

caramel

cinnamon

citrus	**TOMATILLO**	banana
melon	berry	caramel
pear	citrus	chocolate
tropical fruit	mango	cinnamon
vanilla	prickly pear	nectarine
THYME	tropical fruit	peach
chocolate	**WALNUTS,**	pear
citrus	**BLACK**	plum
lemon	apple	pumpkin
raspberry	apricot	rum

Pastry Chefs' Use of Ingredients

Nancy Silverton tries to hit the bull's-eye of flavor in her use of ingredients. "I take the flavor of the ingredient and see how it best suits itself. For me, it's important to be able to close my eyes and know what I'm eating. There are certain strong flavors like chocolate, coffee, and lemon that people either love or hate. I try to cater to people who love those flavors." Continual learning is important no matter how long you've been in the business. There's always something more to learn about flavors and specific ingredients, perhaps how flours are milled or how certain fruits are grown. This knowledge can often lead to inspiration in the kitchen.

> In my days at his restaurant, Charlie Trotter constantly told us to taste our mise en place, not only before service at five o'clock but throughout the evening. We tasted all the food we served in order to ensure there would be no mistakes.
> —Andrew MacLauchlan

"Each time we go into another season and have huckleberries or rhubarb, we learn more. Each time I challenge myself with new ways of working with the same seasonal fruits," says Elizabeth Falkner.

Richard Leach reveals his process of creating, over time, a mental ingredient dictionary of the usage of a full range of items. "I think seasonally, and just from having experimented with things and ending up with nice combinations, which I keep in the back of my head. The combinations repeat, but I always try to use them in a different form. I may see what other people do or see a recipe and choose to try just two of its components together instead of the entire dish. Flavors are oddly linked—for example I like basil with pineapple. To me, both go well with cinnamon. Also, certain foods taste or smell like other foods. For example, a watermelon rind smells to me like kaffir leaf, so I might combine them because the smells are similar."

Working with other people who love food or who share their enthusiasm for a newly available product or way of working with a familiar product is inspiring; their enthusiasm is often contagious. "More often than not, chef Roland [Liccioni, chef of Le Français in Wheeling, IL], on one of his trips to the market, finds something that intrigues him," says Jim Graham. "He has a wonderful eye for novelty and quality and he'll just bring it in. He'll buy a handful of something, not expecting that I'll do something with it necessarily, but in his enthusiasm, he'll come back to where I'm working and say, 'Look what I've found.' That often sparks an idea in me for a new chocolate. This is an exciting time to be a chocolate maker because some really great products are coming out onto the market. Very often, in tasting a new variety of chocolate, I see possibilities in terms of flavor associations. I haven't really changed my ingredients much over time, but I certainly exercise greater subtlety with flavors, paying more attention to balancing them."

Frais de bois
(wild strawberries)

Tasting those ingredients that make up our desserts is a part of the job that can't be ignored. In my days at his restaurant, Charlie Trotter constantly told us to taste our mise en place, not only before service at five o'clock but throughout the evening. He asserted that over relatively short periods of time, the flavors of delicate sauces or other items could possibly be sour or not at their peak. We tasted all the food we served in order to ensure there would be no mistakes.

Jackie Riley discusses her developing outlook. "I'm definitely more knowledgeable now than I was at the beginning. By reading and by exposing myself to different types of cuisine and working with different people, I'm constantly learning. I'm more likely to use ingredients that are less common because I am much more comfortable using them."

Roland Mesnier insists on only fresh ingredients for the White House. "When salespeople call me and say 'I have a great new flavoring compound,' I say you can send it if you want but you're wasting your time. I won't buy it. I don't care how good it is. Everything I use is fresh. That's my job. That's what keeps me here. I use fresh ingredients and do things from scratch. If you tell me that tomorrow I have to use compounds, I'm going to buy a big truck and ride the highway. I will no longer be a pastry chef."

Mangoes

Dan Budd's teaching experience at The Culinary Institute of America has brought him to a new level of understanding about ingredients and their interactions. "I'm definitely becoming more intelligent about it as an instructor. Before, I was inspired by ingredients, but I didn't understand them as well as I do now. It's almost like the students force me to learn because mistakes happen everywhere and I realize where the most common mistakes are. Then I have to find out why and put that into words in a lesson. I try to make sure that the answer is simple and easily understood so the mistake never happens again. That's forced me to look at the ingredients and really learn more about how to put them together."

Bill Yosses sees a natural evolution in an attitude of respect for ingredients. "I think when people first come into this business, they crave recipes. 'What's the recipe?' 'Did you get the recipe?' and they write them down. Certainly recipes are important and you develop your skills that way, but I think my experiences taught me to emphasize the quality of ingredients. As long as you respect certain physical laws, it doesn't matter if you change the ingredients a little bit. I guess I came to that realization after trying the best recipe with second-rate ingredients. You don't get what you want."

Bruno Feldeisen recalls his changing attitude toward ingredients. "I think I'm more aware of ingredients than I was ten years ago. At first, you think chocolate is just chocolate, sugar is just sugar, and flour is just flour. Then you understand the quality of chocolate and the quality of flour. Even the mint you use is so important."

Sherry Yard describes ingredients as one of the unfolding intricacies of this business that one learns over time. "When you start off, a wealth of things are going on. Just when you figure out the difference between all-purpose flour and pastry flour, then comes high-gluten flour. You can overwhelm yourself if you try to figure out all those things at once. When I came into the business, I was naive, but slowly I figured things out. Then I started to read. To this day, when I find something I'm interested in, I research it and find out what it's all about. I don't like compromising the restaurant by using products that are not of the highest quality. If I go to the farmers' market and a farmer gives me a peach and it's kind of mealy, I might buy it and make sorbet. If the farmer has a crispy peach, then I can make cobblers. That's how ingredients affect things. Sometimes the flour isn't exactly the same and you call the purveyor on the phone and find out what's wrong. Ingredients are the magic of pastry. Mother Nature can really affect what we do, but if you buy only the best ingredients and you know how to use them, then you have the key to the magic. If you have that magic and the foundations and you know how to be the conductor of all that, then you are really a pastry chef."

Michelle Gayer explores ingredients' versatile, multifaceted nature by using fruit in many ways. "I don't just cut up fruit, I use different fruits as a purée, a thickener, a crispy chip, a dried ingredient, a sorbet, an ice cream, or a fruit-flavored caramel."

Mary Bergin notes how her understanding of the use of ingredients influenced her development as a pastry chef. "I understand why things work and why they don't. I think learning this has been a natural progression. I tend to get less complicated as I get older. I keep things much simpler now than when I was first starting out. I have been spoiled over the years. At Spago, we use the best

> Students force me to learn because mistakes happen everywhere and I realize where the most common mistakes are. Then I have to find out why and put that into words in a lesson.
>
> —Dan Budd

chocolate, vanilla beans, and high-quality everything. This is what I have used over the years, so this is what I prefer to use. It's a matter of taste more than anything else."

Emily Luchetti describes her development as a pastry chef. "In the beginning, when I first started doing pastry, I did much simpler presentations. Then I could do a really good cobbler or a really good pie because people had them in their childhood but they hadn't had them in a restaurant. Now they've had them in a restaurant, so I have to take both the flavor and the presentation to the next level. I might use caramel to make it interesting on the plate. Cost comes into it too, though. You can't be naive and think you can use only the most expensive things. If the most expensive things are the best quality, then definitely use them, but if you can use something cheaper that's just as good, use that too."

Gale Gand researches the sources of specific products by doing a little private investigation. "I often work closely with the people who sell ingredients. I'll go visit the factory where whatever it is is produced. I'll go to the Valrhona chocolate factory and observe how they're making chocolate or I'll go to the Ravi-Fruit factory and see if the fruit is really picked at its prime ripeness. I like to go as often as possible to inspect the places where products are made. Unlike commercial bakers, I'm not afraid of using the real thing to get the flavor, the vanilla bean instead of the extract. When I first started as a pastry chef, everyone was pushing compounds and using liqueurs for flavoring. I did that a little bit at the beginning of my career; for example, using Grand Marnier to get orange flavor. Later, I thought, why not just use an orange? I started out with things that were easy, like orange zest, but went on to grinding up oranges, reducing them over low heat, and sieving them and using the actual fruit."

> Ingredients are your tools. You must know your product, and know what goes with what.
> —Sherry Yard

Sherry Yard emphasizes restraint as you attain greater understanding of ingredients. "Sometimes people go off on these creative tangents and then figure out that they needed to learn puff pastry really well before altering it. The ingredients I use have changed as I have grown as a person. I'm always looking to the next level. I would put my passion fruit sorbet up against anyone's in the country today because it's the best and the reason it's the best is because I taste the passion fruit and I ask myself, 'What's in here?' When I do a dessert, I ask myself, 'How do I bring that flavor out? How do I enhance it and not mask it?' Ingredients are your tools. You must know your product, and know what goes with what."

Structure of the Pastry Kitchen

Knowledge of the structure, design, and layout of pastry kitchens is crucial information for anyone interested in or intimately involved in pastry, baking, and desserts at all levels. Work flow, refrigeration, expediting service area, the temperature of the room, and equipment choice and placement are critical factors in the makeup of a successful pastry kitchen. As a pastry chef, I have been consulted many times for my ideas regarding the layout of the pastry production area, as it is where I have to work. Who better to talk to than the pastry chef? Richard Leach's approach is to set up part of the pastry area much like the hot line or garde manger so dessert service is done à la minute. "All the mise en place is laid out, organized, counted, tasted, and ready to go. Between the pastry staff and the waitstaff, you need to organize the kitchen space in order to maximize the flow."

Charlie Trotter's approach follows the example of other parts of the kitchen. "Since the early days, we've always approached our pastry department much as we would the hotline setup. Where mise en place is organized, things are cut up, everything is ready, and a team of pastry people is ready to cook something off, flash the plate if it's supposed to be a warm, put the elements together on the plate, scoop the ice cream, drizzle the sauce around, add the nuts around or whatever is relevant, and time it so all the desserts for each table are finished at the same time."

> All the mise en place is laid out, organized, counted, tasted, and ready to go. Between the pastry staff and the waitstaff, you need to organize the kitchen space in order to maximize the flow.
> —Richard Leach

Gray Kunz adds his ideas for the attention and delicacy required in the production of fine desserts. "I think there is a drastic need for improvement in the work spaces for pastry chefs. The environment that a pastry chef needs is very different from the rest of the kitchen. The pastry kitchen needs different temperatures for the different ingredients they use and products they work with. The design of the pastry kitchen is an important element. For example, the area where chocolates are made cannot be next to the open oven doors. I think this needs to be looked at closely and fine tuned."

Peanut Butter Shortbread

by Ann Amernick

Yield: 30–35 shortbreads

1 cup butter, unsalted, cold

⅔ cup sugar

2 cups flour

1 cup peanut butter

1 teaspoon vanilla

1. In the bowl of an electric mixer equipped with a paddle, combine the butter and sugar. Mix on low speed for 10 seconds.

2. Add the flour, peanut butter, and vanilla. Mix on low speed for about 2 minutes. Turn the dough out on the work surface and finish mixing by hand to be sure the ingredients are evenly and thoroughly mixed.

3. Preheat the oven to 250°. Dust the dough and work surface with flour and roll the dough to ¼-inch thick.

4. Using a cookie cutter or a knife, cut the cookies into simple shapes and place them 1 inch apart on a nonstick tray or a sheet tray lined with parchment. Chill for ½ hour in the freezer.

5. Bake for 45 minutes or until firm. Cool on the tray and serve. The cookies are best stored in an airtight container refrigerated.

Creating Pastry Menus

A menu, in its simplest form, is a customer wish list of ideas about what's to come. It is vitally important that the menu accurately represent what is served. For instance, if a flavor is listed on the menu as part of a particular dessert, then that flavor better be pronounced enough in the dish for the customer to experience it. I've noticed that the agreement between menu descriptions and the desserts that follow is one area where inexperienced pastry chefs can falter. If you

> It is the tweaking of subtle flavor nuances that in the end displays your talent as a pastry cook.
> —Andrew MacLauchlan

describe something as a browned butter tart, for example, then you absolutely must be sure to brown the butter dark enough so that flavor really comes through. If you describe a chilled fruit soup as one infused with star anise, then that flavor must come up without an overwhelming taste. This is where refinement, skill, and experience as a pastry chef come into play and where the pastry chef can truly shine. It is the tweaking of subtle flavor nuances that in the end displays your talent as a pastry cook.

The decisions made to create the menu also reflect your judgment and dedication. Can you wait for the right moment when the melon is picked, when it is at its peak sweetness and flavor, to feature it on your menu? Can you use those Santa Rosa plums when they hit the market at their best, then move quickly on to other fruits of spring and summer as they arrive?

"I believe in visualizing the menu first," says Bruno Feldeisen. "If I can't see it in my mind, then I don't do it. I try to use influences that are around me—the weather, the season, and the fruits. I never do a menu from scratch. There's always an evolution from the past menu and I rarely do desserts that I did five years ago. It's a step-by-step evolution."

Emily Luchetti acknowledges a similar process. "I never say, 'On Friday, we are going to change the entire menu.' People ask how we come up with our desserts. I don't sit down and come up with a bunch of new desserts. I wish it were that easy, but it's not. You just have to be around it all the time and you have to have your hands in the flour. Going to other restaurants also feeds your creativity. Menu evolution is something that happens all the time. Sometimes I come up with desserts quickly and other times I have to fight for them. Sometimes I'll be doing a really simple dessert that I've been doing for a couple of years and then suddenly decide I don't like it anymore."

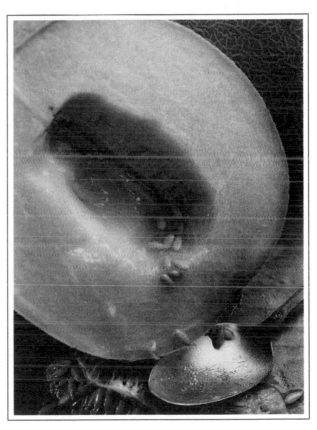

Juicy, ripe honeydew melon

From Emily Luchetti
(Farallon)

··

DESSERT MENU

Hot Chocolate Fudge Cake

With chocolate chunk malt ice cream

Pomegranate Granita

With Tahitian vanilla bean crème
and pirouette cookies

Chocolate Nib Stack

Layers of chocolate nib wafers and Valrhona custard
with chantilly and milk chocolate sauce

Meyer Lemon Souffle Cake

Served in a pool of anglaise

Apple Pithivier

With crème fraîche ice cream
and bourbon vanilla bean caramel sauce

Persimmon Pudding Cake

With rum raisin ice cream and orange sauce

Small Endings

A selection of housemade confections, cookies
and other luscious things

A Selection of Artisanal Cheeses

Served with brioche toast, sliced apples and roasted nuts
3 cheeses   5 cheeses

Roland Mesnier asserts that the pastry chef should be a dreamer. "You should be an artist. That's how you should come up with your designs. You should be able to sit at a table and visualize the menu as if you are eating it at the same time as you are making it, imagining the flavor, imagining the color. You can imagine everything that you do. Then come back to the techniques of how to do it. I don't think that comes at age twenty or twenty-five years old. When it does come, I would say that is when you have arrived as a pastry chef."

Dan Budd reflects on his own development in his approach to menus. "I think my early approach with dessert menus was kind of lucky. We worked hard at it, but we didn't analyze it very much. Here at the school, I've had to analyze it and teach the students about menus in every class I've had. Every student writes a dessert menu for one of their projects. I make a list of different aspects they should think about, including flavors, textures, temperatures, seasons, holidays, celebrations, presentation, eatability, and execution. All these things are important about the menu. You can come up with some really great things, but unless it can be executed well all the way to the customer, then it's not going to work."

Gray Kunz was at the forefront of promoting fruit soups. "I was doing that back in Hong Kong. I think it is a great way of leading from something very, very cold after the main course back into something warm again. That was really the format that struck me as working the best."

Nancy Silverton conceives a menu in terms of intensive flavor options for the guest. "If you really like lemon, then I'm going to make my lemon dessert really lemony. It's not overkill; it's a matter of taste and a matter of doing it right. If it's the chocolate dessert on my menu we're talking about, it isn't faintly chocolate or almost chocolate, it's truly chocolate. This dessert is geared for the chocolate lover. Others are geared for the lemon lover or the coffee lover. With respect to making and creating a menu that is balanced, for

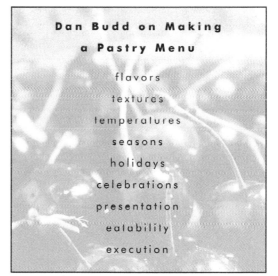

> You should be able to sit at a table and visualize the menu as if you are eating it at the same time as you are making it, imagining the flavor, imagining the color.
> —Roland Mesnier

Dan Budd on Making a Pastry Menu

flavors

textures

temperatures

seasons

holidays

celebrations

presentation

eatability

execution

From Dan Budd

....

THIS EVENING'S DESSERTS

Milk Chocolate Crème Brûlée

Passion Fruit and Yogurt Parfait with
Tropical Fruit Salad

Crisp Apple Tart with Tahitian
Vanilla Ice Cream

Opera in the Park

Chocolate-Caramel Cake with
Caramel Ice Cream

White Chocolate Gratin over
Champagne Soaked Berries

Hawaiian Vintage 1993 Chocolate
and Banana Tart

Pink Lemonade Granité

A Selection of Petit Fours and
Handmade Chocolates

Fresh Seasonal Fruits

House-made Ice Creams and Sorbets

Cheese

Grilled Sheep's Milk Camembert with Greens, Grapes, and Walnuts
Danish Blue and Warm Pear Tartlett
Camembert Fondue with Truffle Essence

From Jim Graham
(Le Français)

··

THE CHOCOLATS LE FRANÇAIS
COLLECTION OF CHOCOLATE BONBONS

Framboise

*A purée of ripe raspberries gives this ganache
an intense fruitiness.*

Earl Grey

*Flavored by an infusion of Earl Grey tea. The bergamot and
tannins of this tea harmonize beautifully with chocolate.*

Orange

A buttery cream of mandarine and bitter orange.

Mi-Amère

*A silky smooth ganache. A hint of rich milk chocolate,
with a refreshingly bitter finish.*

Pur Caraïbe

*Made exclusively with the aristocratic "Trinitario" cacao
of the Caribbean islands. A wealth of complexity.*

Gianduja

*A creamy mousse of gianduja (roasted hazelnuts ground
with chocolate to a smooth paste).*

Mint Leaf

*Fresh mint leaves from our garden infused in cream
impart a marvelous "leafy" note to this ganache.
Taste the difference.*

Spice

A unique and surprising blend of six fresh-ground spices. Fills the mouth with warm aromas.

Palet Or

The perfect marriage of fine chocolate and real "bourbon" vanilla bean. Refined and generous. Crowned with a fleck of pure gold.

Caramel

A buttered caramel blended with milk and dark chocolates.

Moka

An airy mousse of milk chocolate and coffee. Reminiscent of a frothy cappuccino.

Nougat

A traditional French honey and nut meringue, with macadamias, pine nuts, hazelnuts and pistachios.

Noix

Walnuts bound with buttery milk chocolate and honey.

Trio

Ultra-thin squares of finest marzipan, naturally flavored with ginger, cherry, and apricot.

Lemongrass

A white chocolate mousse infused with a delicate hint of lemongrass.

me it is keeping those flavors limited and separate. I do want a chocolate dessert but I don't want a chocolate-lemon dessert, so I keep them separate. I try not to overlap too much because I have seven or eight other items on the menu to work with. I try to create a dessert menu with a particular flavor for everybody."

From Richard Leach
(Park Avenue Café)

....

DESSERT MENU

Bittersweet Chocolate Mousse

With chocolate tea ice cream

**Warm Strawberry Angel
Food Cake**

Fresh berries with sour cream ice cream

Banana-Rhubarb Strudel

Carmelized bananas and banana-rhubarb sorbet

Frozen Lemon Torte

With Lemon Curd Fresh Lemon Thyme

Roasted Pineapple Tart

Basil ice cream and pineapple curd

Chocolate Cube

Filled with frozen espresso mousse and nougat

Pecan Mille-Feuille

Crisp layers of strudel and peach-caramel ice cream

Fresh Mangoes

Mango sorbet and tangy lemon-coconut sauce

Parfait of Canteloupe and Musk Melon Granite

Chilled yellow watermelon-lime leaf coulis

Classic Crème Brûlée

With warm berry and plum compote

Citrus Poached Peaches

Peach sorbet, sour cream ice cream and hysop

Blackberry and Crème Fraîche Cheese Tart

Lemon verbena sabayon and blackberry sorbet

Sorbets and/or Ice Cream

Fresh Raspberries and/or Strawberries

From Elizabeth Falkner
(Citizen Cake Patisserie/Cafe)

....

CAKES
(ANY ONE OF THESE CAKES CAN BE MADE LARGER OR SMALLER TO FIT YOUR NEEDS)

Carrot Cake

Classic spiced cake made with carrots, coconut, currants and walnuts with "spiked" cream cheese frosting and toasted fresh coconut strips.

Lemon Kir Gateau

Lemon cake layered with lemon mousse and kir syrup.
Decorated with torched meringue and garnished with lemon slices.

Laurel's Cake

Fresh banana cake with pecan-caramel filling
and passionfruit buttercream; garnished with white
chocolate curls and ruffles.

After Midnight Chocolate Cake

A moist buttermilk chocolate cake layered with milk chocolate mousse,
glazed with bittersweet ganache and finished with chocolate scrolls
and triangles and gold leaf accents.

INDIVIDUAL DESSERT TARTS

Warm German Chocolate
Cake Tart

A sweet pastry shell filled with coconut caramel and Scharffen berger
cake batter with toasted walnuts. We can bake it for you here or
we suggest you take it home and bake it in your oven and serve it warm and gooey
at the table. (Bake 350 degree oven, 10–12 minutes on a baking sheet.
Let the tart sit out of the oven for 2 to 3 minutes, then dust
with powdered sugar or serve with ice cream.)

Rosebud Brûlée Tart

Delicious vanilla custard with a hint of rose water in a lemon
pistachio crust. We can caramelize the top for you or you can do it
at home with your own torch or broiler.

Blood Orange Tart

A sweet pastry shell filled with blood orange curd and topped
with paper thin blood orange slices.

In his experience as a chef, restaurateur, designer, menu conceptualizer, and food lore expert, Mark Miller has discovered some important boundaries and goals a pastry chef should be mindful of in creating menus. "In creating a dessert menu, you need to follow the same sensibility as the rest of the restaurant—putting the twists and turns of its cuisine into the elements of the desserts. If I go to a French restaurant, I expect to see a classic dessert menu with crème brûlée and tarte tatin. I would be shocked to see Middle Eastern pastry come out after a French meal. There has to be some attention to the basics. Maybe you don't have good texture in your sorbet. Get the texture right before you start creating interesting flavors.

> To me, the top tier of pastry chefs think on a more complex level. They are able to unify, diversify, and create within a framework or category.
> —Mark Miller

"The things that are most interesting to me," says Miller, "are themes on a plate. These are desserts that I always remember. The last time I was at Jean Louis Palladin's Napa restaurant in Las Vegas, there was a chocolate theme. They did a chocolate mousse that was denser and richer than anything I have ever had, a pot de crème, a chocolate crème brûlée. He had four chocolate desserts, all made with cream, and all different textures and tastes. Another theme I had in France was grapefruit—grapefruit sorbet, grapefruit napoleon, caramelized grapefruit. It was a theme being played out, reiterating a single ingredient, playing with it rather than just having a lot of one thing on a plate. That is one thing people never have at home. To me, the top tier of pastry chefs think on a more complex level. They are able to unify, diversify, and create within a framework or category.

"Another interesting thing," says Miller, "is when you find a familiar flavor in something you don't expect. For example, if the customer finds licorice or anise flavor in your chocolate cake, they may like it or they may not, but it shocks them. I think that creates memorable desserts. Eye appeal does it. Being homier and better than mother's best does it. Variation on a single ingredient does it by creating palate echo and complexity within itself. Diversity is created subtly rather than grossly. For example, I can appreciate the difference between three kinds of ginger more than I can appreciate the difference between three completely different spices."

From Elizabeth Falkner
(Rubicon)

....

D E S S E R T S

Rose Petal Crème Brulée

Apple Tart with Apple Sorbet

Lime in the Coconut

A Trifle Outrageous

Mayan Mocha Pyramid

Suddenly Last Summer

Chilled Fruit Soup with Sorbet and
Black Sesame Wafer

Assorted Ice Creams with
Pizzelle Cookies

Assorted Cookies

A Selection of Cheeses
by Janet Mason of Oakville Grocery

From François Payard
(Payard Pâtisserie & Bistro)

....

Viennoiserie

Croissant   Almond and Fruit Danish   Cannelle   Mini Kougelhopf
Scones   Pain au Raisin
Almond Croissant   Pain au Chocolat
Brioche   Brioche au Sucre

Tea Cakes

Lemon cake   Pumpkin cake
Winter apple cake   Banana cake
Summer apricot cake   Carrot cake

Seasonal Tarts

Apple tart   Peach tart   Pear and almond tart   Berry tart   Lemon tart
Walnut and caramel tart   Apricot tart   Rhubarb tart
Chocolate tart   Passion Fruit tart   Plum tart   Fig tart

Individual Traditional

Mille-feuille   Eclair au chocolat, au café, au vanille   Opéra
Religuese (chocolate, café)   Sacher   Baba au Rhum
Paris-Brest   St. Honore   Tropezienne

Fancy Pastries

Chocolate	Fruit
Le Louvre	New York, New York
Le Notre Dame	Le Chambord
Le Trianon	Le Chinon
Le Fountainbleau	Le Checonceau
Le Sacré Coeur	Le Chantilly
Le Versailles	Le Mont St .Michel
L'Amboise	

Gateaux

(6″, 8″, 10″, 12″ and larger sizes available by special order)
Choice of 12 different seasonal cakes, Special occasion cakes,
Theme cakes, Signature cakes

Petits Fours
Macarons

(raspberry, coffee, chocolate, pistachio, vanilla)

Pâte de Fruits

(raspberry, strawberry, cassis, orange, lemon)

Pistachio

Bouchons de Bordeaux

Hand Made Chocolates

Palette d'or   Muscadine   Praline wafer
Chocolate almond bars
Chocolate nut clusters   Nougat
Ganache flavored with Earl Grey or orange
Chocolate candied orange peels
Chocolate nut clusters   Selection of truffles

Ice Creams & Sorbets

Gale Gand discovered a creative plane for herself that borders on a dream state. "Right before I fall asleep, when I'm sort of thinking about the day, that's when I get my great ideas. Usually they start with something really simple like marshmallows, or I'll draw from something that I miss from when I was little ."

"I try to go seasonally," Mary Bergin says. "In the wintertime, when there's not a lot of fruit, I have more nut desserts and chocolate desserts, and in summertime, I focus on three or four fruit-based items for my menu—fresh fruit granitas, sorbets. I try to keep it interesting. I look at the overall menu like I would look at a dining room savory menu. I want to have something for everyone. At Spago, I have two different menus. I have the café menu, on which I keep more informal, more rustic desserts, like brownie sundae; in the dining room, I have more elegant desserts, smaller and fancier."

From François Payard
(Desserts from the Bistro)

....

Chocolate Bombe

*Chocolate dome filled with a caramel center and
served with a chocolate sauce.*

Warm Bittersweet Chocolate Soufflé
with Toasted Hazelnut Ice Cream

Warm Waffle topped with
Fresh Berries and a Star Anise Sauce

*Waffles served with a fresh berry marmalade and
a sauce flavored with star anise.*

Warm Apricot Tart Tatin with Caramel Ice Cream

A caramelized upside-down tart.

Traditional Floating Island

*Light egg custard topped with egg whites whisked with sugar,
shaped and poached in milk.*

Warm Traditional Crème Brûlée

*Vanilla custard that is sprinkled with sugar before serving,
then placed under a broiler to caramelize the sugar.*

Chocolate Mousse

Old-fashioned chocolate mousse.

Chocolate Tart with Chocolate Nougatine Tuile

Sweet dough with a ganache filling.

Sacré Coeur

*Biscuit Sacher (chocolate biscuit), white chocolate bavarois
(white chocolate custard lightened with gelatin and whipped cream)
and a coulis of raspberries.*

Amboise

*Coconut dacquoise, chocolate mousse, rum flambéed bananas,
banana mousse, chocolate decoration.*

Summer Fruit Salad with Mint Infusion

*Seasonal summer fruit salad with exotic fruit
served with a light mint syrup.*

Poached White and Yellow Peaches
in Light Verbena Syrup

Berry Tart

Sweet dough, almond cream and fresh berries.

Lemon Bergamot Tart

Sweet dough, lemon curd filling flavored with bergamot.

Apricot and Almond Cream Tart

Puff pastry, almond cream, and fresh apricots.

Chambard

*Almond dacquoise (almond meringue), caramel mousse,
Williams pear mousse, pear decoration.*

....

French butter pear sorbet
with pomegranate sauce and
citrus pirouettes

Butter pecan ice cream sundae
with dark chocolate brownie

Warm Gravenstein apple tart
with cinnamon ice cream
and caramel glaze

Wild huckleberry brown butter tart
with vanilla bean ice cream

Marin wildflower honey
cheesecake with warm figs
and port wine glaze

Warm pumpkin brioche pudding with caramel
currant sauce

Vanilla bean crème brûlée in puff
pastry with fresh berries

Assorted homemade cookies

Postrio dessert sampler
for 2 or more

Selection of cheeses

From Nancy Silverton
(Campanile)

....

DESSERTS

Bitter Almond Panna Cotta

with espresso gelèe and almond bark

Broken Napoleon

with montmorency cherries and mascarpone sauce

Warm Gingerbread

with applesauce and dried fruit compote

Bittersweet Chocolate Mousse

with nougat and candied cocoa nib (limited)

Blum's Cake

with coffee crunch and chocolate sauce

Oro Blanco Sherbet

with ruby red grapefruit and lemon petit four

Michelle Gayer discusses the effect she looks for in the dessert experience at Charlie Trotter's. "It builds as a progression, from something light and delicate, perhaps a sorbet course or cheese, to a custardy, fruity item, to maybe a heavier fruit and ice cream concept, ending with a chocolate dessert." So many approaches to dessert menu creation are the culmination of the experiences and ideas of the pastry chef. You must always remember to stay true to those words on the menu, and attempt not only to meet but also to exceed the customers' expectations in every way.

Menu Balance and Change

If a dessert is a construction, then, to the guest, the menu is the blueprint of what they will experience. Description can be detailed and straightforward or purposefully poetic and vague. "When I start planning a menu," says Gray Kunz, "I look at the in-between factors. Every part of a menu is important. Often I turn a menu upside-down and begin planning ideas for the petit fours, then work my way up the meal, creating everything in between. It's a different approach, but I feel the first thing you get on your plate and the last thing you get before you walk out creates your overall perception of the meal."

Piping bag applying a dessert's bottom layer

"I'm really cognizant of menu balance," says Gale Gand. "You must have a no-fat dessert. Usually you need two chocolate desserts, one that is really intense chocolate and one that is more subtle. I always like to have some kind of custard or cream. It's difficult for me to offer only one. I want to have a rice pudding, a crème brûlée, and a bread pudding because I'm a custard person. I always have some fruit that is in season. You also have to have an ice cream and sorbet selection. In addition, I always like to offer some kind of cheese."

Key guidelines on balancing a menu, while highly personal, become the public choices of the pastry chef. The menu should embody the chef's knowledge of his or her customers, the cuisine of the establishment, and the chef's own creative direction for the food. It should reflect the fine-tuned culmination of the chef's personal history, passion, and talent. "I think when you do a dessert menu, there always has to be balance," asserts Emily Luchetti. "If you do something with almonds in it, don't put something else on the menu with almonds. Being in the kitchen all the time and being around it so much feeds your creativity. I like to have a couple of chocolate desserts on the menu. I have to have something killer chocolate and then I like to have something lighter chocolate. I always have a couple of fruit desserts. In the summer, with all the fresh fruit, I'll have some contrasting heavier selection. I like having a combination of textures, tastes, and lightness."

According to Jacques Torres, balance is a little bit of everything. "Think about winter and you start to think that there are going to be pears, chestnuts, chocolate, and exotic fruits, and each one is going to be a dessert. What is winter for you? Combine all of these items and work them into a menu. I think I let myself define changes according to my taste, but I have a pretty strong foundation of classic pastry. I follow those classics and I build on them. I don't think you can make many mistakes after that."

"We should definitely offer a nice variety and we should look at our menu for sales," says Dan Budd. "We should always have chocolate and involve caramel or butterscotch and some earthy flavors and sugars. We should also have light and fruity things, nutty things, and citrus things. We need to remember our customers and that they buy what they are familiar or comfortable with. Then we make it better than any they've ever had." Budd also thinks a menu should not be too large. "In general, six to eight desserts is a pretty good selection," he says. "If you go with more than that, not only is it hard to execute, but you will have such a low sales percentage on some of it that sometimes it's a waste of food. Six to eight desserts executed well is enough choice for any customer."

Chocolate Polvarones (Mexican Wedding Cookies)

by Wayne Brachman

Yield: 3 dozen

2 cups all-purpose flour

½ cup confectioners' sugar, plus additional for dusting

3 tablespoons cocoa powder

1 cup walnuts, finely chopped

¾ cup butter, room temperature

1 large whole egg

1 tablespoon coffee extract

1 tablespoon vanilla extract

Continued on next page

1. Preheat the oven to 375° and set a rack in the middle of it.

2. In a mixing bowl, combine the flour, sugar, cocoa powder, and walnuts and begin mixing, adding the butter bit by bit.

3. Add the egg and extracts and beat until the dough is blended and masses together.

4. Roll the dough into walnut-sized balls, place on a baking sheet at least 2 inches apart, and bake for 14 to 16 minutes or until golden brown.

5. Remove the polvarones from the oven, and, while they are still warm, roll them in confectioners' sugar. Let cool, then roll them in powdered sugar once more. Serve.

Nancy Silverton agrees. "We keep a limited dessert menu at Campanile. We try to change it every day or every other day, but we don't change everything because of the seasonal items coming in and going out. I make one out of eight items chocolate. There's always something chocolate, there's always something citrusy, there's always something nutty. You have to have those things in there. You always have to have something chocolate because customers love it, but don't make it so easy that they only order chocolate. I do that by only having one chocolate item on the menu. My response to my customers is, if it is going to be a limited menu, have the variety. Not everyone likes citrus, not everyone likes coffee, so have those flavors, but try to have only one of them. So that's how we try to plan our menu—by the flavors."

"I always try to balance my menu," says Richard Leach. "I use a couple of hot items, a couple of cold or frozen items, maybe a couple of fried items, seasonal items, not too much chocolate, a couple of familiar things customers always look for, a nice balance of acidic desserts, warm desserts, chocolate desserts. I look for a nice mix so there's something for everyone."

"It's primarily fruit," says Claudia Fleming of her dessert menu. "You need to have a couple of chocolates, then one hot dessert, one cold, one that can get out of the kitchen very quickly."

Leading pastry chefs all agree that menus must change, they must evolve—but why? What are they searching for? When is it critical that they change? Why work to rearrange classic desserts? Silverton discusses why and why not. "I do it because I try to make something classic taste better. What I do isn't wildly different from other pastry chefs. I don't do it to make it taller or more wild. I've never created to impress—never, never, never. I've created to make it better. I try to tweak the classics. Last year, for example, I did something that was so simple. I called it a broken napoleon with fruit purées. I love the idea of napoleons, but sometimes I hate the way they taste. So I thought, why do I love them? Because I love puff pastry, but I don't like napoleons that taste like the refrigerator, that are made up ahead of time. The pastry starts to get soggy and in order to keep it right, you have to add way too much gelatin to the custard. So I got this idea for a broken napoleon where I bake the sheet of puff pastry by itself, sugar on top and fully baked. Then I just construct it on the plate. I use sabayon, fruit purée, and build it up, put spiced nuts on top. It has all the great things about a napoleon, but it's made to order. It's crisp and delicious, but it's so simple and beautiful the way the powdered sugar hits the broken puff pastry. This was my answer to how to make a napoleon better."

Emily Luchetti says, "When we start to get tired of something, it's time for a change. I think, 'We've had this chocolate dessert on there for a long time and we are getting tired of making it, so let's do something new and exciting.' You get to a point where you don't like it any more and you're not going to do it, even though you used to like it and the public liked it and everything was fine." Emily's main sources for a balanced dessert menu are the seasons and their flavors, as she emphasizes here. "I believe that seasonal choices and flavor go together. With seasonal menu choices, we have to be really careful. Peaches and raspberries might be available in the middle of winter, but so often there's no flavor, so I don't want them. You even have to be careful with produce that's available in season. I only take it if it's good. It's all tied to flavor. So when you're designing, making, and tasting your desserts, you have to pay full attention to the flavor. You have to taste all the components. A dessert can't make it when there's too many things going on on the plate. You should be able to get all the flavors of the dessert in one to two bites. If you have to go all around the plate to get the essence of what the dessert is, then you're making the customer work too hard. When you have desserts in front of you, you want to say this looks great and then dig right in. It's the end of the meal. You want to enjoy it and not work too hard to appreciate it."

Richard Leach constantly addresses the need for menu rejuvenation. "Sometimes, something has been on the menu too long and I get tired of making it, but more commonly, I make changes to the menu when something is either going out of season or coming into season. I try not to change more than three items at one time because it messes up my staff and it confuses the waitstaff. You have to remember that, as pastry chef, you're responsible for consistency. Some chefs like to stick to certain things and have common plates that people rely on and come back to the restaurant for again and again. Other chefs think that people want to see something new all the time. So you have to balance those two approaches."

Michelle Gayer says, "I will have a dessert idea but usually sleep on it for about a week because the idea's not quite developed. Then I talk to the chef [Charlie Trotter] to see if he likes it. I've been here long enough that I have a pretty good repertoire of desserts that I can do—substituting fruits, for instance, and making a napoleon of some kind with phyllo and the best fruit I can get. With the book *Charlie Trotter's Desserts* out now, we have a good basis to work from. We've got a lot of things we can go with that he and I have worked out together."

Wire whisk in vanilla bean–infused cream

Markus Färbinger notes, "The first thing to keep in mind is the restaurant or the place where you work, the ambience, what image it has, the style, the client who goes there. That is before you even start putting a menu together. It is so important that the desserts match the style of the food. To me, an apple pie is as exclusive a dessert as anything else if it is really made well. It is all about communication with the chef. Some chefs load up their customers with dishes and at the end the customer has no room for dessert. They don't want anything, which is important for the pastry chef to communicate with the chef. Obviously, in composing a menu it is important to use a variety of textures, temperatures, tastes, and flavors, from the extreme single flavor concepts to the more complex desserts as well. Portion size is also important. I think a lot of people would love a small dessert at the end. And it's better to have eight desserts than fifteen, and better to have them really well thought out, with a good mixture—say, 50 percent standards people like and 50 percent new items you can introduce, so people who come in often can get something new every time."

When it comes to menu change, Sherry Yard believes season is vital. "Sometimes I feel like I'm a crazy artist because I can't create; I get a block. I think everybody does. Then a new season comes along and it's cherries in ten days. I'm on the phone like a stockbroker, saying, 'Okay, how we doing?' Then the cherries arrive and they get me excited, they get me moving. When I'm in the middle of doing something with cherries, I think of something with chocolate, but when I'm sitting there with rhubarb, strawberries, passion fruit, lemon, I can't come up with something chocolate. I always want to appreciate the beginning of the meal too, not just the dessert. Don't just focus on desserts. Make the desserts so they define the end of a meal in relation to the beginning."

Developing New Items

Gale Gand notices that she thrives under pressure. "The development process is reading, thinking about the new item, making it a few times, creating lots of changes, then putting myself in the position where I have to perform. I've learned that I'm one of those people who works best under pressure. I come up with my coolest stuff when I've promised a tasting to the waitstaff but didn't really put all the elements together until right before it went out. So I often put myself in the weeds, change the menu when it's almost too late, and that's when my greatest work happens."

Dan Budd knows the creative pressure factor as well. "Sometimes, under pressure, pastry chefs come up with the greatest ideas, because at that point they have to make sense of everything. Sometimes your style comes when you have no choice but to make it happen, but I think it's still important to relate to the customers. What do Americans want? Shortcakes, rootbeer floats, and ice cream sundaes come to mind. When we opened Park Avenue Café in Chicago, people wanted sundaes. So I thought I could make that a signature—Windy City Sailing Sundae. I did a little cookie boat with ice cream in it and little masts with sails on them. Then it was in the Chicago Tribune the next week. But it was just developed from the inspiration of an American favorite. It's important to remember what people actually want before you even start working on new desserts."

Elizabeth Falkner involves her staff in menu development. "I work with my pastry cooks and we just start the changes. When we feel we are perfecting our current menu and the things we are working on, we start thinking about the next menu, what fruits are coming along, and how we have to use them. Maybe we won't get to use certain things this year. We have to know what the crop is going to be like and figure out how cherries or strawberries are going to fit in."

Richard Leach takes us through his process. "Let's say blueberries are coming around. I think of an accent flavor or two—lemon verbena, for instance. Then I think through the flavor library in my head. Do I make a sauce or an ice cream with the lemon verbena? Do I use the blueberries warm or cold?"

Gray Kunz describes the process of developing new items. "We had a system for generating new presentation or new menus. I talked with Chris [Broberg] and we took the time to invent and plan our desserts; then we'd go to the next stage of plating the dessert and looking at the whole thing. Finally, when we were both happy with the dessert, we'd put it on the menu. We didn't do just one idea for one dish—we did three based on the same idea. Then we'd assemble those three and from those three directions we come up with a great menu item. This system really ignites the intensity and passion for the process. I love to work that way with pastry chefs and it seems to motivate their talents as well."

> I change things constantly, even within a given dish. It's a constant evolution for me. I don't ever stop looking at something. It's never finished for me.
> —Claudia Fleming

For Claudia Fleming, the development process is an ongoing cycle. "I change things constantly, even within a given dish. It's a constant evolution for me. I don't ever stop looking at something. It's never finished for me."

Emergence of Personal Style

The individual strengths, passions, experiences, and dedication of any pastry chef often lead to using ingredients and employing techniques in an increasingly personal way. Without this, the work of the pastry chef would not be nearly as interesting as it is. Think how terribly robotic our work would be if we were all just pumping out pastries that were made to some national specification. Personal style is the part of the equation that makes this business exciting when it works in concert with technical prowess and talent.

Views on this topic vary. How does personal style come about? Can it be sought or does it come from the heart and soul? Can it be risky? I think of one of Sherry Yard's assistants at Spago who asked, while preparing a recipe, "How do I know when it's mine?" How *do* we know? I think the only way personal style emerges is to ignore it as a goal and simply work hard and do your very best to make the food that you love.

"Everybody changes, everybody has an evolution," says François Payard. "I have evolved too. When I look back through my pictures, I see how my desserts are different now. I've become much simpler and much more rational. I think everybody evolves toward maturity. Sometimes pastry chefs want to show off, but when they get older they become more mature. I simply do what I think is the best."

Bruno Feldeisen says, "Some pastry chefs have different styles and ways of doing things, and I respect that. I'm not saying it's right or wrong. We each have our own styles and our own will to choose different ways."

"I think [developing style is] important," says Gale Gand, "but only later in one's pastry career. I've seen young pastry chefs who try to do it too early and things end up clunky and awkward. They're not ready. They don't know enough yet about the elements involved to combine them with finesse. You need that time with ingredients and you need to amass enough recipes. You need a library of textures and a good palate to work from. I've seen pastry chefs doing things before they develop a palate and they lose a lot of dimension." Gale's wisdom comes from an important

> I think the only way personal style emerges is to ignore it as a goal and simply work hard and do your very best to make the food that you love.
> —Andrew MacLauchlan

learning experience in her art background. "When I first took my paintings to the curator at the Museum of Modern Art, I wanted some feedback on what she thought of my work. I was planning to move to New York and get a gallery there. She said, 'Your work is too derivative. You need to stop looking at other people's paintings. You need to stop looking at art because your work is obviously derived from other things. It's not original.' I took that to heart and try to remember it in my pastry as well. I try hard to ignore what everyone else is doing because I don't want that stencil work to get into my pastry. I'm interested in originality."

Dan Budd says, "I wouldn't say to a pastry student, 'You can't copy anybody. You have to do your own thing and then come up to the level of all that stuff you see.' But still I don't think students should copy all kinds of desserts and say, 'I have to have a style like that.' On the other hand, I think that if you're open to your own inspirations, then you can paint your own picture, meaning you can work with the food and bring out great things about it from your own inspirations. I don't think people should make up a personal style in order to become famous. If you're in this business to become famous, do something else. You have to do pastry because you love it. I'm not stifling creativity by saying don't try to copy. I'm encouraging pastry cooks to get inspired by food itself, not style. A style eventually follows and people recognize it and that's good. Your establishment will be rewarded and you will too."

> If you're in this business to become famous, do something else. You have to do pastry because you love it.
> —Dan Budd

"You can't help having a personal style," says Emily Luchetti. "I think it's important to have a personal style, but you also have to be able match it to wherever you're working. If you're in a restaurant that's doing a certain type of food, your style has to blend with that food. So part of it is personal style, but then part of it is the style of that restaurant. You have to look beyond your personal style to the atmosphere you're serving your desserts in and stay true to that."

"Style is a part of you," asserts Mary Bergin. "The way you dress, the way you live, what you like." Jacques Torres agrees. "I think if you develop your own style, that means you are honest. If you don't develop any style, it means you take things from here and there and you put them together, but you always owe the result to other people. If you have your style, that's you. You develop your work. You develop what you are doing."

Bill Yosses thinks personal style is important for everyone. "I think in any profession or in anything that requires creativity, your style will come out. The way you live your life will come out in the way you cook. It's another way to express who you are."

It is stretching it to define the emergence of personal style as a process that requires conscious development. The general consensus of pastry chefs is that personal style is not an appropriate focus for a young, aspiring pastry chef. You really have to go into this business to work hard, do your very best, create high personal standards, and take pride in your work because personal style is not a place to be arrived at. It is part of the development experience of a devoted, conscientious individual in this field. It can only emerge from the heart and soul through the slow processes of assimilating technique and filtering experience through personal and professional choices. "I never tried to have a style," reports

Lindsey Shere. "I think it just happened. It would never have occurred to me to think about having a style. I think you do it by default, by what you like and how you cook. Style is something that you come to; it's not forced. I don't think it is as important to you as it might be to food writers so that they can define you. If what you do makes sense to you personally and if it suits the place you work in, then expressing your style, whatever it turns out to be, is a function of what you put into it—your background, your interests, your all."

Elizabeth Falkner agrees. "If you work with it long enough, you develop your own style. So it's not like you have to say 'God! I have to find my style!' I think it just occurs." Nancy Silverton adds another essential element: "I think you get to it through what you love," she says. "What you love, what excites you, what keeps you going. Once you develop a style based on that, you can't help but stay true to it. You know what you like and that's what you choose. I know what I like in desserts. I'll make something and think that it's delicious but it needs just a little bit more. Then I work on that little something. Now, am I working on that little something so it fits into my style? or am I working on that little something because it's not complete to me? I think I'm working on it because it doesn't fulfill my requirements of what makes a perfect dessert—whatever that might be."

Jackie Riley looks back to her training. "Before becoming a pastry chef, you have to spend a great deal of time learning and absorbing information and knowledge from the mentors, chefs, and pastry chefs you work for. I think style is about absorbing all that, learning as you go, and being able to apply what you learn. Then decide what feels comfortable and work within your capabilities. I don't think people should strive to develop their own food before they are ready because, more than likely, they will fail, whereas if they are patient with a slow process and they draw from knowledge and experience, then personal style is a byproduct of a natural evolution."

Claudia Fleming points to another source of personal style. "I think that it comes from having a strong personality." Markus Färbinger is skeptical of people who claim to have personal style. "I think that we could do a little bit more thinking before we say we have a style. I think it is often overrated. People think they have a style. Where is it? Show it to me. Explain it to me. What is your

> You have to look beyond your personal style to the atmosphere you're serving your desserts in and stay true to that.
> —Emily Luchetti

philosophy? What are the key elements in every dessert you have developed? You still see a compilation of all the things they have learned. It is still a pâte brisée. It is still a nougat ice cream. It is still fresh raspberries or a sabayon. Explain to me what is different about this. I think that in the beginning you should really push the basics. Then you should go out on your own. It is very important, once you have reached a certain level, to develop your own way of creating desserts. I do think it is important to establish that identity when you're ready."

Roland Mesnier reminds us of the importance and impact our naturally attained individuality can have in the marketplace. "I remember growing up in my hometown in France. There were pastry shops on the corner of every street and every one was different. People went to this shop for this cake and that other shop for that cake. Individuality is what makes each pastry chef and his products so interesting. A pastry chef should have his or her own style and stick with it."

Signature Items

Some chefs feel a recognizable landmark dish is vital to an establishment's menu and encourages repeat business. Customers are comfortable ordering the dish each time because they love it and they know what they're getting. This principle is the leading factor in the success of franchise businesses, but it can can also be applied to a single restaurant, pastry shop, or hotel restaurant. Other chefs dismiss the notion of signature dishes and, instead, impress customers with constant menu renovation. Emily Luchetti thinks signature dishes are more important to the public than they are to the chef. "We create a dessert and people either like it or they don't like it. Sometimes the public likes something so much that you can't take it off the menu because they will revolt. I'm happy to leave it on the menu because that's what they want, but I don't design signature desserts. The public discovers them. You never know it's going to be a signature; it's out of your control."

Claudia Fleming agrees. "I don't think anybody sets out to create a signature dessert, but once you have one, it's great. It's great to be known for a particular thing. Signature desserts are always an accent. In a practical sense, it makes the menu easier because you have less to change."

"I think signature dishes are a good idea," says Mark Miller. "I think you identify particular dishes with a restaurant and you will come back for them. Dessert is also the last thing you eat, so it leaves a strong memory impression.

When you ask most people what they've eaten at a restaurant, they can usually tell you about the dessert. They usually remember dessert more than a particular appetizer or entrée. With a signature item, I think one way to go about it is to do something better than anyone else, and that is very hard to do. Maybe you can get better ingredients, the best butter, the best cream, or maybe you have a specific technique. I remember this puff pastry I had at a restaurant in France that was darker than any puff pastry I have ever had. The chef said they used two French iron pans, one on top and one on the bottom, so when the pastry rose it hit the top iron pan and caramelized to an unusual level, browning the butter." Whether we think of Le Cirque's crème brûlée or Park Avenue Café's Opera in the Park, a restaurant's desserts can create a sensation among customers and promote incredible sales. You create something everyone must experience for themselves.

Mary Bergin says signature items are important to Spago. "I think it is especially important when you have restaurants in two locations—one in Los Angeles and one in Las Vegas, like Spago, for example. This way, people familiar with menu items in the Los Angeles Spago can have the same items in Las Vegas. People have their favorites and they want them, but I always try to expand the customers' tastes a little. I always try to send something extra out to people who I know always get the crème brûlée."

A pastry chef's signature dessert dishes might be straight renditions of classic desserts, such as strawberry shortcake, cherry clafouti, apple brown betty, or linzertorte. Desserts like these become personalized with the deft tinkering of a pastry chef intimately connected to the nuances of flavor, someone with the skill and experience to add or substitute ingredients and create something familiar that a particular clientele will embrace, yet unique and maybe even better in some way.

> It has stood the test of time. I used opera cake for the Opera in the Park dessert at both Park Avenue Cafés because I felt that this was a pastry that just couldn't get picked on by food writers.
>
> —Dan Budd

"Don't forget, when we talk about creating a signature dessert, we have to think about audience level," says Mark Miller. "You have to be careful not to go over the public's head." Bruno Feldeisen adds, "If your customers can't relate to an item, then there's no point in doing it. Sometimes if you put some classic desserts on your menu, it gives the unusual item some credibility. There is nothing wrong with a simple, good lemon meringue tart. There is nothing wrong with a scoop of good vanilla ice cream with a good strawberry compote on top."

Featuring a tweaked or reworked classic item on the dessert menu is a difficult thing to pull off well. It is only accomplished by pastry chefs who understand simplicity and the classics and can work with those standbys in exciting, sometimes whimsical ways, yet still hold true to the integrity of the original. "You know, a classic is a classic for a reason," affirms Dan Budd. "It has stood the test of time. I used opera cake for the Opera in the Park dessert at both Park Avenue Cafés because I felt that this was a pastry that just couldn't get picked on by food writers. If I do it right, it's a classic. You can pick on anything you want, but no one is going to do it to opera cake because someone else is going to say, 'How could you write that about an opera cake?' I could just serve it as my own representation of the romance and ambience of the restaurant."

Richard Leach says, "You have to stick to something, whether you get good reviews or bad reviews. You hope to get good ones, but style and signature desserts are important because you become known for a style, and this is directly related to your success. People begin to label things as your signature desserts, but you have to take it all with a grain of salt and do what you believe in, that's all."

> People begin to label things as your signature desserts, but you have to take it all with a grain of salt and do what you believe in, that's all.
> —Richard Leach

Ann Amernick agrees. "I think you have to do what feels right to you," she says. "You need to focus on doing something that feels good, that feels right, and that you are proud of. That should be enough. I think if it becomes a signature, that is fine."

Michelle Gayer dismisses the idea of being pinned down to signature items. "I don't think about that. I like to do so many different things. I would hate to be tied down to one thing because my mood might change, or the fruit for a certain dessert might not be perfect enough to serve."

Jim Graham's insight on the topic of the pastry chef's personal style sounds a note of caution. "It's a minefield. Where do personal style and signature desserts come from anyway? We've certainly gotten very visual. Press has more to do with that than anything. Certainly, in any printed material, the visual element is dominant. That's what brings the fame. If you're going to cut out a niche as one of the big players in the world of pastry, you've got to get press and the visuals that do that for you. This has led to some extremes that I don't think are good for the trade or the pastry chef. When a pastry chef is conceptualizing a new dessert, if he or she feels that a certain line must be followed to make it more visual, it's an abdication of freedom. Certainly, it's a human instinct to try to categorize and food writers and media inevitably do it, but when you start doing it to yourself, I think it is bad news."

Maury Rubin is careful with this subject as well. "I think that style and signature are very important, but there needs to be great perspective on this. You read about a chef and his signature dessert, then you read about another chef and her signature. More people wanting to learn the trade are going to be thinking, 'What will my signature be?' rather than thinking, 'Have I learned the basics like a master?' Take the word signature and throw it out of your mind and keep it out until you are strong with the fundamentals. The notion of signature or personal style should start to speak to you only once you're really a pro, once you can say to yourself, 'I know this work backwards and forwards.' "

Nick Malgieri agrees. "Signature happens over a long period of time. It is the synthesis of many influences and a lot of study, hard work, travel, and reading. All of these things come together to develop a personal style. There is one place I go where I know the pastry chef. He reads, studies, has a lot of experience, and interprets influences in the context of his own style. Now this is very different from the person who just copies stuff. Both of these people act on an influence from an outside source and they both make a dessert that is similarly based on something that comes from this outside source. One pastry chef does it successfully because he applies all his own taste, knowledge, and experience to it; the other one does it and, without that background and depth of experience, just manages to copy it badly."

Working with the Chef or Owner

The position of pastry chef is distinctive in that the majority of us are leaders and managers to various degrees, yet few of us are self-employed. Though our work is highly specialized, we are generally not autonomous. We understand that our work is an integral part of what many restaurant guests and pastry shop and hotel patrons have come to expect as the dining experience. We are an effective force helping to create the public's overall perception of the quality of the establishment we work for. The ability to work closely and personably with the entire staff, kitchen, and front of the house is crucial. The single most important alliance to be forged, though, is with the chef of your restaurant or hotel—or, in some cases, the owner of the business. The working relationship with the chef can be a pastry chef's formula for success or a recipe for failure. As your immediate superior in most restaurant and hotels, your chef will come to rely on your flexibility and responsive attitude and to depend on you as a vital force in the overall performance of the kitchen.

"I feel, as pastry chefs, all we have to do is better ourselves, and we're doing it," says an optimistic Dan Budd. "Pastry chefs are getting better and better. When you are good at what you do, you can have more respect for yourself and from everyone else. When you do a really good job, believe me, the executive chef is going to notice."

Some chefs and restaurateurs focus on the unity of the entire kitchen. Charlie Trotter says, "I look at the kitchen as one entity, not as separate divisions. The pastry area is not something that is taken for granted, as though that department is on its own. I've always had extraordinary relationships with my pastry chefs and pastry team and work closely with them."

Mark Miller adds, "It takes a pastry chef's understanding of the philosophy of the restaurant. The best situations are when the pastry chef has latitude to create things, and the chef has some insight into not changing the direction of the dish but furthering it." Gray Kunz thinks of the relationship as a marriage based on knowledge on both sides. "I think the pastry chef needs to know about savory food and cooks need to know some pastry. If you do not have that cooperation and similarity of approach, then things will never work well. From a chef's point of view, the pastry chef has to be way up there on his team. Those two key people really make an enterprise work. I am also glad to see pastry chefs going into their own fields, having their own personalities, and writing their own cookbooks. It's a different part of the kitchen, but it should not be segregated."

> The best situations are when the pastry chef has latitude to create things, and the chef has some insight into not changing the direction of the dish but furthering it.
>
> —Mark Miller

Chris Broberg summarizes his collaborative process with the chef. "My assistant and I sit down with the chef and talk about what we want to change, what's been on the menu too long, what's coming in or going out of season, how we can adjust a dessert. Can we use a classical French idea or take an American dessert like tapioca and make it Asian instead? How can we change something to get the flavors more intense? How can we reduce it to its essence of flavor? We come up with ideas. Then we work on presentation. I'll give the chef a presentation that is sometimes exactly right or, if not, he'll point me in the right direction. Sometimes I'm not happy with what I've done and sometimes he's not happy with what I've done, so we do two more presentations before we put the item on the menu. We do it as a special to get customer reaction and serve it on the lunch menu before we put it on the dinner menu. To work in tandem with the chef, you have to realize it's usually the executive chefs who create the concept, so you have to work with them. I think you have to earn the respect of the chef. If you can't, then you're not going to be able to work with that person. In the beginning, you need to know your place on the ladder, but the more experience you have, the quicker you earn the trust and gain the respect of the chef."

Roland Mesnier acknowledges that the two must work very closely. "The best situation I've found for menu making in every hotel and restaurant I worked in before the White House is when the executive chef, the sous chef, and the pastry chef all sit down and contribute to the menu. This is when you do the best menu. That's really the way it should be."

"Knowing your place makes a big difference," says Nick Malgieri. "Like any other relationship, the one that exists in harmony and peace is the one that is going to be successful. Where there are suspicions and resentments, it will be unsuccessful. I think the quality of someone's work suffers as a result of that."

Jacques Torres feels there should be mutual respect between the chef and the pastry chef. "Just respect each other, work together, and try to be friends instead of being two people in competition," he advises.

Bruno Feldeisen notes that you need to be ready for problem solving. "It's not a solution to fight and it's not a solution to ignore problems. You need to work together to get the same results in your food together. Conflict is a part of life. With chefs, sometimes there can be an ego problem, especially when one is more successful than the other. Before you start a job, make sure you get along with the chef. Trust is very important. If you have a problem, just put it out on the table and be frank. Sometimes the truth hurts, but you need to get it out and then move on."

Jim Graham's measured approach has served him well in his working relationships. "The critical factor was being able to establish a level of confidence with the chef, where he felt he didn't have to supervise me and double-check what I was doing. It took a certain amount of time before I could be given a project and trusted to come up with something presentable that he wouldn't mind putting his name on. Once that happened, then things moved very smoothly."

The times are changing for America's pastry chefs. In recent years, they have taken a more central role and receive more credit for creating successful restaurants. Desserts have become more important to the American restaurant experience, and America needs good pastry chefs. If restaurants are theatre, then—with all due respect to the chef—the show is not quite complete without the encore of dessert. The changing times have lifted pastry chefs from behind the scenes and into the limelight, where they are respected and applauded for their work. It's a new world, and pastry chefs are still adjusting. Mark Miller says, "A lot of dessert chefs are too serious and not whimsical enough. Because they are not used to being in the public light, they don't talk to their audience. They tend to be like repressed scientists who think they won't get credit for their hard work. They don't have fun."

> A lot of dessert chefs are too serious and not whimsical enough. Because they are not used to being in the public light, they don't talk to their audience.
>
> —Mark Miller

Nancy Silverton agrees. "The chef gets most of the attention. Then there's the pastry chef in the corner who usually comes in really early, works long hours, and then the chef comes in and says, 'Oh, I forgot to tell you, we need a birthday cake in twenty minutes.' So I always feel like pastry chefs are abused. I do think it's important to work together and to have a good connection with the chef. For example, in our kitchen, our flavors are simple and seasonal, and that's reflected in our desserts, which are also simple and seasonal. Our pastry department and chef are working more closely by having a family-style dinner every Monday night. We have a food theme that brings the chef and pastry department together."

According to Sherry Yard, "The relationship between chef and pastry chef is not unlike any other relationship. You're going to dislike each other at some point. If you love what you do and you're really passionate about what you do, then emotions will surface, but let them happen and don't turn on them. Your food is very personal, but you need to remember that the chef can help you grow and get better. Too many pastry chefs say, 'The chef just doesn't appreciate me. He gives me the sheets [banquet or special party information] at the last minute and he doesn't tell me about the parties." If you haven't accepted that as part of your job by now, then you haven't had enough experience. I am the queen of mise en place on the shelf. I have poached apricots and banana purée, so at any given time we have something ready when that person calls up and says, 'We need eighty chocolate cakes to go.' I have them ready. It's all about having enough experience to be ready for the unexpected."

Elizabeth Falkner notes the importance of paying attention to the chef's food. "I think I feel this way because I've watched the kitchen make so many different dishes. I taste them and I think about the seasoning, or I come to realize the direction the kitchen is going in right now. It changes all the time. If you're constantly aware of what's going on, then you're going to be much better at knowing what people want to have for dessert—not just what your little head thinks of as being really cool on the plate, but what really fits the menu at that point."

> If you're constantly aware of what's going on, then you're going to be much better at knowing what people want to have for dessert—not just what your little head thinks of as being really cool on the plate, but what really fits the menu at that point.
> —Elizabeth Falkner

Richard Leach describes a similar necessary synchronicity. "You need to have a link between the chef's style and your own. You don't want to have one style with the appetizers and entrées and something completely different or absurd with your desserts. So they do have to be linked, but that is also usually why a chef and a pastry chef end up in the same restaurant. I also try not to double up when the chef begins to use seasonal items, because no one wants to eat three courses of pumpkin. You have to set up and provide service the same way that the chef does, get things out with the same flow, the same speed."

Whether you work in a pastry shop, hotel, or restaurant, it is food that you are working with. If you really want to be a good pastry chef, you should be a decent cook. It is very important to know salt as a seasoning, let alone sugar. You need to understand the chef's aims and the emotion of their food on a personal level. Gale Gand works with her husband, who is the chef at Brasserie T and Tru. "My chef is my husband and I've chosen that. I've chosen to work with someone I'm intimate with. I would find it hard to work for a chef I was not married to because, for me, doing pastry and designing desserts that follow someone else's food is a really intimate experience. I have to be in tune with that person and close to them in order for me to truly do their cuisine justice and feel like I'm creating an appropriate finale for their food. It was almost an incomplete experience for me working with chefs other than my husband. So I have a high degree of respect for the relationship. I think it's a careful and precious relationship."

> I have to be in tune with that person and close to them in order for me to truly do their cuisine justice and feel like I'm creating an appropriate finale for their food.
>
> —Gale Gand

Mary Bergin addresses the relationship between chef and pastry chef. "I think mutual respect has everything to do with any relationship you have. I take myself seriously, therefore Wolfgang [Puck] takes me seriously. There is also a hierarchy in a professional kitchen that you really have to respect. It's obvious when someone starts in this kitchen and that hierarchy and respect hasn't been a factor in their work history."

Knowing and anticipating what particular preparations or what flavor combinations the chef likes and being flexible with the style of your desserts can lead to a successful, cooperative vision. It is a great responsibility to collaborate with the chef and use your own vision to benefit the menu and dining experience. Emily Luchetti finds common working ground easily when working with chefs. "That's never been hard for me because there's always been a common vision, a common underlying belief of what the food should be. We are a team and everyone has to be in it together. There has to be that mutual respect. I let them do what they do, and they let me do what I do, but the goal is the same and we are both working toward the same thing. You're always going to fight over plates, but that's the fun part."

"I've had dining experiences where the hot food is one thing and the desserts are a completely different style and I can tell that the chef and pastry chef aren't working together," says Dan Budd. "As a pastry chef, you need to relate to the chef and the chef's food. To be a great pastry chef, you really should understand cooking principles and apply them to pastry. When you have to work with the executive chef, the most direct result is the menu, where all the food goes together. You can use some of the same techniques, some sautéing, some roasting, and you can bring this into your desserts. Not only does the customer appreciate it but the chef does as well. The chef can understand and relate to how you're working and you can build a really good, positive relationship like that. It has to be a team effort to make it happen." Bill Yosses echoes the cooking view. "For a pastry chef, I think it's good to have some general culinary background. From that, you can value the whole process of the meal, how it is prepared in the back of the house, and how it arrives on the table. This way, you can harmonize what you are doing with the rest of the meal—but again, you have to look at the customer's experience first. You want to create an enjoyable ending, so you need to look at what's going on in the meal so you can plan your desserts to finish that."

Good communication can help avoid problems with the chef. While that can be easy in the short term, communication really needs to be maintained and used to further the chef's goals. Jaquy Pfeiffer says, "Lack of communication can be the thing that separates a pastry chef from the chef, but the pastry chef can be very valuable to the chef. For example, if something goes wrong in the hotel, management will call the pastry chef and say, 'We need something really nice to give to this guest.' "

Markus Färbinger thinks that most of the miscommunication happens between chef and pastry chef because they aren't clear with each other, like in a marriage. "Look at the ambience or the decor and the food we serve and the message we want to get across. Can we see opportunities to work together to create the appropriate experience for the guest? I think the chef and pastry chef need to communicate and to make expectations clear on both sides. The chef who hires the pastry chef needs to take the time to ask questions and to inform him or her of what events are coming up, so the pastry chef knows what to expect. It also helps to have three-month, six-month, and yearly evaluations. I am a guy who doesn't like evaluations, but as supervisor of my colleagues, I appreciate how important they are today. People want feedback. They want to know how they are doing, how they can improve. Sometimes there is too much negativity in communication because it is too late and often not enough. People need to value each other more as people and not just as laborers."

> People want feedback. They want to know how they are doing, how they can improve. Sometimes there is too much negativity in communication because it is too late and often not enough. People need to value each other more as people and not just as laborers.
> —Markus Färbinger

Marketing and Self-Promotion

How important is marketing and self-promotion for today's pastry chefs? I think it is important to be able to explain your thought processes about the creative realm, to be able to explain to someone who may not know anything about food about what you do and why you do things a certain way. You must be able to express your views in a clear, eloquent manner. Charlie Trotter always said to me,

Mixer whipping a meringue

"If someone asks to interview you or get some information or a recipe to them, do it immediately." Get it to them right away because they will notice and appreciate it. Very few chefs do that. So often, if a magazine or newspaper wants a recipe from a chef, the writer may have to call several times to remind them. If you make the effort to honor the request, set the time aside, and get the recipe to them, then the next time those writers are writing an article or speaking with other journalists, your name may come up because you will have developed a reputation as someone who is prompt and easy to work with.

Though the time demands of being a pastry chef can be enormous, this prompt can-do attitude can only help you in the present and future. Taking the initiative to write a recipe or article for a culinary periodical is also a good step. You can't make the mistake of thinking you'll be discovered or have the attitude that the public will come to you.

Timothy Moriarty raises his thoughts on the subject. "People have come to us and said, 'You know, you've never heard of some of the best pastry chefs working out there.' These pastry chefs are laboring at their bakeries or in their restaurant kitchens but are content to turn out perfect pastries—not pastries made for show-business, just great cannolis or great chocolate cakes. If a pastry chef's objective is to work his way up from a small restaurant or a country inn to a Ritz-Carlton in a major city or a great restaurant in New York, well, then, publicity is key. We have no way of knowing about a chef unless someone brings that person to our attention. I don't think you need a public relations person. It's just a matter of sending us recipes with a photograph, because we do like to see the presentation. Getting into print is possible for anyone who takes the time. You can't wait to be discovered. I respect the people who are content doing the food and taking pride in that. I respect people who don't want publicity, but I can also see how chefs can use it to get better jobs."

> If it is in your interest to increase your status, then it's important to self-promote.
> —Michael Schneider

Michael Schneider has seen many changes in the pastry world. He seized an opportunity and created *Pastry Art and Design,* the only magazine in the United States devoted solely to professional pastry chefs and their desserts. This significant step was precipitated by a rising tide of interest in spectacular desserts and a behind-the-scenes look at those who create them. He's bold, outspoken, and not afraid to take a chance on what he calls "an industry in its infancy." Michael enjoys personal and professional relationships with many of the country's brightest pastry chefs and receives significant interest and participation from pastry chefs. "It is extremely important to self-promote," he says. "We have never had any sources to go to, for example, to get a list of all the pastry chefs in this country. The lists don't exist. There's no real source of information, so we get it by being exposed to the pastry world. We find most people because they contact us, by having them send us recipes, by having them tell us about themselves. If it is in your interest to increase your status, then it's important to self-promote. It's also helpful to me as an editor, of course. The downside is that a lot of people in this industry take it as a personal affront when pastry chefs outwardly praise their own accomplishments."

Gathering Ingredients for Success

A career as a pastry chef is a recipe of many ingredients. Knowing intimately the building blocks of flavor—such as strawberries or apricots, chocolate or honey— is as important as understanding menu creation, emphasis of style, and working closely with many important people. No matter what level of success is achieved, being a pastry chef requires a tactile closeness with your raw products that can become fantastic desserts. Developing a repertoire of these desserts and compiling a dictionary of dessert ideas is ultimately based on knowledge and awareness of the ingredients involved. To be a good pastry chef, you must get out and experience all the wonderful ingredients you can work with. You must know the flavor profile of a pomegranate. You must know how much ginger root begins to make a dessert pungent and how much is just right. You must not only know how to sculpt and change the form of chocolate, you must know how to taste it, to understand the range of bitter to sweet. This is only the beginning. You must also understand the palate of others. Taste, explore, and work with the world of flavor. This takes precedent over form. The shape and beauty of your desserts can develop over time, but if you don't address flavor as your number-one priority, you have no solid ground from which to develop and integrate a personal approach. Keep a journal of flavor ideas that strike you. This way, you develop and record vital information that can become a reference book throughout your career. Divide it by season or by month and note your favorite flavors and those of others. Interview your grandmother; ask her what her favorite dessert is. You have the ability, ambition, and the inspiration to gather these ingredients, to measure and weigh them, to simmer them and mold them into your own sweet success.

> To be a good pastry chef, you must get out and experience all the wonderful ingredients you can work with.... You must not only know how to sculpt and change the form of chocolate, you must know how to taste it, to understand the range of bitter to sweet.
>
> —Andrew MacLauchlan

CHAPTER six

RADITIONS, TRENDS, FUTURE

The Classics

When the pastry chef's profession is passed from one generation to the next, classic desserts, recipes, and techniques are brought through time from their invention to the present. Through scrapbooks, recipe files, and other writings as well as through the oral traditions of apprenticeships and stages, we have inherited an entire language of desserts and sweets. These are the classics. This what we learn from. This is our foundation. "You can build on the classical," says Jacques Torres, "but your base stays the same. If you don't have some good classical training, I don't think you have a very strong background."

> When pastry chefs build lots of things on the plate, you can strip them away and usually find that what is left underneath is a classic dessert.
> —François Payard

François Payard likes to get to the root of the dessert. "I like classic American and French desserts" he says. "When pastry chefs build lots of things on the plate, you can strip them away and usually find that what is left underneath is a classic dessert." Claudia Fleming says, "There is always a role for the classic because that base and standard is always needed. When classics are done well, they're incredible, but they're very often done poorly. I think that, technically, they give us a base from which we can express ourselves freely. For me, learning French pastry was like a musician learning the scales and classical music before playing jazz. I was classically trained as a dancer for fifteen years and then I became a modern dancer. Without that original base training, I don't think I would have been any good at modern dance."

Emily Luchetti is passionate about the classics. "My desserts are renditions of classical European and American desserts, so I love to look to the classics for inspiration. Here is a dessert that's been done forever and ever; what can we do to make it taste better? What should we leave in it that makes it true? I like to carry on a tradition, to keep something just the way it was created except for a little twist here and there. You can always improve on the flavor."

Jim Graham says, "The classics certainly have their place. There are many that I enjoy. I like the more rustic, regional pastries in the classic European repertoire, not so much the style associated with Paris of the 1940s and 1950s. Those traditions stay around for a long time because of the training process in

France. Some wonderful regional pastries are not necessarily appropriate for a restaurant but they certainly have their place, more in French society than in ours. In France, there are niches, such as holiday traditions, and regional ingredients for specific kinds of pastry that don't really exist here."

Berries in Champagne Jelly

by Lindsey Shere

This is a simple, beautiful, and festive dessert. The jelly can be made a day ahead and layered with any combination of berries at serving time.
You can also layer it with sections of blood orange, oranges, grapefruits, and tangerines and garnish it with a little candied citrus peel for a refreshing winter dessert. Use only a champagne that you like to drink.

Yield: 6 servings

3½ teaspoons unflavored powdered gelatin

1 cup cold water

¾ cup plus 2 tablespoons sugar

1 bottle (750ml) dry champagne, room temperature

1½ pints mixed berries, such as blackberries, strawberries, red and black raspberries, mulberries, blueberries, boysenberries

1. Sprinkle the gelatin over the water in a stainless steel saucepan and soften for 5 minutes or until well moistened.

2. Add ¾ cup of the sugar and place over low heat until gelatin and sugar dissolve.

3. Remove from the heat and slowly pour in the champagne while stirring gently. Pour into a bowl and chill, covered, for at least 6 hours or overnight.

4. If using strawberries, slice them and stir with remaining 2 tablespoons of sugar. Let them sit for a few minutes until they appear juicy.

5. Layer the champagne jelly and the berries in wine or parfait glasses, ending with the berries. Drizzle any remaining juices over the tops. If you are preparing them ahead of time, add the last layer of berries just before serving.

Michelle Gayer comments on the profound influence of the classics in her work. "It affects everything I do because it has affected the customer and what they have been expecting to eat for the last hundred years. The crème brûlée is still the most popular dessert."

Gale Gand's reasoning from a customer's standpoint helps explain why. "The classics are important to me. Those are things that really speak to the people who come to our restaurant. So many times I draw from those to have a kind of dialog and shared language with my customers."

Dan Budd says, "Some of these things are classics because there are great, unique things about each of them. It's important that we teach the classics and that we idolize the great things and be sure to carry them along. Maybe what we are doing is giving ourselves the chance to create a new classic. Maybe thirty, forty, or fifty years from now, something that we did could become a classic because we respected the ones before."

Lindsey Shere agrees with Budd that classic desserts are classics for a reason. "I think anything that's made well and tastes good deserves to be called a classic. It should be something that fits with everything that's come before. I don't have a lot of patience with desserts that have no relevance to the meal itself, unless you're having tea in the afternoon—then it doesn't matter."

> It's important that we teach the classics and that we idolize the great things and be sure to carry them along. Maybe what we are doing is giving ourselves the chance to create a new classic.
>
> —Dan Budd

Classic desserts are so connected to people's experience that to do them really well is not a simple task. The last thing you want to do is to change a classic dessert by adding components and making it more complex for no good reason. You'll wind up making something that you realize was better off before anything was changed, something no one understands anymore. Placing a classic dessert on the menu conjures up a preconceived notion. A customer reads that description and recreates a picture of flavor in his mind based on a past experience with that dessert. He may not be impressed with your interpretation; then the flavor impact of the original has been lost. "I love a great apple pie with vanilla ice cream," says Sebastien Canonne. "The flavors are there; there's no need to mess around. The flavors are real—apples, cinnamon, vanilla. If it's a pie or a tarte tatin that's been glazed with caramel in the same way, the less you mess around with it, the better."

Caramel
Pots de Crème

by Emily Luchetti

*Emily Luchetti says that this simple yet elegant dessert is one of her favorites.
Caramel custards are the epitome of all custards. The rich, intense
caramel flavor creates a totally satiating dessert.*

Yield: 6 servings

6 large egg yolks

1 cup sugar

¼ cup water

1 cup milk

2 cups heavy whipping cream

1. Preheat the oven to 300°. Place the yolks in a large mixing bowl and lightly whisk them. Set the bowl aside.

2. In a heavy-bottomed 1½- to 2-quart pot, dissolve the sugar in the water over low heat. Increase to high heat and cook until the sugar is a golden amber color.

3. While the sugar is cooking, pour the milk and cream into a heavy-bottomed saucepot. Scald the mixture over medium-high heat.

4. As soon as the caramel becomes a golden amber color, carefully and slowly pour the hot cream and milk into it. Using a long-handled spoon or whisk, mix them together. The caramel will bubble as you begin to combine the ingredients.

5. Whisk the caramel cream into the egg yolks. Strain and refrigerate the custard base until cool. Skim any air bubbles off the surface of the custard base.

6. Pour the custard base into six 6-ounce ramekins. Place the ramekins in an ovenproof pan and put it in the oven. Fill the pan one-third to one-half full with hot water. (It is easier to fill the pan when it is already in the oven.) Cover the pan with aluminum foil.

7. Bake the pots de crème for about 50 minutes. When gently shaken, they should be set around the edges, yet have an area in the middle, about the size of a quarter, that is not completely firm. Refrigerate for several hours or overnight.

Respect for the classic repertoire of European, American, and many other dessert traditions is paramount to every pastry chef I interviewed. Pastry chefs must be careful with the wording on menus which describe their renditions of classic desserts that have been somehow made better or adapted to the restaurant setting by breaking the components down and assembling the dessert at the last minute. Pastry chefs are also searching for ways to showcase the characteristics of particular classic desserts they like and to enhance those features by going for more crispness, more lightness, more creaminess, more crunch. "To me, a classic is something you don't want to mess with," offers Nancy Silverton. "Apple brown betty should be served warm with chunks of apple and the topping. Now does it come with ice cream? No. So I think if you put ice cream with it, you're adding something to it. But would you want to completely change it around and put the apple brown betty in a crust and serve it in a slice? I think if you get too far away from something that is classic, then why not just make up another dessert? Right away, you get into problems if you call something by its original name and somebody's grandmother made it better, or they made it better themselves, and they let you know it. So you're already setting yourself up for a problem."

Classic French Soufflés

by Sebastien Canonne

Yield: Five 6-ounce soufflés

For the soufflé base:
¼ cup butter
½ cup sugar
¾ cup high-gluten bread flour

For the soufflés:
1½ cup milk
Soufflé base (from above)
4 egg yolks

Flavoring:

For chocolate soufflés: ¼ cup dark cocoa powder, sifted

For raspberry soufflés: 1 cup raspberry purée

For orange Grand Marnier soufflés: ½ cup orange juice concentrate *and*

several pieces of ladyfinger biscuit or spongecake soaked

in Grand Marnier

2 tablespoons cornstarch

¼ cup plus 2 tablespoons sugar

6 egg whites

Pinch of salt

Confectioners' sugar for sprinkling

To make the soufflé base:

1. In a mixing bowl equipped with a paddle, mix the butter with the sugar.

2. Add the flour and mix for a few seconds. The mixture should be sandy in appearance.

To make the soufflés:

1. Preheat oven to 375°. Brush soufflé ramekins with melted butter and dust with granulated sugar, tapping out the excess.

2. In a saucepot over medium heat, bring the milk to a boil. Add the base and whisk rapidly for 20 seconds.

3. Transfer the mixture to a large mixing bowl. Whisk in the egg yolks and chosen flavoring. (For orange, add only the concentrate at this point.) Set aside.

4. Stir together the cornstarch and the sugar. Whip the egg whites to soft peaks, adding the pinch of salt at the beginning of whipping. Do not overwhip the whites. Fold in the sugar and starch mixture.

5. Fold the egg whites into the flavored base mixture until smooth. (At this point, for the orange soufflés, fold in the Grand Marnier–soaked biscuit pieces.) Fill the ramekins and, using a spatula, scrape across the top of the ramekins to create a full ramekin and a level surface.

6. Place the soufflés on a tray and bake in the oven for 3 minutes. Dust the tops with some confectioners' sugar, then quickly return tray to the oven for 12 to 16 minutes or until the soufflés are well risen and golden brown. Serve immediately.

Silverton describes her process of transforming the classics as a way of growing as a pastry chef. "I got bored making the same strawberry shortcake, so I changed the ingredients in the recipe. I took James Beard's idea of putting sieved, hard-boiled egg yolk into a dough, which gives the shortcake this crispiness that I really like and gives the dessert a little bit more character. I was bored with the rawness of what a shortcake was tasting like. So I did that and then I played around with browned butter, which I love. I made browned butter, chilled it, and then incorporated it into the recipe as you would regular butter. Now it had so much more flavor, a different flavor. I changed it enough that I don't call it a strawberry shortcake. I call it strawberries with a brown-buttered biscuit. So I think I made it different, more interesting, but the respect for the original is still there and, with the new name, I'm covering myself; I'm not disappointing anybody."

"You will always see that body of classic pastry," says Nick Malgieri. "You see the way-out new stuff, but then you go to a pastry shop and you see the

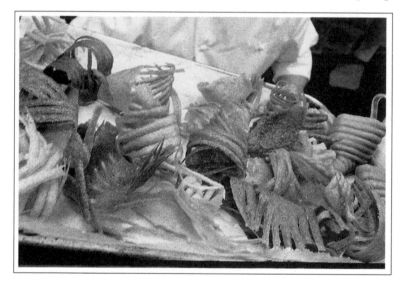

"Tumbleweed" tuile cookies

brioche and croissants and those things that really haven't changed at all. I think a lot of what is happening now is that the most talented pastry chefs are making a phenomenally good version of a classic pastry or doing new twists on it. Also, a lot more European regional specialties are becoming known to a wider public.

Maury Rubin respects the classics. "I don't screw around with them. When people come in to City Bakery and see the croissant and ask, 'Is there anything in that?' I have to stop and think, 'Oh yeah, some people put stuff in their croissants.' Pastry is a pure thing for me. 'No,' I say. 'It's a traditional croissant.'"

The classic recipes and desserts teach methodical processes and outcomes, which form a cataloged memory for the experienced pastry chef, who can reach into and use this store of information in many ways. Its value is immeasurable.

Sebastien Canonne reminds us, "You need to have food science knowledge from the classics to be able to be creative. Otherwise, how can you change a recipe and make it work? You need to know how to change ingredients that react with other ingredients."

Why Do People Want Dessert?

A fundamental question close to the heart of chefs, pastry chefs, and anyone who works with food is, why do people want desserts, sweets, baked goods, and chocolates? We are talking about a pastry chef's livelihood here. Why people indulge in desserts is a good question to ponder when considering how they support the skills and talents of so many pastry chefs across the country. Certainly people need food to live, but the truth is, they really don't need dessert. Dessert is a reward that people give themselves or a pleasure they allow themselves.

Mark Miller takes a psychoanalytical approach to considering why people want dessert. "It's tempting. We live in an affluent society where people feel they can afford dessert. There's a certain amount of self-reward going on. By eating something you really like, you reward yourself. Desserts have always been a part of the reward system. Parents say, 'If you're good, you can have an ice cream cone.' Dentists hand out lollipops. Doctors give children a little candy after a shot. Go into any supermarket in America and you'll hear, 'Mommy, Mommy, can I get this? Can I get that?' The kids have their hands on six different treats and the parents only let them have one. So when you ask grownups why they order dessert, it's a little bit of 'I am feeling good about myself and want to give myself something good.' People feel better when they eat desserts and identify with childhood and their memories."

Lindsey Shere observes, "From the beginning of your life, you are offered treats that are sweet. You're not offered steak as a treat."

Jim Graham sees the childhood factor firsthand in his own children. "It sure starts early. I have two children and it's fascinating to me from a sociological standpoint, to watch their attitudes toward food develop. Right from the beginning, dessert is in a predominant position in their diet. It's fundamental; it's not cultural."

Charlie Trotter recalls a classic bribe from the dinner tables of our American youth. "'If you eat your vegetables and beef brisket, you can have your dessert.' How many kids get this reward dangled in front of them? Very few kids need to be coached to eat dessert, but many need to be coached to eat their dinner. I personally have a love affair with chocolate things, a love affair with custardy things, with ice creams and sorbets. I have a love affair with all kinds of fruits in season, with nuts. I have a sweet tooth. I don't like things overly sweet or rich, but I want the natural flavor of whatever it is to explode. I believe that almost everybody enjoys that aspect of a meal as a reward."

Dan Budd places desserts' emotional appeal over actual necessity. "When we look at a dinner's nutritional analysis, we are often completely satisfied before dessert. It's not an easy sell, because most people are already full and they don't really need that food. Dessert signifies a celebration time, and we think of those childhood memories and it's a very happy thing. That's one of the big things I like to bring to my classes, that desserts are happiness. I saw, at Park Avenue Café, not one time but every night, people coming in to the restaurant with stress. They come to the restaurant to be entertained and to have a great time. So maybe the appetizers are five minutes late and they're really hungry and to them it seems like two hours. Then maybe the steak comes at the wrong temperature—it was medium and they ordered it medium rare. It seems like when desserts come down on the table, people finally smile. Even if we gave them a fruit soup, that could change their whole attitude. This is the reason people want desserts: it makes them happy."

> Dessert signifies a celebration time, and we think of those childhood memories and it's a very happy thing. That's one of the big things I like to bring to my classes, that desserts are happiness.
>
> —Dan Budd

Jacques Torres emphasizes the fun of dessert. "For most people who go to restaurants, it's festive and sweets are a satisfying way to end the meal. I believe you have to do something fun with desserts because after people have had a lot of food and wine, you have to wake them up, to excite them, to give them a little bit of the unexpected at the end with desserts that have an amusing edge."

How health-conscious are people when it's time to order dessert? There certainly has been a public debate for many years over the healthfulness of fats and sugar. Somehow, though, the opportunities for pastry chefs continue to be many, which calls into question what people really want, despite the spread of the idea that low-fat is more healthy. Nancy Silverton considers the desires of her customers. "I think when people go out, they tend to let themselves go. At our restaurant, our largest-selling entrée is the prime rib. Now, with all the talk about staying away from meat, staying away from fat, why do we sell so much here? It's good, yes, but I think when people go out, they also think, 'Well, I don't make steak at home.' It's the same with dessert. How many people make desserts from scratch at home? Very few."

Nick Malgieri adds, "Now that people are more health-conscious, I think they look upon dessert as a reward. When they do go to a nice restaurant, they want to reward themselves for those twenty days when they haven't had anything more caloric than a cucumber. Isn't there a human genetic need for sweets? Everybody wants them. You might have the best recipe for liver the world has ever seen, but I think if you have the best recipe for devil's food cake, more people are going to like you."

The last dish the guest has is the pastry chef's chance to send the customer off happy, and that can be the difference that fosters both repeat and word-of-mouth business. Roland Mesnier says simply, "I think it's always beautiful, at the end of the meal, to slow it down, to end it on a high note." Chris Broberg adds, "I think dessert reminds a lot of people of their childhood. Dessert might be unnecessary, but it tastes good, it's such a comfort. That's why, in America, the most popular desserts are the ones that remind us of our childhood, maybe with a little bit of added sophistication, like something that's gooey chocolate but now it's more bitter, a custard now with an herb flavor rather than just vanilla, or even cookies that, when you were a

Ecstatic customer

child had walnuts, but now are bursting with macadamia nuts. Fruit that you couldn't even get as a child we can serve for dessert. As a child, my father saw only oranges once a year, in his Christmas stocking."

Three-Point Peach Tarts with Peach Compote and Preserved Ginger

by Charlie Trotter
and Michelle Gayer

According to Gayer and Trotter, this tart is somewhat rustic, but it is actually a very elegant dessert. The cream cheese dough melts in your mouth, almost like puff pastry, yet it maintains a nice crispiness. The entire concoction is enhanced by the addition of ginger and sage. This tart is fairly versatile. It works well with a variety of fruits—plums, figs, apples, pears, or strawberries. It can be served hot out of the oven or at room temperature. When served warm, the peaches explode like molten jam. A scoop of ice cream can be added to provide additional richness.

Yield: 6 servings

For the cream cheese dough:
½ cup cream cheese, cold, cut into chunks
½ cup butter, cold, cut into chunks
½ cup all-purpose flour

For the preserved ginger:
½ cup julienned ginger root
½ cup granulated sugar
1 cup water

For tart filling and compote:

4 white peaches

5 tablespoons granulated sugar

⅛ teaspoon cinnamon

¼ cup crème fraîche

1 egg, beaten

Confectioners' sugar for dusting

2 tablespoons water

¼ cup freshly squeezed lemon juice

2 tablespoons preserved ginger

2 tablespoons tiny fresh sage leaves

To make the cream cheese dough:

1. Mix the cream cheese, butter, and flour until the dough just comes together. There should still be streaks of cream cheese.

2. Remove the dough from the bowl. Pat it into a disk, cover with plastic wrap, and refrigerate for at least 1 hour before use.

To make the preserved ginger:

1. Blanch the ginger in boiling water for 10 seconds. Drain and blanch in boiling water twice more.

2. Bring the sugar and 1 cup of water to a boil. Add the ginger and simmer for 20 minutes. Refrigerate the syrup until ready for use.

To make the tarts:

Roll the cream cheese dough to ⅛-inch thick and cut six 3-inch circles; refrigerate on a parchment-lined sheet pan for 15 minutes.

To make the filling:

1. Peel and dice 2 of the peaches and toss together with 2 tablespoons of the granulated sugar, the cinnamon, and the crème fraîche.

2. Brush the dough lightly with the beaten egg and spoon a generous tablespoon of the filling in the center of each circle. Lift up three edges of the tart and pinch

Continued on next page

three points of the tart about halfway to the filling to form the sides of the crust.

3. Preheat the oven to 350°. Refrigerate the tarts for 30 minutes. Brush the sides of the crust with egg and sprinkle lightly with 1 tablespoon of granulated sugar. Pinch the points again to make sure the tart is sealed tightly. Freeze for 10 minutes.

4. Remove the tarts from the freezer and immediately bake for 20 to 25 minutes or until golden brown. Let cool slightly and dust with confectioners' sugar.

To assemble:

1. Mix 2 tablespoons sugar with 2 tablespoons water and simmer until dissolved. Dice the remaining 2 peaches with the skin on. Toss with the simple syrup and lemon juice and warm in a sauté pan slightly.

2. Spoon some of the diced peaches and juice around the plate. Place a tart in the center of each plate and sprinkle with the preserved ginger and sage leaves. Serve.

Sherry Yard takes another point of view about why a diner orders dessert. "I think there's something sexual about it. It's an indulgence. People think there's some kind of discipline they are avoiding by having desserts. It's sex on a plate. It's tempting and exciting. I love it when I make a dessert and someone says, 'God, that's sexy.'"

Markus Färbinger makes a similar comparison. "I don't want to be too frank, but asking why people want dessert is the same as asking why people want sex. I think it has a lot to do with passion, pleasure, sin, and having something they can't have all the time. Some people do it out of sheer indulgence, and other people have dessert out of the pleasure of doing something they feel they shouldn't be doing, everything from the physical craving for sweets to the mental and emotional side of indulging in it. Aside from that, food and bread are always important, basic things to have, while dessert is something extra. It's not something you need to have. It's not even nutritionally sound, but it's something we grew up with and want. It reminds us of childhood, of comfort and safety, special moments, and birthday cakes. Pastry is very spiritual—not

> People think there's some kind of discipline they are avoiding by having desserts. It's sex on a plate. It's tempting and exciting. I love it when I make a dessert and someone says, "God, that's sexy."
>
> —Sherry Yard

religious, but spiritual in the sense that it evokes certain feelings. Food can do it too, but I think pastry has much stronger emotional content."

Buchteln

by Markus Färbinger

Buchteln, or "pockets," are delicious the next day as a snack with a glass of milk. They break apart nicely because they are dipped in butter before baking. Fillings other than blueberry, such as cream cheese, ricotta, nut, or poppy seed, work wonderfully in this recipe.

Yield: 36 buchteln

For the dough:
1 cup milk, lukewarm
2½ teaspoons dry active yeast
4 cups flour
4 tablespoons granulated sugar
3 eggs
1 teaspoon salt
Zest from 1 lemon, finely grated
2 teaspoons vanilla extract
¼ cup plus 1 teaspoon butter

For the filling:
2 cups blueberry jam
½ cup butter, melted

To finish:
¾ cup milk
2 ½ tablespoons sugar
Confectioners' sugar for sprinkling

Continued on next page

1. Preheat oven to 375°. Dissolve the yeast in the milk and add enough flour to make a thick paste.

2. Pour the remaining flour on top and let the mixture sit for 1 hour or until the paste breaks through the flour.

3. Add the remaining ingredients, except the butter, and mix until smooth, about 12 minutes. During the last 4 minutes of mixing, add the butter. Transfer the dough to an oiled bowl and cover with plastic wrap. Allow to rise for 30 minutes.

4. Roll the dough into a 12 × 12-inch square, then cut it into 2 × 2-inch squares.

5. Place a spoonful of jam in the center of each square and fold up the corners to make a pocket.

6. Roll the pocket in the melted butter and place into a 12 × 8 × 2-inch pan. Continue with the remaining pockets. Cover loosely and allow to rise for 20 minutes. Bake for 16 minutes.

To finish:

1. Whisk together the sugar and the milk. Pour this over the baking buchteln and return the pan to the oven for 8 more minutes.

2. Remove the buchteln from the oven. Sprinkle with the confectioners' sugar and serve with vanilla ice cream or enjoy them on their own.

Emily Luchetti cites the soul-stirring power of desserts. "People want desserts for emotional fulfillment. What do people have at the end of a bad day? A chocolate chip cookie or a chicken breast? Sweets fulfill a real emotional need and create an emotional satisfaction."

> We are selling dreams, you know. Customers don't need dessert; usually they've already eaten.
> —Bill Yosses

Bill Yosses quotes an influential mentor who ties the dessert experience to something otherworldly when he says, "We are selling dreams, you know. Customers don't need dessert; usually they've already eaten. They're not hungry, but they want to dream."

Chocolate Walnut Brownies

by Bill Yosses

This simple brownie recipe is a signature Bouley Bakery item.
Be sure to use a high-quality bittersweet chocolate. Pleasant dreams!

Yield: 8 servings

8 ounces bittersweet chocolate, chopped small

1 cup butter

4 eggs

1 cup sugar

1 cup flour

1 cup walnuts

1. Preheat oven to 350°. Place the chocolate and butter in a large bowl over hot water to melt.

2. When melted, remove bowl from hot water and whisk in the eggs.

3. In a separate bowl, stir together the sugar, flour and walnuts and add this dry mixture to the chocolate mixture, stirring until combined.

4. Pour into a greased 10 × 12-inch pan and bake for 20 minutes. Brownies should still be soft in the middle.

5. Allow to cool. Cut and serve at room temperature.

What's Ahead?

Pastry chefs have come a long way. No longer hidden within the maze of kitchen walls, pastry chefs, like chefs before them, have developed strong opinions about their business, the day-to-day realities of their work, and the future of their livelihood. Pastry chefs realize that the food they make is considered extra but somehow still central to our individual identity, culture, and enjoyment of life. We would feel incomplete and unsatisfied without dessert after a fine meal, whether formal or casual. Without pastry shops, bakeries, and the hard work of hotel and restaurant pastry chefs, the world would be a different place. Pastry chefs are not only here to stay but also to face their individual challenges, grow as professionals, and prosper as much as their abilities and aspirations allow. The roads are many, and opportunities for pastry chefs continue to broaden.

Michael Schneider's work with pastry chefs over the years has provided him with unique insight into their world. "It takes a special breed because they know, going in, that they have virtually no chance to rise through the ranks and become the executive chef. They can rise through the ranks and become executive pastry chef, but they are never going to take over the kitchen. A pastry chef can buy his own place and take that route, but compared to the mindset of an ambitious line cook who's thinking, 'I want to rise to be number one in the kitchen,' the pastry chef doesn't really do that. So it's a whole different demeanor and one that I think is wonderful because pastry chefs, by and large—and I've met so many of them over the years—are younger, with a great sense of humor and a willingness to share. There's a sense of beauty about the people in the business that's just great."

Glazed chocolate mousse

The Profession

I believe that many pastry chefs in this country are at a turning point. We've reached an era of recognition and opportunity. As we look back, we see a long road of hard work—quiet, countless hours, days, and nights of perfecting our methods, techniques, and ideas, adhering to the highest standards of quality, turning out great pastries, cakes, and desserts in relative obscurity. There is greater opportunity now for the pastry chef as a business owner or a partner in restaurants, bakeries, and pastry shops. Being part pastry chef, part businessperson makes a split personality that Maury Rubin lives daily. "These are really two different fields: one baking, the other business. Half of my world here is about payroll. Thirty-two people work here. I'm responsible for everything—managing public relations, creating business strategy, collecting the bills, managing the front office, establishing and maintaining a standard of professional conduct. What I have spent more time on in the last few years is growing the company, turning it into a legitimate, professional company. That's not a part-time job. I don't care how good a pastry you can make, running a business requires a person's total devotion."

Lindsey Shere, Chez Panisse's long-time pastry chef, is also part owner of the restaurant. "I think partnership is an ideal situation, but it does mean you have to get along. I am lucky that I found someone [Alice Waters] with whom I still get along after so many years, but I imagine there are situations where it could be difficult. Obviously, if you have the same philosophy about food, you should be able to make it work. I think that's why it has worked for us. Alice wanted the people who worked in the restaurant to be partners because she felt we would give more to the restaurant. I don't know if that's true or not. I don't know if that would have made any difference in how hard I worked, but feeling like I'm part of something makes it a personal activity."

If you want to be famous, pastry is probably not the profession for you. As Dan Budd says, "You have to love it." If you love it, you might decide to own a restaurant. That is how the business of restaurants has developed for executive chefs. The chef went from being leader of the kitchen to running the restaurant, from overseeing the front of the house to being in charge of the accountant. I can see that happening for good pastry chefs. Why not? When they become valuable assets to the chef and vital to the balance of the menu, then they are a true value to customer satisfaction and the business as a whole. Being an owner or partner may not be the goal of all pastry chefs, but I see it as a way for them to take full responsibility for their work, to stand up and be heard, to reach their full creative potential and generate more income for themselves. It also creates employment opportunities for others whom they might hire.

Mark Miller says, "Pastry chefs need to be a little bit more entrepreneurial in thinking about the restaurant, rather than just pastry, as a career. They need to become partners in restaurants, learn to do more management, learn the intricacies of a restaurant. Then I think their pastries will have more influence. They need to become better speakers, better on television, better with the public, and better representatives of their establishments. They tend not to look at the responsibilities of creating a great restaurant. One of the reasons more people become chefs rather than pastry chefs is that pastry chefs tend to be hidden away. Becoming more involved in the business requires pastry chefs to change mentally. Pastry chefs should take the time to work on the line and learn the complexities of cooking. They should work the front of the house. Pastry chefs tend to be less knowledgeable about many aspects of the restaurant industry. They tend to be more specialized. I think that hinders their long-term career potential. While chefs want to own their own restaurants, most pastry chefs want to be pastry chefs, so chefs generally have higher goals and aspirations. Pastry chefs tend to move on, but if they were partners in the restaurant, the restaurant would become better-known for a style of pastry and the food and the desserts would develop together. It makes the restaurant weaker if every two years the pastry chef leaves and the style of the desserts changes. It would be better if the pastry chefs had the opportunity to become partners earlier on and chose to evolve themselves with the restaurant."

> There are always restaurant customers who are going to be impressed with the razzle-dazzle stuff, sleight-of-hand tricks, things constructed. I always think these are the people who really don't know much about food, the people who are just beginning to dine out, who are impressed with those sorts of things.
>
> —Charlie Trotter

Miller's viewpoints on the professional potential of pastry chefs are worth examining. While the scenario he describes is both possible and exciting, it is important to remember where we came from and to continue to create consistently good products that add value to our establishments for our customers.

Gale Gand notes the increasing need for good pastry chefs in order for restaurants to compete successfully for customers. "I think restaurateurs and chefs are finally putting pastry in the budget and understanding how important having a pastry chef can be and how much integrity it can give a restaurant. They realize, too, how much money can be made from original pastry that is made in-house. So I see more and more places for pastry chefs in the future."

Charlie Trotter looks optimistically at the future for pastry chefs. "There is a lot of possibility out there; don't forget that pastry chefs can be involved in bread baking. When you put dessert and bread together, it's an extraordinary world of flavors and things that you can serve to people. I think we're going to continue going down the path of people wanting to eat healthful, flavorful food. I think both of those things are equally, mutually obtainable. You can make something that is unbelievably flavorful and delicious, yet very healthful. We're going to see more and more of that. There are always restaurant customers who are going to be impressed with the razzle-dazzle stuff, sleight-of-hand tricks, things constructed. I always think these are the people who really don't know much about food, the people who are just beginning to dine out, who are impressed with those sorts of things. They are more taken by the visual aspect and already think it's great without having the ability to decide for themselves, in terms of flavor, really how good the food is. Many pastry chefs who work in this style are extraordinary craftsmen, but if someone said you had one dessert left in your life, would you really want some big, hollowed-out frozen tube with a bunch of hollowed-out frozen sponge cake sticking twelve inches off the plate? A lot of it takes great organization on behalf of the chef. It takes creativity and technical skill, but most of that stuff has nothing to do with flavor, the most important feature of food. When I think of the pastry chefs who are sensualists versus the pastry chefs who are architects, the sensualists offer something much more appealing."

Judy Contino sees many more possibilities now than in years past. "I remember thinking that pastry chefs only worked in hotels and now they're in so many wonderful restaurants, both fine dining and casual. Dessert has become a more important part of the meal in more casual restaurants. Pastry chefs can have a casual style and still do great pastry. It's not as though they do whatever they want. They want to finish off the meal with a dessert that fits the style of the restaurant and the menu."

Dan Budd thinks it's a great time to become a pastry chef, but he cautions that you have to be happy with what you do. "You can't get into this to be famous; you have to love it. There is a demand out there because Americans are developing a more sophisticated palate for desserts. There are all these hearth-oven breads and great pastries and coffee houses, so I think the business opportunities are endless. Every level of being a pastry chef is growing, both the business side and in the ingredients being offered to us, like better chocolate. It's an inspiring time."

Maury Rubin expects to see more and more bakeries as start-up businesses and Chris Broberg agrees that the time is ripe for pastry chefs in business. "I think it's a good time to be a pastry chef," he says. "Look at all the pastry shops in New York! If you're willing to do the best possible product, then you're always going to have customers. People are more knowledgeable than ever before about fine desserts. They want to experience them more and think it's a nice way to splurge without doing a whole meal outside. I think people are interested in having dessert at their own pace. They might make dinner at home and then go out for dessert. They might eat out in one restaurant and then go somewhere else for dessert. The learning possibilities are great right now as well, with so many pastry chefs willing to share their knowledge through books and schools. You can learn from very good people right now."

Jacquy Pfeiffer is contagiously optimistic about the future. "I think, in this country, this is the best time ever to become a pastry chef. For the past five or ten years, pastries and desserts have emerged from nowhere. We have a lot of talented pastry chefs and it's going to become bigger and bigger because so many of us aren't going anywhere else and we aren't going to stop working, teaching, and evaluating. Compared to executive chefs, there are actually not enough of us, so that creates a need for more pastry chefs."

Gray Kunz agrees. "I think that we will see pastry chefs evolving in the years to come, because there is a great need for them. There certainly is a lack of them at the top, professional level, more so than chefs, and for simple reasons. It is such a specialized area and such an interesting one, yet I think you have to have both ambition and talent. Pastry chefs have a different feel for food than chefs have."

Jacques Torres looks at what's in store for this business. "I think the quality is going to be pushed even further. I think ingredients are going to keep getting better, fruits are going to be better. We already see fruits being handled better so that they come in ripe. Chocolate is better than it used to be. Quality is going to be more accentuated. There are a lot of good professionals, a lot of schools across the country. There's big development in pastry and a lot of talented pastry chefs. I see better-quality work in restaurants, pastry shops, and bakeries."

Emily Luchetti remembers the power of the marketplace when thinking of the future. "It's an exciting time to be a pastry chef. It took a long time to get the American dining public to value desserts and the development of the dessert menu. I think that pastry chefs, in the last four to five years, have attained a new respect."

Michelle Gayer sees the detailed, intricate responsibilities of a pastry chef as an opening for someone inclined to focus in that direction. "I think it's a growing field with great opportunities. So many executive chefs don't know a lot about pastries. There's so much more to it than throwing a few things together and, if you are a chef, how are you supposed to handle all of your other responsibilities and do pastries too? Even though pastries aren't the highest seller or the biggest part of the menu, they are still a whole different world. I think some people who come from a savory cooking background don't understand that in pastry everything has to be carried out with precision. You can't expect something to come out great if you start it in a half-hearted way, even if it's simple syrup."

Jackie Riley notes the specialist nature of pastry chefs. "I think it's a better time than ever to become a pastry chef. The field itself is growing. In restaurants, people are eating desserts and wanting desserts that are more interesting. Also, more positions are open for pastry chefs because restaurant owners and chefs realize that dessert making is a complex process and that they need someone with skills that the chef either doesn't have or doesn't have time for."

Elizabeth Falkner foresees a higher profile for good pastry chefs. "From a media standpoint, I think this is an exciting time for pastry chefs. People are recognizing that there is a major person in the kitchen who actually influences a lot of the cuisine. So we are getting more attention these days as a pastry chefs."

Sherry Yard agrees. "Pastry chefs are going to be doing what they are doing no matter what. Then all of a sudden the press plucks you out of nowhere."

Banana Salzburger Nockerln
by Sherry Yard

Yield: 8 servings

For the banana base:
1 tablespoon butter
¼ cup light brown sugar
2 tablespoons sugar
2 ripe bananas, finely chopped
2 tablespoons rum
1 tablespoon lemon juice

Continued on next page

For the soufflé mixture:

8 egg whites

¼ cup sugar

2 tablespoons all-purpose flour

4 ounces bittersweet chocolate, chopped into ¼-inch chunks

To make the banana base:

1. In a thick-bottomed saucepan over high heat, combine the butter and sugars. Allow the mixture to caramelize to a deep amber color.

2. Add the chopped banana. Stir and carefully add the rum. (It will flame.) Cook for 1 minute, then turn off the heat.

3. With a spatula, scrape the banana mixture into a blender and add the lemon juice. Purée, then transfer to a bowl. Refrigerate the mixture until cool.

To make the soufflé mixture and to assemble:

1. Preheat the oven to 400°. Brush eight 6-ounce soufflé ramekins with melted butter and coat with granulated sugar, tapping the excess out of each.

2. Whip the egg whites to soft peaks, then sprinkle in the sugar while continuing to whisk to medium peaks. Sift the flour over the whites and fold it in gently.

3. Fold the chopped chocolate into the banana base, then fold the whipped whites into the banana mixture until just mixed. Be careful not to overmix and risk deflating the whites.

4. Spoon the mixture into the prepared ramekins and bake for 12 to 14 minutes or until browned on top. Serve at once, placing the ramekins on plates lined with folded napkins.

Jim Graham points out a disturbing trend. "Pastry chefs in some hotels are being pressed to the maximum. They feel tremendous pressure to perform. In some places, if they use any prepared ingredients, they fear that their job could be taken by someone with less skill. For a restaurant pastry chef, the picture might be a little more optimistic. Pastries are a profitable component of the meal, often more so than the other areas of the menu. A good reputation for pastry alone can draw people to a restaurant. So on that level, I think there is always opportunity."

Markus Färbinger hopes for clearer communication between culinary educators and people in the industry and a standardization of pastry terminology. "There is a tremendous enthusiasm here in America, a growing-up period. I'm hoping it grows into something solid and we can really move on to create a profession in this country that is respectable, that has a force and a language. We still need to write a book in the United States that defines pastry making. We need to define techniques, skills, and methods to give American pastry chefs and bakers a common language. If you were trained in France, you use French terminology. In Italy, it's different. So it's a *biga* in Italian (fermented dough for bread baking) or it's a *pouliche* in French and we're trying to talk about the same thing. Things get all confused and everyone is using different words when talking about the same things. Standardization is needed—to provide a common language to everyone. I think that The Culinary Institute of America, for instance, and other large institutions have the responsibility to produce such a language. That is part of what education should provide. It should do what the industry itself cannot do. Industry cannot do as much research as a university can do. Industries can provide the money, but it is still the universities that do the research for the future."

Finished desserts en route to pickup area

Food and Dessert Trends

Where is the craft of pastry going? What does the future hold for techniques, methods, and finished products? Is it better to look into the past and into traditions to discover the future? The future lies in the hands of those practicing the art. The pastry chefs of today are the teachers and mentors of new generations of pastry chefs. Some are concerned that the integrity of pastry chefs is in jeopardy. Richard Leach feels there is too much focus on showpieces, and pastry chefs have become more model makers than cooks. "There are too many inedible things on plates," he says. "It seems like the future could go two ways: pastry chefs who use all-natural ingredients and start with raw product to make their desserts, and pastry chefs who buy premade products, assemble them, and put them out. There are too many premade products out there these days. It's not cooking to me anymore. It takes the fun out of it."

Paying attention to and using dessert trends can be a way of pleasing the customer. "Customers will tell you what they're looking for," says Bill Yosses. "I see a trend of more and more concern for flavor and texture. If you make the simplest tart and the bottom is crunchy and there's a layer of cream and fruit that is fresh, the texture is part of the pleasure of eating as well as the flavor. I would say those two things are becoming foremost in the customer's mind. More ingredients will be available that aren't available now, with the way international borders are breaking down. A lot of products will be brought into this country that aren't available now, perishable fruits in particular, so there will be a wider variety to choose from." People are really concerned with the source of food, not only for safety reasons, but for nutritional reasons as well. I think that will become very large.

Nancy Silverton acknowledges that pastry is always a few steps behind food. "I think we are in the middle of this architectural thing that actually started with architectural savory food," she says. "I think we are still there because it impresses people. Where will it go? Perhaps back to more simple presentations."

Ann Amernick agrees. "We are seeing a lot of great technical stuff now. I think we have hit the edge of it and there is a backlash in motion. We seem to be driven now by fad. We are driven by what attracts attention and what gets press. That's what seems to thrive in restaurants."

Nick Malgieri believes the creative end of any pursuit is always going in a million directions. "You have the people who are way out and successful at it. Good and bad taste is always going to be with us and it's great that people are going in all these directions. If some of them don't succeed as admirably as others, I still think it's great. Certainly it is a lot better than thirty years ago, when there was only one pastry chef for every thirty restaurants. I still think that we will live to see the day when, as in France, there can be two pastry shops right next door to each other and each can survive."

Dan Budd looks at ingredients and equipment. "We're going forward and backward with ingredients; flours are too refined, and now we're trying to get the organic flours, but in the future we need to look in both of these directions and just bring out better food. I also hope to see better, more efficient equipment technology, things like our batch freezers, ovens, stoves, refrigeration, and shelving. A lot of this could be drastically improved, and I think it will. I see a lot more use of computers in the kitchen and I think that this is only going to help the pastry chef do a good job and arrive at the level that our customers expect much more easily."

Breton Apple Tart

by Nick Malgieri

*This nontraditional version of the classic Gâteau Breton
adds a layer of apple filling to lighten and flavor the pastry.*

Yield: One 10-inch tart

For the Breton dough:

1 cup butter

1 cup sugar

1 tablespoon dark rum

1 teaspoon vanilla extract

4 egg yolks

2 ¾ cup all-purpose flour

For the apple filling:

2 pounds (6–7 medium) Golden Delicious apples

½ cup sugar

3 tablespoons butter

1 tablespoon lemon juice

½ teaspoon cinnamon

2 tablespoons dark rum

Egg wash:

1 egg beaten with a pinch of salt

To make the Breton dough:

1. Beat the butter until soft and beat in the sugar in a stream. Continue beating until the mixture lightens in color.

2. Beat in the rum, vanilla, then egg yolks, one at a time. Beat until the mixture is very smooth and light.

3. Beat in the flour until it is absorbed. Do not overmix. Cover the mixture and set aside.

Continued on next page

To make the apple filling:

1. Peel, core, and slice the apples into a large saucepan. Add the sugar, butter, lemon juice, cinnamon, and rum. Turn the heat to medium, cover, and cook the mixture until the apples exude their juices.

2. Uncover, turn the heat to low, stir, and continue cooking, allowing the juices to evaporate. Remove from heat and cool the filling.

To assemble:

1. Preheat the oven to 350°. Prepare a 10-inch cake pan or springform pan by buttering and lining it with baking parchment, then buttering the paper as well.

2. Divide the dough in half and press one piece of the dough evenly into the bottom of the pan and about 1 inch up the sides of the pan with fingertips.

3. Spread the cooled filling on the dough. Dust the other piece of dough with flour and shape it into a 10-inch round, place it on a sheet tray, and slide it on top of the apple filling.

4. Press the edges into place, making sure the sides are straight and even.

5. Brush the top with the egg wash and poke a decorative pattern on top with the tines of a fork.

6. Bake for 40 to 45 minutes, cool on a rack in the pan for 20 minutes, then unmold and cool completely. Slice the tart and serve.

Elizabeth Falkner cites a few directions. "I think people are paying a lot of attention to all the types of chocolate that are available; I hope that continues, and I hope that it's reflected in desserts. I also think I'm starting to see a lot more sugar work on desserts, which I hope doesn't stay because I think it has its place, but not on the plate. I also hope that pastry chefs across the country use seasonal products available in their region."

Chris Broberg looks at customer requests for signs of change in the demands of his customer base. "Right now, we get requests for less sweet, diabetic, and vegan items. I think people are getting more demanding. We get a lot of vegans who want no milk, no eggs, and no processed sugar. So we use palm sugar or maple syrup or something that isn't as refined as white sugar. Rather than skipping dessert, people are becoming a lot more particular—more knowledgeable, too. They are dining out a lot more and they know chefs can make a dessert without gluten, and if they are diabetic, they don't have to settle for sliced fruit on a plate."

Coconut Tapioca
with Passion Fruit and Coconut Sorbets and Cilantro Syrup

by Claudia Fleming

Yield: 6 servings

For the tapioca:
4 cups milk
1 cup sugar
¼ cup large-pearl tapioca
¼ cup small-pearl tapioca
1 cup coconut milk
¼ cup heavy cream

For the passion fruit sorbet:
1¼ cup passion fruit purée
¾ cup pineapple purée, strained
1½ cup simple syrup

For the coconut sorbet:
2 cups milk
1 cup fresh grated coconut
1½ cups plus 2 tablespoons sugar
½ teaspoon lime juice

Continued on next page

For the coconut tuiles:

2½ tablespoons butter, softened

1¼ cups sugar

6 egg whites, room temperature

2 cups fresh grated coconut

¼ cup all-purpose flour

For the passion fruit caramel:

1½ cup sugar

¼ cup water

2 tablespoons butter

½ cup passion fruit purée

For the cilantro syrup:

1 bunch cilantro

1 cup light corn syrup

To make the tapioca:

1. In a large saucepot over medium heat, bring the milk and the sugar to a boil. Pour half into another saucepot.

2. Put the large-pearl tapioca in one pot and the small-pearl tapioca in the other pot and cook over low heat for about 20 minutes or until soft. The mixtures should not boil.

3. In a separate saucepot over medium heat, bring the coconut milk and heavy cream to a boil and pour it over the tapioca. Refrigerate to chill.

To make the passion fruit sorbet:

Whisk together all ingredients and freeze in an ice cream machine. Reserve in the freezer for final assembly.

To make the coconut sorbet:

1. In a large saucepot over medium heat, bring the milk, coconut, and sugar to a boil.

2. Remove from heat and allow to sit until the mixture cools to room temperature, about 2 hours.

3. Strain the mixture and add the lime juice. Freeze in an ice cream machine. Reserve in the freezer for final assembly.

To make the coconut tuiles:

1. Preheat oven to 300°. In a mixing bowl equipped with the paddle attachment, cream the butter with the sugar.

2. On medium speed, drizzle in the egg whites, a little at a time, until incorporated. In a separate bowl, mix together the coconut and the flour and add to the egg white mixture. Mix for 15 seconds.

3. On a nonstick sheet or a Silpat, spread the batter very thin in circles 6 inches to 8 inches in diameter, or into other desired shapes. Bake for 16 to 18 minutes or until golden brown.

4. While tuiles are still hot, shape and mold them over the back of a glass into cup shapes. Set aside for final assembly.

To make the passion fruit caramel:

1. In a saucepot, combine the sugar and water and place over medium heat. Cook to an amber-colored caramel, about 12 to 15 minutes.

2. Carefully whisk in the butter and passion fruit purée.

To make the cilantro syrup:

1. Prepare a pot of boiling water and a bowl of ice water. Plunge the bunch of cilantro into the boiling water for 10 seconds, then immediately plunge it into the bowl of ice water.

2. Squeeze excess water from cilantro, then purée it in a blender with the corn syrup. Allow to sit for ½ hour. Strain and reserve for final assembly.

To assemble:

1. Place a coconut tuile cookie in the center of each plate and fill with a scoop of the tapioca pudding.

2. Place a scoop or egg-shaped quenelle of each sorbet on the plate against the tuile. Drizzle the passion fruit caramel and the cilantro syrup around the arrangement and serve immediately.

Claudia Fleming thinks we should look realistically at the future. She worries about trends that take the focus off the food. "I am hoping that the trend is for there not to be a trend. The trend should be that we just make great desserts."

Emily Luchetti is philosophical when looking at the future of desserts. "It's like the western frontier, when the pioneers crossed the plains and got to California. Where do you go after that? Where do you go when you've hit the ocean? There's no more land to conquer, no more cuisines to discover at this point. So I think there's going to be a filtering down and rearranging of the ingredients we have. Not to belittle it or to say that there's nothing new and exciting we can pull in. I just think it's going to be harder, and it's going to be interesting to see what new trends in pastry really last. The plating and presentation of desserts is more of a focus. It's more controlled in the kitchen. When we sent a pastry cart go around the room, things were different. Now, desserts are back in our hands and we have the control over presention and quality. Presentation keeps things alive, keeps it interesting and exciting. On the other hand, I think it is bad when it is taken too far, like anything good taken to excess, where the presentation overrides the flavor."

Warm Papillote of Exotic Fruit, Strawberry Sorbet, and Spiced Tuiles

by Jacquy Pfeiffer

Yield: 6 servings

For the papillote:

3 sheets parchment paper

¼ cup butter, melted

2 bananas

½ pineapple

2 limes, zested

2 cups mixed wild berries

½ cup plus 2 tablespoons brown sugar

3 vanilla beans, split

For the strawberry sorbet:

½ cup granulated sugar

3 tablespoons glucose or light corn syrup

½ cup water

2 pints strawberries, washed, hulled, puréed in a blender

For the spiced tuiles:

¼ cup butter

1 cup confectioners' sugar

½ cup egg whites

½ cup cake flour

3 drops bergamot essence

3 drops orange oil

For the tuile filling:

¼ cup honey

½ cup granulated sugar

¼ cup butter, softened

¼ teaspoon ginger

¼ teaspoon cinnamon

¼ teaspoon clove

¼ teaspoon ground nutmeg

1 cup almonds, finely chopped

To make the papillotte:

1. With scissors, cut six 11-inch-diameter parchment paper circles and brush one side of each with the melted butter.

2. Cut the banana and pineapple into small cubes.

3. With a sharp French knife, chop the zest very fine.

4. Divide the cubed fruit and berries among the centers of each parchment circle. Sprinkle the lime zest and brown sugar over each and place a half a vanilla bean on top of each.

Continued on next page

5. Fold the paper in half over the fruit and fold a seam where the edges meet to seal the fruit in the paper. Store the papillotes refrigerated until needed.

To make the strawberry sorbet:

1. Combine sugar, glucose, and water in a saucepot over low heat. Whisk together until dissolved.

2. Remove from heat, transfer to a bowl or plastic container, and refrigerate for ½ hour or until cool.

3. Whisk the mixture with the strawberry purée and freeze in an ice cream machine.

To make the spiced tuiles:

1. Preheat the oven to 350°. In a mixing bowl, cream the butter with the confectioners' sugar.

2. Add half the egg whites and half the flour. Mix well.

3. Add remaining egg whites and flour, continue mixing, and add the bergamot essence and orange oil.

4. Spread 2-inch circles very thinly on a nonstick baking sheet or Silpat. Set aside.

To make the tuile filling:

1. Whisk together the honey and granulated sugar. Whisk in the butter, spices, and chopped almonds. Mix well.

2. Spoon a 1-inch-diameter scoop of the tuile filling into the center of each tuile.

3. Bake for 14 to 16 minutes or until golden brown. Remove from oven and mold the tuile into half-circle shapes in a tuile mold. Reserve for final assembly of dessert.

To assemble:

1. Preheat the oven to 400°. Bake the papillotes for 8 to 10 minutes. Remove from oven and place each on a warm plate.

2. On six separate smaller frozen plates, place a quenelle or scoop of the sorbet and top with a spiced tuile.

3. Serve a papillote and sorbet dish to each guest.

The idea of pastry chefs drawing more ideas, inspiration, and ingredients from different cultural sources or traditions for their desserts is as important as the chef accurately replicating the flavor profile, preparing actual authentic dishes, or including technical aspects of those dishes effectively according to the cuisine of the restaurant. Mark Miller traveled extensively in Mexico, Spain, and Latin America before his foray into modern Southwestern cuisine with the Coyote Café restaurants. These travels influenced every aspect of the restaurants, from the decor, colors, and design to the hearty, rustic, and fiery nature of the food. I traveled with Miller to Japan and China to immerse myself in the cuisine of these lands. In China, we spent entire days walking in markets, sampling street foods, and going to restaurants at night. In Japan, we toured a mochi (rice paste dessert or candy) factory and ate in restaurants that specialized in regional foods. These experiences gave me a feel for the culture and expanded my palate immeasurably. As consulting pastry chef for his Asian restaurant, I was able to access my experiences not only to draw on specific flavors and intensities and subtleties of spice but also to include the nuances of Asian aesthetic in my desserts.

Deep frying a "bunelo" (a traditional mexican pastry)

Miller's constant evaluation of food trends leads him to interesting observations about the future of desserts. "I am disappointed that we are not seeing spicier desserts, that we are not seeing more interesting layers with different spices. Pastry chefs are not looking at Asian or South American ingredients to intensify desserts. We never see more than one level of bitter, sour, or sweet in the same dessert. Generally, desserts are at only one level of sweet and sour, which makes them not as complex to the palate. I don't think enough American pastry chefs know anything about Asian dessert techniques. They don't know how to work with mochis (sweet rice paste) from Japan; there is no schooling in Japanese techniques. They are not prepared to create within the Asian dessert traditions that exist. So I think that it might be up to the Japanese or Chinese coming here to combine their techniques with American ingredients. Middle Eastern things could take off too. The Middle East is one of the only areas that has not been played out in America yet. There is a huge dessert tradition from Persia, Turkey, Lebanon, Egypt, Iran, Iraq. Those places are unpopular to think about today. If that changes politically, the flavors of those places will become more accepted. If you had told someone in 1965 that American supermarkets were going to carry sushi, they would have laughed at you. Here it is."

Pastry sous chef, Stacey Doss

Jackie Riley considers her opportunity to work within the framework of Indian cuisine and how that translates into her desserts. "Being in the position I'm in at Tabla is an awesome situation because people have this preconception of what an Indian dessert is like. They think of an Indian dessert as a dry, almond-pasty rosewater thing or a syrupy sweet sponge cake. Our opportunity at Tabla is to set the standard and create what we want these Indian desserts to be. I want to make desserts that people embrace and can relate to and say, 'Wow! I never thought I would like caramel-coriander ice cream, but I do, and I would like to come back and have that again.' But I want to give people dessert combinations that they can relate to, like chocolate with bananas, and then go out on the edge a little bit and have them try the caramel-coriander ice cream."

Where Will They Be in the Future?

This chapter explores pastry chefs' beliefs about the future of the profession and of the craft. But what do pastry chefs want? Where do they want to be? Where do their dreams take them? What do they want to leave as a legacy? These chefs have worked so hard to get where they are—I wonder where they'll be in the future. Let's look at the long-term ideas of pastry chefs in order for those starting out in this field to find their place among us and to find their own pathways in the world of pastry. Dedication is one of the pastry chef's keys to success in the business, as is persistence in the face of many obstacles along the way.

Bruno Feldeisen offers some words of wisdom. "The next step for me is to make my own business a success," he says. "I don't pretend to be the best pastry chef, because I think that is the wrong way to go. It doesn't matter if you're number one or number two; that's not the point. The point is to be happy. Life is a journey from point A to point B and in between you have to do some learning."

Jacques Torres looks ahead. "I have a ton of things going on right now. I'm interested in television, I'm interested in writing, and I'm interested in developing a product for a big company. I would like my legacy to be, 'I have helped you, now you go and help another person.' It's not the chocolate work or the perfect pithivier or the pulled sugar flower—it's more personal and fundamental things. To be someone who helped people and asked in return that they help other people, that's important. That's my legacy."

Judy Contino has an eye toward her future. "I would love to travel. I'm working this hard now so that I can travel and see more and learn more. I'm a little bit like a teacher. I feel I am helping to mold hard-working, creative people. I like to think that we have sent a lot of good pastry people out of this shop. I also want to expand my business by having another small shop that we can take orders from and transport pastry to sell in another location and make it more convenient for our customers."

Gale Gand is reluctant to predict where it might go for her. "Pastry is such an expanding field that I am not smart enough to know. Five years ago I would never have been able to imagine that I could have a cookbook, work on television, be on the radio, have my Gale by Mail mail-order business, and have my own brand of root beer distributed nationally. That is not the kind of stuff that we knew was available to us. I've been cooking for twenty-two years now and it was a blue-collar job when I started."

Emily Luchetti sees more of the path she's on in her future. "I would say I will be doing the same thing I'm doing now—a combination of being in the kitchen, writing, teaching, and promoting good desserts, also somehow widening the sphere of opportunities in baking for other people. I think when you get more involved in projects, then more and more opportunities come along, and the more you get out there, the more you learn."

Claudia Fleming stresses continued learning as well as other ambitions. "I'm thinking about a book and a venture of my own, and I have no idea what form that will take. I want to do more training. I want to learn. There is so much to learn, but it's difficult when you get to this point to take time off and do it. I always hope to be better at what I am doing."

Vanilla Butter Buttons

by Ann Amernick

These cookies are irresistible.
No bigger than one bite, they melt in your mouth.

Yield: Approximately 24 cookies

¾ cup unsalted butter, room temperature

⅓ cup sugar

1 large egg

1 teaspoon vanilla extract

¾ cup all-purpose flour

1. Preheat the oven to 350°. Fit a pastry bag with a ½-inch plain round tip.

2. With a mixer using the paddle attachment, cream the butter and sugar on low speed until pale and fluffy.

3. Add the egg and vanilla while still mixing. Gradually add the flour. Mix for 30 more seconds or until well blended.

4. Fill the pastry bag halfway with the dough and pipe ½-inch balls 1 inch apart on nonstick cookie sheets or sheet trays lined with baking parchment.

5. Bake on the middle rack of the oven, turning the tray around after 5 minutes. Bake until the edges begin to brown and the centers are set, about 10 minutes. Watch the cookies carefully because they can brown very quickly.

6. Let cool, remove from the trays, and serve. Cookies can be stored refrigerated in airtight containers.

Training those less experienced in the kitchen has always been a responsibility of the pastry chef. There is the daily level of getting the job done, putting your vision into action, and making sure people stick with it. On a wider scale, by working with others you can give something back to the pastry profession. I think this is an admirable goal and something that a successful pastry chef should be involved in, whether it's routine or special technique training, taking on extern students from culinary schools, conducting classes, writing, or setting a good example for others who strive for similar success.

Nick Malgieri is one such pastry chef. "Certainly I think it is good to contribute to a field and not just reap whatever benefits are there. I feel very strongly about that because I'm always in touch with people in the field here in New York and, to a lesser extent, all over the country, because I do placements for our extern students. It's amazing, sometimes, how often chefs, owners, and pastry chefs have this insular mentality of, 'I have my work to do and I can't have any students mucking around with it.' I understand that it's hard to do that and put yourself out, but you have got to put something back into the field that is rewarding you by giving you a living. I feel strongly that it's important for chefs to be willing to give as well as to take. So many of us have been fortunate in this field and ridden the crest of the popularity wave that has made us so successful. It would be a shame not to be giving anything back."

Sebastien Canonne explains his aim of giving something back through The French Pastry School. "I am someone who enjoys giving back what I learned myself, to pass on the knowledge." Sebastien's business partner, Jacquy Pfeiffer, agrees. "When people come to our classes, they are apprehensive and seem a little afraid, but when they leave the school, they remember how we explained and shared. We get a lot of comments from our students on how easy we make it to understand. I feel we are just at the beginning. We want to keep passing on the knowledge by writing books and coming up with new products. All this is to improve pastry. There's so much to do. There are so many techniques to be learned and improved upon."

Nancy Silverton says she doesn't like writing her cookbooks, but something drives her to them. "I like to share and I get so excited. When I figured out how to make a loaf of bread, I said, 'I've got to do a book on this. I've got to show someone else."

Roland Mesnier considers a way to give something back to the profession as well. "I have a lot of interest in young people. I think young Americans are fascinating to teach. They are much better students than the Europeans are at this point. The Europeans have been totally spoiled. I taught the first pastry program in Washington, D.C., for ten years. I opened up the class myself and put the whole thing together. When I handed out my program, there was a waiting list to get in. I love teaching Americans. I think they are devoted and hard-working. A lot of good people came out of my classes and are still around here in many jobs. In the future, I would like to try to influence, in a positive way, young people about the pastry business."

Dan Budd also feels a strong pull to share his knowledge. He found that opportunity at The Culinary Institute of America. "When I came here, people said to me, 'Wow! You're in the spotlight in New York and you've just been nominated for the James Beard Award and you're doing all this stuff. Why don't you keep going?' Well, I never did this to get all that. That was a great bonus, and in the beginning it was hard because I didn't know what to do. I always said that if I get the opportunity to have an impact on people, to help other people, then I should do it. When you say things from the heart, people benefit from it. I hope to help this industry grow and help people realize that they can have a great career doing this. When they get into it, I'd like to be there to support them in any way I can. The world of pastry has been good to me and I think a lot of other people can have that too."

> I hope to help this industry grow and help people realize that they can have a great career doing this. When they get into it, I'd like to be there to support them in any way I can.
> —Dan Budd

Budd continues to plot ideas for the future. "If there's something I do next, it's probably going to be along the lines of a product idea. I would like to be involved in product development or writing books. I also think of a chain or franchise business where I could do great pastries. Very, very simple. It could be only one product and that's all I would do and sell it nationally. That would be a challenge for me."

Among the challenges a pastry chef faces is the idea of making a creative contribution. "I'm rebellious about styles that are almost set in stone in the pastry world," says Elizabeth Falkner. "With the holidays and the marzipan, everything seems to be too cute and I'm trying to make things a little more expressive. I want to pay attention to what works and I want to expand it."

Maury Rubin is not content to remain fixated on standard bakery fare. "In a bakery context, I think things are really tired. European bakery pastry is so tired, if you blew on it, it would fall over. Cars are redesigned every year, and theatre and dance introduce new productions every year—it is like fashion. Designers come out with a new line every year. Life pours through all these creative fields. Why doesn't that exist in pastry? I think, on one hand, a croissant should be a croissant. On the other hand, I think the making of food in America is a young industry. I think there are so many opportunities and that it just takes a thoughtful mind to say, 'There are the boundaries for what is classic here,' then, 'There are the limits for opportunity over here,' then start working on the space in between."

> Life pours through all these creative fields. Why doesn't that exist in pastry?
> —Maury Rubin

Rubin looks at his bakery as a link between bakeries of the past and his vision of what a bakery can be now and in the future. "I think that City Bakery poses some questions. I think bakeries in New York are of two generations. There is the old generation with the great, fabled names in the history of New York food, and a new generation of bakeries that we're just now beginning to experience. My work is to push the limits on quality. I think City Bakery was the first neighborhood bakery in a generation in New York to take quality to a new level, to make it as interesting as what is going on in savory kitchens. City Bakery is making a major contribution to the idea of a bakery featuring only seasonal fruit and produce in its pastries and products. We're contributing to a more sustainable agricultural system that serves bakeries. We've made an investment in that. I have spent 46 cents a pound on organic flour for seven years, although now I've got a discount, as opposed to 18 to 22 cents a pound for regular flour. We can't get that difference back from our customers. We charge more, but the quality is high—plus it's organic. My work is about putting fresh ideas into the bakery genre. As for the future, City Bakery is evolving into a series of companies with a single pursuit. For example, I'm opening up a hot chocolate and lemonade business in Grand Central Station. We're beginning a package line selling cookie dough regionally, then nationally. Everything's all natural and primarily organic. I see myself working on the concepts, developing the products, then producing them for my customers."

Bill Yosses's ideas for the future of pastry chefs represent a look at the development of cooks and chefs in the recent past. "Cooks went through an evolutionary stage about twenty years ago and reinvented their role. Pastry chefs have yet to do that, but I think it's just starting. I think pastry does need to be reinvented in the sense of how it fits into the meal, what the experience is, and what role the dessert chef has in the business. Pastry chefs have always been the stepchildren of the restaurant family. Sometimes they encourage that themselves, but I think one of the responsibilities of a pastry chef is to assume the role and be part of the team. Having said that, I don't see why they can't be equal partners with a good chef.

"Looking ahead for myself, I'll still be making desserts. I still like this profession. It offers many challenges; that's why it's so satisfying. Creativity, the ability to work in a team environment, the interest in talking with customers, and even math skills are important skills for a pastry chef. I like to be involved in bringing great recipes and experiences to a wider audience and letting them participate in it."

> This is your chance to be part of the present and future of this wonderful profession, the chance to build on your experiences and transform precious ingredients into great works that lift the spirit, brighten memories, and celebrate a passion for life.
> —Andrew MacLauchlan

There has never been a better time in America to pursue a career in pastry. It is a challenging profession and even the most successful pastry chefs continue to set new goals for themselves. Whether that goal is to learn new techniques, start and run their own business, develop and promote a product, write cookbooks, or directly affect the lives of pastry students as culinary instructors, pastry chefs have worlds of possibility open to them.

The opportunities are ripe and the skills of pastry can be applied to the needs of the market in self-directed, highly personal ways. With every dessert you put out, every hand-dipped chocolate, every wedding cake, every breakfast pastry, you affect the lives of many people. This is your chance to be part of the present and future of this wonderful profession, the chance to build on your experiences and transform precious ingredients into great works that lift the spirit, brighten memories, and celebrate a passion for life.

ANN AMERNICK is pastry chef and owner of Amernick in Wheaton, Maryland. She is the author of *Special Desserts* and co-author of *Soufflés*. Ann has been the assistant pastry chef at the White House, and pastry chef at Jean-Louis at the Watergate and Citronelle in Washington, D.C.

MARY BERGIN is pastry chef of Spago Las Vegas at Caesar's Palace in Las Vegas, Nevada. She began working in a restaurant as a prep cook by day, while working nights assisting a pastry chef at La Toke in Los Angeles, California. She began at Spago in West Hollywood, California, as a pastry cook in 1982, and became executive pastry chef in 1987. She is the author of two cookbooks: *Spago Desserts* and *Spago Chocolate.*

WAYNE BRACHMAN is pastry chef at Mesa Grill and Bollo in New York, New York. Wayne has an eclectic background, including stints as a musician, performance artist, and record producer. He has also worked in all stations of the restaurant kitchen. Former pastry chef at New York's Odeon and Arizona 206, he is the author of *Cakes and Cowpokes: New Desserts from the Old Southwest.*

CHRIS BROBERG is pastry chef at Lespinasse in New York. Broberg was a pre-med student when he decided to follow his passion for baking and pastry. His first pastry chef position was at Odeon in Philadelphia, Pennsylvania then at the Ritz Carlton Hotel in Philadelphia, Pennsylvania, and Caesar's Tahoe Resort in Lake Tahoe, Nevada.

DAN BUDD is an assistant professor of pastry arts at The Culinary Institute of America. After graduating from the The Culinary Institute of America in 1987, he served as pastry chef at such restaurants as the Park Avenue Café in both New York and Chicago and at River Café and Adrienne in New York before returning to the The Culinary Institute of America in 1996 to teach future pastry chefs. Budd also serves on the board of directors for the United States Pastry Alliance.

SEBASTIEN CANONNE is co-owner and instructor at The French Pastry School in Chicago, Illinois. Sebastien apprenticed in France and worked at Michelin three-star restaurant La Côte St. Jacques, and at hotels in Geneva and Basel, Switzerland. He was pastry chef at Palais de l'Élysée for French President Francois Mitterrand and at the Ritz-Carlton Hotel in Chicago, Illinois. A member of the 1996 and 1997 World Pastry Cup teams, Sebastien has created many winning pastry sculptures.

JUDY CONTINO is pastry chef and owner of Bittersweet Bakery in Chicago, Illinois. She has served as assistant pastry chef and pastry chef at Chicago's Ambria, and pastry chef at Printer's Row. Contino was corporate pastry chef for Lettuce Entertain You's numerous Chicago restaurants before opening her own shop in 1992.

ELIZABETH FALKNER is pastry chef and owner of Citizen Cake in San Francisco, California. Elizabeth holds a degree in fine art from the San Francisco Art Institute and has worked in some of the cities finest restaurants, including Masa's as assistant pastry chef and Elka and Rubicon as pastry chef.

MARKUS FÄRBINGER is chocolatier and co-owner of L.A. Burdick Chocolates in Walpole, New Hampshire, and Cambridge, Massachusetts. Färbinger holds a Masters degree in pastry and confectionery management from Meisterschule für das Konditorenhandwerk in Wolfenbüttel, Germany. He served as team leader for curriculum and instruction in baking and pastry arts at The Culinary Institute of America for nine years. He trained throughout Europe and is the former pastry chef of Marquet Patisserie in Brooklyn, New York, and Le Cirque in New York, New York.

BRUNO FELDEISEN is pastry chef and owner of Senses Bakery & Restaurant in Washington D.C. and executive pastry chef of Senses Bakery & Restaurant in Toronto, Canada. Bruno served as apprentice chocolatier at Les Palets d'Or in Moulins, France, and as chocolatier for Alain Ducasse at hotels in St. Jean de Luz and Monaco. He worked with Joachim Splichal as pastry chef at Patina and Pinot Bistro in Los Angeles and as pastry chef at the Four Seasons Hotel in New York, New York.

CLAUDIA FLEMING is pastry chef at New York's Grammercy Tavern. Trained in modern dance, Claudia supported herself as a dancer by working in restaurants, and was drawn to the kitchen. She left New York's Union Square Café for an intensive training period in Paris where she worked at Fauchon. Upon returning to New York, Claudia was pastry chef at Montrachet, Tribeca Grill, and Luxe.

GALE GAND is pastry chef and co-owner with her husband, Chef Rick Tramonto, of Tru in Chicago and Brasserie T in Northfield, Illinois. Gale trained as an artist and then took pastry classes at La Varenne in Paris. In New York she was pastry chef at Gotham Bar & Grill, and in Chicago, at Carlos, The Pump Room, Café 21, Bice, Bella Luna, and Charlie Trotter's. She has also served as pastry chef at Stapleford Park in London.

MICHELLE GAYER is pastry chef of Charlie Trotter's restaurant in Chicago. She attended The School of Culinary Arts at Kendall College in Evanston, Illinois, and worked for Nancy Silverton at La Brea Bakery and Campanile restaurant in Los Angeles. She co-authored *Charlie Trotter's Desserts* with Charlie Trotter.

JIM GRAHAM is chocolatier for Chocolats Le Français in Wheeling, Illinois. Trained as a draftsman, Graham turned his attention to pastry and confectionery arts with classes at Le Cordon Bleu cooking school in Paris, France. He worked at a branch of Lenôtre's patisserie in Houston, Texas, and returned to Paris to work at Maison du Chocolate.

GRAY KUNZ is the former executive chef of Lespinasse in New York, New York. Kunz worked in the kitchen of Girardet in Switzerland and was the chef of the Hong Kong Regent's Plume and the Peninsula Hotel in New York, New York.

RICHARD LEACH is pastry chef of Park Avenue Café in New York, New York. Leach graduated from The Culinary Institute of America and began his career as a line cook at the River Café. He was pastry chef at Aureole, where his desserts first gained a national reputation. He later became pastry chef at Lespinasse, One Fifth, Symphony Cafe, and La Côte Basque in New York.

EMILY LUCHETTI is the executive pastry chef of Farallon restaurant in San Francisco. A graduate of the New York Restaurant School, Emily was pastry chef at Stars in San Francisco for seven years. She opened Starbake, a wholesale and retail bakery, and has authored *Stars Desserts* and *Four Star Desserts.*

NICK MALGIERI is director of the baking program at Peter Kump's New York Cooking School. A graduate of The Culinary Institute of America, Nick has served as pastry chef at Windows on the World and assistant pastry chef at the Waldorf Astoria. He is the author of *Chocolate, How to Bake, Nick Malgieri's Perfect Pastry,* and *Great Italian Desserts.* Nick serves as an advisor and trustee for several national and international professional culinary boards and foundations.

ROLAND MESNIER has been the pastry chef at the White House since 1980. He trained in France and worked in Paris and Germany. In London, he was pastry sous chef at the Savoy Hotel, then, in Bermuda, became executive pastry chef and corporate pastry chef for Princess Hotels International. In Paris, he was Pastry Chef for the George V Hotel and consulting pastry chef for the Michelin three-star restaurant Vivarois. Roland moved to the United States in 1976 and was pastry chef of the Homestead Resort in Hot Springs, Virginia. Chef Mesnier has won many awards for his pastry creations and has been active in training future pastry chefs.

MARK MILLER is the chef and owner of Coyote Café restaurants in Santa Fe and Las Vegas, as well as Red Sage in Washington, D.C., Miller worked at Chez Panisse before opening his Fourth Street Grill and Santa Fe Bar & Grill in San Francisco. He is the author of several books including: *Coyote Café, The Great Chile Book,* and the *Red Sage Cookbook.*

FRANÇOIS PAYARD is pastry chef and owner of Payard Patisserie & Bistro in New York City. Francois apprenticed in his native France and was pastry chef at Tour d'Argent in Paris and for Chef Alain Senderens at Lucas Carlton. In the United States, he was pastry chef at Le Bernardin and Restaurant Daniel where he formed the partnership for his current venture with chef Daniel Boulud.

JACQUY PFEIFFER is co-owner and instructor at the French Pastry School in Chicago, Illinois. Jacquy apprenticed in France and has worked in several renowned pastry shops. He has served as pastry chef for Saudia Arabia's royal family, the sultan of Brunei, Hyatt Regency Hotel Hong Kong, and Chicago's Fairmont Hotel and Sheraton Hotel and Towers. He was captain of the silver-medal-winning 1996 U.S. World Pastry Cup team and has won numerous pastry sculpture competitions.

JANET RIKALA is pastry chef at Wolfgang Puck's Postrio in San Francisco, California. Rikala began her career baking at a country inn in Maine. She was assistant pastry chef at Kuleto's in San Francisco and pastry chef at Rancho Valencia Resort in San Diego.

JACKIE RILEY is pastry chef at New York's Tabla. Riley is a graduate of The Culinary Institute of America and has worked in the pastry kitchens of Chicago's Drake Hotel and Four Season Hotel, and as pastry chef of the Park Hyatt. In Washington, D.C., she was pastry chef at Kinkead's; she returned to Chicago to become pastry chef at Charlie Trotter's.

MAURY RUBIN is the owner and creator of City Bakery in New York's Union Square neighborhood. He is the author and designer of the award-winning *Book of Tarts: Form, Function and Flavor at The City*

Bakery. Rubin continues to create new ventures under the umbrella of City Bakery, including nationally distributed packaged foods and a hot chocolate and lemonade business called "Drink City."

LINDSEY SHERE is the co-owner and former pastry chef of Chez Panisse in Berkeley, California. In her 26 years at Chez Panisse she has influenced countless chefs and pastry chefs. She is the author of *Chez Panisse Desserts.*

NANCY SILVERTON is pastry chef and owner of Campanile restaurant and baker and owner of La Brea Bakery in Los Angeles. She attended Le Cordon Bleu cooking school in London and École Le Notre in France. She was pastry chef at Wolfgang Puck's Spago and is the author of *Desserts* and *Nancy Silverton's Breads from La Brea Bakery.* She is also co-author with her husband, Chef Mark Peel, of *Mark Peel and Nancy Silverton at Home: Two Chefs Cook for Family and Friends* and *The Food of Campanile.*

JACQUES TORRES is pastry chef at New York's Le Cirque 2000 and serves as dean of pastry arts at The French Culinary Institute in New York, New York. Torres apprenticed in his native France and was pastry chef at the Hotel Negresco in Nice. In the United States he served as corporate pastry chef of Ritz Carlton Hotels and has been pastry chef of Le Cirque since 1989. He is the author of two books, *Dessert Circus* and *Dessert Circus at Home* and is the host of his own PBS television program.

CHARLIE TROTTER is the chef and owner of Charlie Trotter's in Chicago, Illinois. He holds a degree in political science from the University of Wisconsin-Madison. Trotter is the author of a series of cookbooks:

Charlie Trotter's, Charlie Trotter's Vegetables, Charlie Trotter's Seafood, Gourmet Cooking for Dummies, and *The Kitchen Sessions with Charlie Trotter.* He and pastry chef Michelle Gayer have authored *Charlie Trotter's Desserts.* Trotter created and stars in his own PBS cooking show.

SHERRY YARD is pastry chef at Spago in Beverly Hills, California. A graduate of The Culinary Institute of America, Sherry honed her skills at New York's Rainbow Room, Montrachet, and Tribeca Grill. In San Francisco, she was pastry chef at Campton Place Hotel, and in Napa Valley, at Catahoula.

BILL YOSSES is pastry chef at Bouley Bakery in New York, New York. Yosses holds an M.A. in French literature from Rutgers University and a degree in hotel management from New York City Technical College. He worked in Paris at Le Bistro d'Alex, Fauchon, and La Maison du Chocolate. With Bryan Miller, he co-authored *Desserts for Dummies.*

Bastyra, Judy and Julia Canning. *The Fruit Book.* London: Salamander Books, 1989.

Berolzheimer, Ruth. *The United States Regional Cookbook.* Chicago: Consolidated Book Publishers, 1947.

Black, Maggie. *The Medieval Cookbook.* London: British Museum Press, 1992.

Brierley, Joanna Hall. *Spices: The Story of Indonesia's Spice Trade.* Oxford: Oxford University Press, 1994.

Chaitow, Leon. *Stone Age Diet.* London: MacDonald & Co., 1987.

Dornenburg, Andrew and Karen Page. *Becoming a Chef.* New York: John Wiley & Sons, Inc. 1995.

Dornenburg, Andrew and Karen Page. *Culinary Artistry.* New York: John Wiley & Sons, Inc. 1996.

Filippini, Alexander. *The International Cookbook.* New York: Doubleday, Page & Co., 1907.

der Haroutunian, Arto. *Sweets and Desserts from the Middle East.* London: Century Publishing, 1984.

Jones, Evan. *American Food.* (2nd edition) New York: Random House, 1981.

Montagne, Prosper. Jennifer Harvey Lang, editor. *Larousse Gastronomique.* New York: Crown Publishers, 1988.

Roux, Michel and Albert Roux. *The Roux Brothers on Patisserie.* New York: Prentice Hall Press, 1986.

Santa Maria, Jack. *Indian Sweet Cookery.* London: Rider & Co., 1979.

Tannahill, Reay. *Food in History.* New York: Crown Publishers, 1989.

Torres, Jacques. *Dessert Circus.* New York: William Morrow, 1998.

Trager, James. *The Food Chronology.* New York: Henry Holt & Co., 1995.

Trotter, Charlie. *Charlie Trotter's Desserts.* Berkeley: Ten-Speed Press, 1998.

Vence, Celine and Robert Courtine. *The Grand Masters of French Cuisine.* New York: G. P. Putnam, 1978.

Wheaton, Barbara Ketchum. *Savoring the Past.* London: The Hogarth Press, 1983.

Willan, Anne. *Great Cooks and Their Recipes: From Taillevent to Escoffier.* New York: McGraw-Hill, 1977.

THE MAKING *of a* PASTRY CHEF

Blood oranges, 219

Blueberries, 219

Books, 143-146

The Boston Cooking School Cookbook
(Fannie Merritt Farmer), 24

Boulud, Daniel, 161

Brachman, Wayne, 192, 253, 317

Braker, Flo, 145

Brazil nuts, 219

Bread, 3

   spice, 9

Breton Apple Tart, 301

Brinkley, Jimmy, 34

Broberg, Chris, 97-98, 117, 145-146, 160,
168, 174-175, 178, 190, 258, 266-
267, 295-296, 302-303, 318

Brownies:

   Caramel Fudge, 172

   Chocolate Walnut, 291

   S'more, 163

Buchteln, 289

Budd, Dan, 21, 35 36, 52, 60-62, 64, 68,
71, 84, 92-93, 100, 112-113, 133-
134, 140-141, 146-147, 151, 165-
166, 185, 197, 208, 213, 230, 231,
237, 238, 253, 257, 259-260, 263,
264, 266, 270-271, 278, 293, 295,
300, 314, 318

Bugat, Paul, 143

Bunelo, 309

Burke, David, 71

Buttermilk Panna Cotta with Lemon
Jelly, 182

C

Cajeta, 52

Cakes, 11

The California Culinary Academy (San
Francisco), 114

Canonne, Sebastien, 28, 42, 65, 79, 84,
118, 141-142, 161, 278, 280, 282-
283, 313, 318

Caramel:

   and Coriander Ice Cream, 210

   Fudge Brownies, 172

   Pots de Crème, 279

   Sauce, Apple Mousse on Walnut
   Crust with Apple Crisps and, 198

Cardamom, 219

Career development, 132-152. *See also*
   Training

   changes, career, 94, 97-102

   and choice of career, 88-94

   and future need for chefs, 310-316

   marketing and self-promotion, 272-
   273

   negative experiences, learning from,
   133-137

   new positions, moving to, 146-152

   reading for, 143-146

   travel for, 139-143

Carême, Marie-Antoine, 12-16

Carrots, 219

Cashews, 219

Catastrophes, 133-135

Catering, 165

Catherine de Medici, 10

Challenges, 177-178, 181-185

Farmer, Fannie Merrit, 24

Feijoa, 222

Feldeisen, Bruno, 35, 69, 138, 139, 159,
        161, 171-172, 190-191, 200,
        203, 231, 235, 259, 263-264, 267,
        311, 319

Fennel, 222

Feuillantines, 10

Figs:

    Fiori, Persian Mulberry-Poached, 51

    flavor combinations with, 222

    Glazed Ricotta Cheese with Port and,
        131

    in Tropical Fruit Spring Rolls, 72

Filippini, Alexander, 22

Financier, Pear, with Hazelnut Praline Ice
        Cream, 28

Fiori Figs, Persian Mulberry-Poached, 51

Flavor combinations, 216-220, 222-228

Fleming, Claudia, 50, 56, 61-62, 70, 80,
        88-90, 99-100, 110-111, 124, 132,
        135, 142, 144, 147, 154, 167,
        182-184, 200-201, 208, 215, 218,
        254-255, 258, 261, 262, 276,
        303, 306, 312, 319

Foley, Michael, 133

Food Arts, 37-38

Forgione, Larry, 31

Formal training, 104-116

464 Magnolia (Los Angeles), 126-127

Four Seasons, 155

France:

    apprenticing in, 121-123

    as culinary influence, 21-22, 26-27

and history of sweets, 9-18

Franchin, Louis, 122-123

Frangipane, 10

The French Pastry School (Chicago),
        117-118

Friberg, Bo, 143

Fritters, Apple, 22

Frumenty, 7

Fudge, Chocolate, 25

Future, the, *see* Trends

G

Gand, Gale, 21, 40, 49, 50, 53, 58, 65, 66,
        76, 85, 93, 99, 125, 127-128,
        136-137, 140, 144, 152, 161, 175,
        197, 218, 232, 247, 252, 257, 259,
        269-270, 278, 294, 311, 320

Gautheron, Gerald, 74

Gayer, Michelle, 49, 58, 61, 109, 129-130,
        155, 156, 174, 183, 218, 231, 251,
        256, 264, 278, 286, 296-297, 320

Gelatin:

    in Berries in Champagne Jelly, 277

    in Buttermilk Panna Cotta with
        Lemon Jelly, 182

    in Champagne Strawberry Gratin,
        Pistachio Ice Cream, and Banana
        Crisp, 178

Gender discrimination, 127-128

Genghis Khan, 5

Ghorayebah, 6

Ginger:

    flavor combinations with, 222

    Preserved, Rhubarb Napoleon with

Vanilla Mascarpone, Rhubarb
Sauce and, 156
Preserved, Three-Point Peach Tarts
with Peach Compote and, 286
Glasse, Hannah, 19, 20
Glazed Ricotta Cheese with Figs and
Port, 131
Gooseberries, 222
Gouteyron, Eric, 134
Graham, Jim, 56-57, 61, 73-74, 86-87, 90,
99, 119, 128-129, 135, 137, 139-
140, 152, 176-177, 185, 196, 218,
221, 239, 264-265, 268, 276-277,
283, 298, 320
Grapefruit, 222-223
Grapes, 222
Greece, ancient, 3-4
Guava, 223
The Guide to Cooking Schools (Shaw),
113

H

Hayden, Jerry, 71, 92
Hazelnut(s):
in Baked Apple-Hazelnut Tart with
Chocolate Chantilly, 120
flavor combinations with, 223
Praline Ice Cream, Pear Financier
with, 28
Healy, Bruce, 143
Heatter, Maida, 33-34, 144
Hinduism, 5
Hiring, 110, 150-151
History of sweets, 2-44

in ancient Egypt/Greece, 3-4
in China, 5
in colonial America, 19-21
and Crusades, 7
earliest uses, 2-3
in India, 5
Middle Ages, 7-11
in Middle East, 6
in nineteenth-century U.S., 22-23
in post-Renaissance Europe, 11-19
in Roman empire, 4-5
in twentieth-century U.S., 23-44
Hoecakes, 20
Hotels:
responsibilities when working in,
118-119
working environment in, 160-161
Huckleberries, 223

I

Ice cream:
Caramel-Coriander, 210
Hazelnut Praline, with Pear Financier,
28
in Peach Melba, 18
Pistachio, with Champagne
Strawberry Gratin and Banana
Crisp, 178
Pistachio-Rosewater Ice Cream
Sandwich on Espresso Pizzelle with
Chocolate Sauce, 192
in Viennese Café Glace, 43
Iced Raisin Squares, 47
India, 5

Influences, food:

    cultural, 60-62

    family, 65, 67-69

Ingredients, 215-233

    and flavor combinations, 216-220,
        222-228

    as inspiration, 79, 80

    pastry chefs' use of, 228-233

Inspiration, 79-81

    ethnic, 141

    from reading, 144

    travel as source of, 139-143

J

Jefferson, Thomas, 21

Johnson and Wales University
    (Providence, RI), 114

The Joy of Cooking, 144

K

Kaffir leaf, 223

Kitchens, pastry, 233

Kiwis:

    flavor combinations with, 223

    in Tropical Fruit Spring Rolls, 72

Kumin, Albert, 73

Kumquats, 223

Kunz, Gray, 150, 159, 208-209, 233, 237,
    252, 258, 266, 296, 320

L

Leach, Richard, 24, 46, 68, 70-71, 74-75,
    79, 87, 91-92, 108-110, 128, 130,
    131, 134-135, 141, 144, 154, 176,

    201, 207, 218, 228-229, 233, 241,
    254-256, 258, 264, 269, 299, 320

Lemon, 223

Lemongrass, 223

Lemon verbena, 223-224

Lenôtre, Gaston, 18-19, 144

Liccioni, Roland, 229

Lime:

    and Apple Mousse, 188

    flavor combinations with, 224

Longan, 224

Loquat, 224

Luchetti, Emily, 21, 36-37, 39, 53, 60,
    64-65, 74, 75, 78, 88, 92, 98, 106,
    133, 138, 141, 145, 155, 181,
    191, 203, 218, 232, 235, 236, 255,
    260, 261, 270, 276, 279, 290, 296,
    306, 311-312, 321

Lychee, 224

Lynn's Apple Crisp, 55

M

Macadamia, 224

Macaroons, 10

MacLauchlan, Andrew, 12, 17, 41, 55, 72,
    88, 112, 126, 228, 234, 259, 274,
    316

Malgieri, Nick, 27, 37-38, 53-54, 70, 100-
    101, 106, 148, 160-161, 184, 190,
    194, 202, 265, 267, 282, 295, 300,
    301, 313, 321

Mamaey Sapote, 224

Management styles, 186-187, 190-191,
    194-195

Pine nuts, 226

Piñon nuts, in Chocolate Piñon Cookies, 41

Pistachio:

    flavor combinations with, 226

    Ice Cream, with Champagne Strawberry Gratin and Banana Crisp, 178

    -Rosewater Ice Cream Sandwich on Espresso Pizzelle with Chocolate Sauce, 192

Pizzelle, Espresso, with Pistachio-Rosewater Ice Cream Sandwich and Chocolate Sauce, 192

Plantain, 226

Plum, 226

"Pockets" (*Buchteln*), 289

Polvarones, Chocolate, 253

Pomegranate(s):

    flavor combinations with, 226

    Sauce, Tangerine Sorbet with, 212

Poppy seed, 226

Pouding de Cabinet, 14

Prickly pear, 226

Professional development programs, 117-119

The Professional Pastry Chef (Bo Friberg), 143

Puck, Wolfgang, 136, 154, 184

Pudding:

    Coconut Tapioca, with Passion Fruit and Coconut Sorbets and Cilantro Syrup, 303

    Raisin, 14

Pumpkin, 226-227

Pumpkin seeds, 227

R

Raisin(s):

    in Dried Fruit and Nut Scone, 8

    in Iced Raisin Squares, 47

    Pudding, 14

Raspberries:

    flavor combinations with, 227

    in Orange Brûlée with Julienne of Orange, 214

    in Peach Melba, 18

Reading, 143-146

Relationships:

    with customers, 195-197, 200-201

    with mentors, 69-71, 73-78

    with staff, 186-187, 190-191, 194-195

Restaurants:

    responsibilities when working in, 119

    working environment in, 154-155, 159

Rhubarb:

    flavor combinations with, 227

    Napoleon, with Preserved Ginger, Vanilla Mascarpone, and Rhubarb Sauce, 156

Richard II, 10

Ricotta Cheese, Glazed, with Figs and Port, 131

Rikala, Janet, 21, 172, 212, 250, 322

Riley, Jackie, 59, 108-109, 155, 160, 185, 209, 210, 229-230, 261, 297, 310, 322

Ritz, Cesar, 17

Splichal, Joachim, 203

Spring Rolls, Tropical Fruit, 72

Staff:

    hiring, 186-187, 190

    relationships with, 186-187, 190-191, 194-195

Starfruit, 227

Strawberry(-ies):

    in Blackberry Soup with Noyau Ice, 32

    Gratin, Champagne, with Pistachio Ice Cream and Banana Crisp, 178

Style, personal, 70, 258-262

Success, requirements for, 111-112, 206-209, 211, 213, 273-274

Sugar, 10-11

Sugar cane, 2-3, 5

Syrups:

    Apple Apple Apple, 77

    cilantro, with Coconut Tapioca, Passion Fruit and Coconut Sorbets, 303

T

Tamarillo, 227

Tamarind, 227-228

Tangerine(s):

    flavor combinations with, 220

    Sorbet, with Pomegranate Sauce, 212

Tart(s):

    Baked Apple-Hazelnut, with Chocolate Chantilly, 120

    Breton Apple, 301

    Three-Point Peach, with Peach Compote and Preserved Ginger, 286

    Zinfandel Marinated Cherry-Cocoa, 95

Three-Point Peach Tarts with Peach Compote and Preserved Ginger, 286

Thyme, 228

Tomatillo:

    flavor combinations with, 228

    Sorbet, 126

Torres, Jacques, 40, 58, 63-64, 76, 77, 80-81, 84, 85, 90-91, 99, 109-110, 122-123, 135-136, 147-148, 151, 166-167, 178, 196, 207, 218, 253, 260, 267, 276, 296, 311, 323

Tour de France, 122

Tower, Jeremiah, 26, 74, 88, 133

Trager, James, 2

Training, 104-119, 121-130, 132

    American vs. European, 123

    European apprenticing tradition, 119, 121-123

    formal, 104-116

    by individuals vs. experience, 123-130, 132

    mentoring vs., 74

    pastry degree programs, 113-116

    professional development programs, 117-119

Tramonto, Rick, 161

Travel, 139-143

Trends:

    food and dessert, 299-300, 302-303,